MIR Series in International Business

Series editors
Michael-Jörg Oesterle
Stuttgart, Germany

Joachim Wolf
Kiel, Germany

Stefan Schmid
Berlin, Germany

Klaus Macharzina
Stuttgart, Germany

The MIR Series in International Business is an excellent platform for scholars in International Business and International Management that features state-of-the-art research in the form of monographs and contributed volumes. The series also publishes outstanding English-language PhD dissertations. Its primary goals are the advancement and dissemination of research in the fields of International Business/International Management, and its scope includes all major topics within these fields including Cross-Cultural Management, and Comparative Management. The series is affiliated with the journal Management International Review.

More information about this series at http://www.springer.com/series/13480

Björn Röber

Escalation of Commitment in Internationalization Processes

The Role of Bounded Rationality in the Uppsala Model

Springer

Björn Röber
University of Stuttgart
Stuttgart, Germany

ISSN 2511-2244 ISSN 2511-2252 (electronic)
MIR Series in International Business
ISBN 978-3-319-69101-5 ISBN 978-3-319-69102-2 (eBook)
https://doi.org/10.1007/978-3-319-69102-2

Library of Congress Control Number: 2017954947

Printed on acid-free paper

This Springer imprint is published by Springer Nature
The registered company is Springer International Publishing AG
The registered company address is: Gewerbestrasse 11, 6330 Cham, Switzerland

Foreword

Research on internationalization processes (IP research) is traditionally characterized by a close link to the field of behavioral management studies. This stream of research has been ongoing for decades and shows a particular interest in the decision-making of managers under real-world conditions. Respective studies employ the perspective of bounded rationality to describe and explain decision-making processes and outcomes. At the same time, they refrain from idealizing premises and concepts such as states of perfect rationality or the paradigm of the economic man. In the field of IP research, the respective course of action was founded by the most prominent internationalization process theory—the Uppsala Model. Yet despite its behavioral character, the Uppsala Model is built on the somewhat implicit assumption of consistently and purposefully acting decision-makers. The model thereby neglects behavioral research insights, which indicate the inaccuracy of the corresponding assumptions.

Against this background, Björn Röber's study reviews the behavioral assumptions of the Uppsala Model critically by confronting the idea of consistently and purposefully acting decision-makers with the theoretical and empirically proven concept of escalation of commitment. Based on a thorough analysis of the constructs of rationality and bounded rationality, the relation between bounded rationality and escalation of commitment serves as a blueprint for a theoretical framework for the underlying study. This framework reflects the challenges of escalation of commitment for a firm's internationalization process as it is postulated by the Uppsala Model. The empirical analysis of the framework as well as of the respective hypotheses via randomized experiments shows impressively that the Uppsala Model does not mirror basic behavioral assumptions in all elements. In fact, decision-makers do not necessarily internationalize the firm's activities in a consistent and purposeful manner as they can be heavily biased by an escalation of commitment. Additional case studies of real internationalization processes deliver further supporting arguments.

Finally, Björn Röber's study discusses possibilities of how escalation of commitment could be reduced so that the managers concerned do not necessarily follow their inclination to "throw good money after bad" in the future. Thanks to its topics as well as to its sound conceptualization and analyses, the study is a must-read for all who are interested in internationalization processes and/or in the general hows and whys of managers' decision-making. I sincerely hope that the study will find a lot of readers and wish the author all the best.

Stuttgart, Germany — Michael-Jörg Oesterle
August 2017

Preface

The aim of this study is to present a critical review of the role of bounded rationality, i.e., limited information availability and limited cognitive capabilities, of decision-makers in internationalization process (IP) research. Despite the circumstance that the internationalization processes of firms have been subjected to scientific debates for several decades now, it is questionable whether behavioral research insights are sufficiently acknowledged in this academic discipline. Respective theoretical frameworks tend to build on the assumption of consistently and purposefully acting decision-makers. In doing so, they show a certain neglect of behavioral research insights indicating the limited applicability of these assumptions. A consideration of behavioral research insights, however, would be a necessary precondition for the development of realistic and fruitful abstractions of the internationalization processes of firms.

Against this backdrop, this study questions the behavioral assumptions of the Uppsala Internationalization Process Model (U-Model). This particular theoretical approach is commonly considered to be the pivotal approach in internationalization process research, and therefore, it can be treated representatively for the research field altogether. A closer examination of the model yields the insight that it builds at least implicitly and partially on the assumption of rationally proceeding decision-makers. In this regard, it recognizes incomplete information availability, while cognitive dispositions and behavioral biases are not addressed. According to the U-Model, decision-makers are expected to possess the cognitive capacity to assess their actions purposefully and consistently under the restriction of limited information availability. Yet as mentioned above, this expectation contradicts behavioral research insights, which show that administrators act on no account on such a rational basis. Therefore, the behavioral assumptions of the U-Model can be doubted. In this context, this study aims at a demonstration of a display of escalation of commitment in internationalization process decision-making. Escalation of commitment presents a specific manifestation of the limited cognitive capabilities of decision-makers. Concerned administrators show the inclination to adhere to current decision paths despite ongoing negative results. As a consequence, they act beyond the grounds of reason and facts, and they tend to "throw good money after bad" (in an economic context at least). Thus, escalation of commitment represents a concrete example for the cognitive dispositions that constitute the form of bounded rationality that is somewhat neglected by the U-Model. A demonstration of a respective decision-making display in internationalization processes would indicate a major shortcoming of this pivotal theoretical approach in IP research.

In order to meet the research objective empirically, this study is built on a mixed-methods approach. As a quantitative-empirical research method, a randomized experiment is conducted under the laboratory circumstances of a simulated internationalization process. In comparison to other quantitative-empirical research methods, randomized experiments possess the distinct benefit of allowing reliable statements regarding the causality of effects since dependent and independent variables are commonly kept under control. Despite this advantage, experimental research presents a relatively novel approach in the sphere of international business. As a qualitative-empirical research method, the research topic is additionally addressed with a descriptive case study as an illustration of escalation of commitment in business reality. In this regard, the merger of Daimler-Benz and Chrysler as well as the attempted production offshoring to China by the German manufacturer of plush toys Margarete Steiff GmbH is discussed. At large, this study shows in a hypothesis-confirming manner that escalation of commitment can be a critical factor for the internationalization processes of firms. Thus, it becomes clear that the bounded rationality of decision-makers, particularly their limited cognitive capability, presents an issue that internationalization process research, including the U-Model, should give greater consideration to.

Stuttgart, Germany
August 2017

Björn Röber

Acknowledgements

Several people have contributed to the successful development of the present doctoral thesis. I would like to thank the following persons for their great support:

- First, I wish to express my particular gratitude to my doctoral supervisor and reviewer Prof. Dr. Michael-Jörg Oesterle for his challenging yet always constructive and supportive comments. His dedication to faultless academic workmanship has benefitted not only the present thesis but also myself a lot.
- I would like to thank the second reviewer, Prof. Dr. Birgit Renzl, for her critical evaluation of the present study. Furthermore, I wish to thank the chairman of the examination committee, Prof. Dr. Bernd Woeckener.
- The opportunity to publish my work in "MIR Series in International Business" is greatly appreciated, and I would like to thank the editors very much.
- I would like to thank my former and current colleagues at the University of Stuttgart. I am particularly grateful to Dr. Nikolai Kramer, who provided outstanding comments on the empirical section of the present study.
- I also wish to mention Mr. Ian Clover, who I would like to thank for the time and effort that he invested in order to proofread this study.
- Above all, I would like to express my deep gratitude to my family, especially my parents Annette and Manfred Röber. Without their relentless support for my personal as well as professional development over the past decades, this thesis would have not been possible, and I cannot thank them enough.

About This Book

This book reviews the role of bounded rationality in internationalization process (IP) research. More specifically, it questions the behavioral assumptions of the most influential internationalization process theory today, the Uppsala Model. Despite its behavioral roots, this pivotal approach builds at least implicitly and partially on the assumption of rationally proceeding decision-makers. Contrary to this assumption, the author aims at a demonstration of bounded rationality in the form of escalation of commitment in IPs, i.e., an inclination of internationalization managers to "throw good money after bad." The author builds his investigation on an empirical mixed-methods approach, put together from a randomized experiment as well as a descriptive case study. This book contributes to IP research as it shows that bounded rationality in the form of escalation of commitment can be a critical factor for the internationalization processes of firms. It is an indispensable read for specialists as well as students.

Contents

List of Abbreviations

ANOVA	Analysis of variance
DF	Degrees of freedom
DM	Deutsche Mark
EUT	Expected utility theory
FDI	Foreign direct investment
IB	International business
ILS	Israeli New Shekel
IP	Internationalization process
JDM	Judgment and decision-making
MNE	Multinational enterprise
PT	Prospect theory
ROI	Return on investment
SUV	Sport utility vehicle
U-Model	Uppsala internationalization process model

Chapter 1
Bounded Rationality and Internationalization Process Research: An Introduction

1.1 Distorted Judgment and Decision-Making Capabilities Due to Bounded Rationality

In the past as much as today, questions of judgment and decision-making (JDM) present a key issue in business and economics. Scholars have contributed to a large and ever-growing body of literature with the aim of supporting decision-makers prospectively in order to take rational actions or of explaining retrospectively previous decision paths.[1] For decades, orthodox economic approaches to JDM have prevailed in this field. These approaches share the characteristic that they are marked by a prescriptive nature and that they build on the neoclassical premises of the model of the *homo economicus*. As such, they expect decision-makers to act according to a consistent logic and along the lines of systematic and coherent considerations.

However, one cannot help but notice clear inconsistencies as well as violations of the axiomatic foundations of these traditional economic models in reality. As a matter of fact, empirical studies regularly show that decision-makers tend to systematically break the rules of rational economic behavior.[2] The reason for this discrepancy between the assumed and the factual behavior can be found in the bounded rationality of decision-makers. Bounded rationality refers to their distorted assessment of risks and opportunities. On the one hand, decision-makers often lack the necessary information in order to take fully justified and consistent decisions. On the other hand, they do not possess the necessary cognitive capabilities in order to process the available information properly. As a result, administrators in JDM processes expose various behavioral biases, which distort their judgment and decision-making capabilities and which hamper rational decisions from an orthodox economic point of view. Against the background of an increasing influence of

[1] Cf. Wolf (2013, pp. 125 ff.) and van der Pligt (1996, pp. 30 ff.).

[2] Cf. Kahneman (2003, pp. 1449 ff.).

B. Röber, *Escalation of Commitment in Internationalization Processes*, MIR Series in International Business, https://doi.org/10.1007/978-3-319-69102-2_1

peripheral research areas in business and economics (e.g., psychology and other social sciences), the bounded rationality of decision-makers has found its way into economic research programs since the 1950s and 1960s.[3] Especially under the roof of the 'Carnegie School', scholars began to consider the bounded rationality of decision-makers in JDM processes and turned away from traditional economic beliefs.[4]

From a scientific standpoint, the recognition of distorted JDM processes is decisive in order to arrive at realistic insights about managerial decision-making behaviors in business practice. This decisiveness is not restricted to any particular research area in the fields of business and economics. Since bounded rationality can affect practitioners in any functional position, every researcher addressing matters of managerial decision-making could be concerned by the subject of distorted JDM processes.

1.2 Questionable Recognition of Bounded Rationality in Internationalization Process Research

Despite the circumstance that distorted JDM processes may present an issue for various matters of business and economics, the consequences can be particularly grave in the context of internationalization process (IP) decision-making. For a start, one could say that IPs have judgement and decision-making at their essence as they consist of consecutive decisions regarding inter alia location choices as well as market entry modes.[5] Furthermore, one must also see that internationalization decisions present a critical subject in business and economics due to their substantial importance for the growth and long-term success of firms. Therefore, internationalization research should recognize the potential consequences of distorted JDM processes, and any scientific attempt of an abstraction of IPs should reflect the bounded rationality of decision-makers in order to be realistic. Hence, bounded rationality should not only be a relevant topic in general JDM literature, but it should be equally present in the IP-sphere of international business (IB).

There is room, however, to be skeptical concerning the amount of recognition that bounded rationality currently enjoys in IP-research. Actual managerial decision-making mechanisms, for example, are commonly not sufficiently included in many cases of IP-related research.[6] As a consequence, researchers' knowledge about strategic decision-making in IP-reality is limited and does not necessarily

[3]Cf. Kunz (2013, p. 206).

[4]Cf. Cyert and March (1963, pp. 114 ff.), March and Simon (1958, pp. 137 ff.), and Simon (1955, pp. 99 ff.).

[5]Cf. Buckley et al. (2007, p. 1069).

[6]Cf. Buckley et al. (2007, p. 1086).

include matters of bounded rationality.[7] Also, there is a deficit of scientific contributions—with only a few exceptions[8]—that turn to failed internationalization processes and consider bounded rationality as a cause of IP-failure. The questionable recognition of bounded rationality applies to IP-research in general and even includes its pivotal approach, the Uppsala Internationalization Process Model (U-Model). Respective theories tend to apply an understanding of decision-makers, which is marked by the assumption that they are rationally reflecting their decision alternatives.[9] Bounded rationality—and behavioral biases in particular—seem only to be insufficiently included. The questionable recognition of bounded rationality presents IP-researchers with a need for further research because the current understanding of decision-makers is possibly not realistic and, therefore, respective theories are not necessarily applicable in reality. Against this background, the present study aims at an exploration of bounded rationality in the context of internationalization processes.

For this purpose, the U-Model has been selected for further study. Among the different theoretical approaches to internationalization processes, it has been chosen because of its unmatched popularity among scholars and because of its high count of citations.[10] Partly, the U-Model owns its popularity to the claim of being a particularly realistic abstraction of internationalization processes. Indeed, it assumes that decision-makers are confronted with incomplete information. Furthermore, the U-Model postulates that they proceed as rationally as possible, i.e., step by step, in response to this limitation. It is only due to an initial internationalization investment that further iterations are carefully fostered. In this process, the target for decision-makers is to maintain a balance between perceived and tolerable market risks. In a nutshell, the U-Model acknowledges the importance of organizational learning and provides a processual perspective for the internationalization of firms.[11] Yet even the supposedly realistic and pivotal U-Model falls short of sufficiently explaining why internationalization processes sometimes take unforeseen paths. One could argue, for example, that so-called 'International New Ventures' or 'Born Globals' leapfrog over the different evolutionary steps of the U-Model.[12] More importantly for the context of the present study, however, are failing internationalization processes of firms. If the internationalization process according to the postulate of the U-Model was true, IP-failure would not be a reality. The obvious contradiction between theory and practice is possibly linked to

[7]Cf. Matthyssens and Pauwels (2000, pp. 697–698) and Papadakis et al. (1998, pp. 115–116).

[8]Cf. Oesterle (1999, pp. 225–229) and Benito and Welch (1997, pp. 7 ff.).

[9]For respective theories cf. for example Luostarinen (1979, pp. 173 ff.) and Vernon (1966, pp. 190 ff.).

[10]Hutzschenreuter et al. (2007, pp. 1055 ff.); as of 2017, a short search with Google Scholar revealed that a total of 11,246 publications cited Johanson's and Vahlne's initial study—many of which from the current year (cf. Sect. 3.1).

[11]Cf. Schmid (2002, pp. 389–390).

[12]Cf. Oviatt and McDougall (1994, pp. 45 ff.).

the questionable recognition of bounded rationality in this particular IP-theory. At first, this assumption seems surprising because of the U-Model's consideration of incomplete information mentioned above. However, bounded rationality is not only constituted by limited information availability, but also by a limited cognitive capability of decision-makers to process the given information. As it will be shown in Sect. 3.2 of the present study, this aspect, however, is not fully reflected in the U-Model and presents a point of concern because it means that the theory is possibly not as realistic as it is often said to be. This potential shortcoming calls for a critical review and for further research on the role of bounded rationality in the Uppsala Internationalization Process Model.

1.3 Escalation of Commitment as a Suitable Representative for Bounded Rationality in Internationalization Process Theory and Practice

In order to conduct a critical review of the matter of bounded rationality under particular attention to the limited cognitive capability of decision-makers in the U-Model, the present study will take a closer look at the issue of escalation of commitment. Escalation of commitment describes the cognitive disposition of decision-makers to allocate additional resources to an already initiated course of action despite ongoing negative results. Concerned decision-makers do not acknowledge the negative feedback from previous decision periods and tend to reinforce their "failing course of action"[13] by allocating further capital, time, and effort. Escalation of commitment therefore describes the inclination of decision-makers to adhere to current decision paths and to throw "good money after bad".[14] From an orthodox economic point of view this should not happen. A rational administrator would consider the involved information at each decision period respectively and come to a justifiable conclusion based on the prospects of the available alternatives and regardless of the previous decision path. Escalation of commitment, thus, presents one of the earlier mentioned behavioral biases that distort managerial judgment and decision-making capabilities due to the cognitive limitations of administrators. Therefore, it can be considered as a suitable representative for bounded rationality in this regard.

In the theoretical context of internationalization processes, Benito and Welch mentioned escalation of commitment relatively early as an inhibitor for the de-internationalization of firms.[15] Furthermore, it has also been identified as a relevant topic by Matthyssens and Pauwels.[16] The authors followed a comparative

---

[13]Brockner et al. (1986, p. 122).

[14]Brockner et al. (1986, p. 110).

[15]Cf. Benito and Welch (1997, pp. 14–17).

[16]Cf. Matthyssens and Pauwels (2000, pp. 697 ff.).

case study approach in order to discuss strategic flexibility as a response to escalation of commitment in international market exit dilemmas in a marketing-psychological related context. Most notably for the present study, Matthyssens and Pauwels raise attention to the subject of escalation of commitment as a possible cause for erroneous judgments in internationalization processes. As the authors identify a series of research limitations in their own work, they consider their article as a "first step in gaining insight into international market-exit decision making",[17] and call for further empirical research.

This topic, however, does not only present a merely academic and theoretical issue. In the past, IP-failure was frequently observable in business reality. In some instances, it is possible to associate the failure with typical decision-making patterns in situations of escalation of commitment. One might consider, for example, the North-American activity of the British retailer Marks & Spencer, which could overall be described as an "inglorious failure".[18] By 1972, the firm began to operate its first stores in Canada, and by 1988 it entered the USA. It expanded its activities henceforth despite a poor economic performance in both countries.[19] Regardless of the disappointing internationalization result, Marks & Spencer waited until 1999 (Canada) and 2006 (USA) until it withdrew from the North-American market. Likewise, the international experiences of Wal-Mart in South Korea and Germany can be seen as typical in this regard since the American retailer fell some way short of its initial targets.[20] Nevertheless, Wal-Mart clung to its internationalization strategy for a total of almost 10 years before it decided to sell its stores in 2006 in both countries. Furthermore—and without anticipating too much of the course of investigation of the present study—it is also worthwhile to note two exemplary cases that will be discussed as part of a cross case analysis in Sect. 4.3 of the present study: The reversed merger of Daimler-Benz and Chrysler as well as the attempted production offshoring of the German manufacturer of plush toys Margarete Steiff GmbH to China bear a certain resemblance to typical decision-making patterns in situations of escalation of commitment.

In this theoretical and practical context, the present study picks up the thread of escalation of commitment in internationalization processes in order to test the U-Model. An empirical demonstration of such a behavioral bias in IP decision-making would constitute a contradiction to the internationalization process as it is postulated by this theory because it would highlight that decision-makers do not necessarily proceed as rationally and carefully as foreseen.

[17]Matthyssens and Pauwels (2000, p. 702).

[18]Burt et al. (2002, p. 192); see also Mellahi (2003, pp. 150 ff.).

[19]Burt et al. (2002, p. 204).

[20]Cf. Gandolfi and Strach (2009, pp. 187 ff.) and Christopherson (2007, pp. 451 ff.).

1.4 Point of Departure, Research Objective, and Structure of the Present Study

The argumentative point of departure of the present study lies in the questionable recognition of bounded rationality in internationalization process research. Principally, respective theories have gained complexity in the past and have come closer to the target of satisfactorily describing and explaining the internationalization process of firms. All the same, one must notice that motives of bounded rationality are insufficiently considered as drivers for the internationalization of firms. This concern refers primarily to the limited cognitive capability of administrators. Within internationalization process literature, judgment and decision-making seems to be predominantly considered as the result of rational reflections. This could mean, for example, that decision-makers supposedly focus consistently on economic benefits when it comes to the pursuit of international activities.[21] The concern applies equally to the U-Model, which can be regarded as the state-of-the-art model among internationalization process theories considering its continued prominence in IB research.[22] It postulates that decision-makers possess the cognitive capability to maintain a balance between perceived and tolerable market risks.[23] Therefore, it considers them, at least implicitly, to be rationally proceeding actors. Yet, this assumption contradicts business reality, in which IP-failure presents a frequent factual reality. It also conflicts with behavioral research streams according to which decision-makers act on no account persistently along the lines of rational reflections. This contradiction between theory and practice indicates the already outlined need for further research.

Against this background, it is the overall objective of the present study to contribute to international business literature with an exploration of bounded rationality in the context of internationalization processes. For this purpose, the discipline's pivotal U-Model is subjected to a critical review in the following. The review challenges the theory's implicit assumption of rationally proceeding decision-makers. In this regard, the present study aims at a demonstration of a display of escalation of commitment in IP decision-making. Such a display would constitute a contradiction to the U-Model's postulate of decision-makers, who possess the cognitive capability to balance perceived and tolerable market risks. In this research setup, escalation of commitment presents a representative for the limited cognitive capabilities of decision-makers under bounded rationality. In consideration of the argumentative line outlined here, the research problem of the present study can be summarized by the following question: Is there substantial evidence for the display of bounded rationality in the form of escalation of commitment in IP decision-making?

---

[21] Cf. Oesterle et al. (2016, p. 1115) and Schotter and Beamish (2013, p. 538).

[22] Cf. Welch et al. (2016, pp. 783–784), Hadjikhani et al. (2014, pp. 155–157), Meyer and Thaijongrak (2013, pp. 1126–1129), and Hutzschenreuter et al. (2007, pp. 1055–1056).

[23] Cf. Sect. 3.2 for an in-depth presentation of the U-Model.

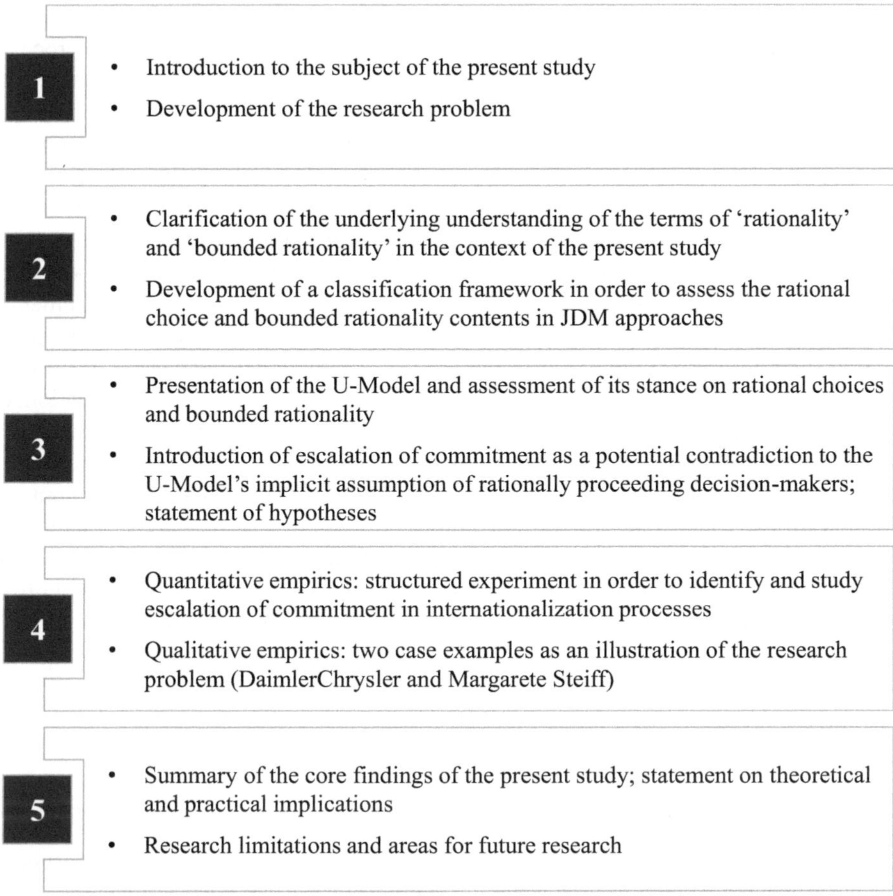

Fig. 1.1 Structure of the present study. Source: Own figure

In order to meet the research objective, the present study covers the analysis of the research problem in five chapters (cf. Fig. 1.1). After this introduction to the subject of the study, the second chapter deals with the criterion of rationality for the evaluation of judgment and decision-making approaches. For this purpose, Sect. 2.1 clarifies the underlying understanding of the terms of 'rationality' and 'bounded rationality' for the context of the present study. Thereafter, Sect. 2.2 introduces a classification framework in order to assess rational choice and bounded rationality contents in JDM approaches. The third chapter, which deals with the key issue of the present study, begins with the presentation of a broad overview of internationalization research in Sect. 3.1. Hereafter, the previously developed framework serves as a basis for an assessment of the U-Model's attention to bounded rationality (in Sect. 3.2). The aim of this section is to clarify whether or not the U-Model is actually as realistic as supposed, to discuss its stance with regard to bounded rationality contents, and to highlight its implicit assumption of rationally proceeding decision-makers. In this context, Sect. 3.3 discusses escalation of commitment as a potential contradiction to the postulated decision-making process according to the U-Model. Ultimately, this section concludes with a statement of hypotheses. The empirical investigation of the research problem is the subject of the fourth chapter. As it is outlined in Sect. 4.1, a mixed-methods research approach has been selected in this regard. This approach is based on two pillars. Section 4.2 consists of a randomized experiment, which has been conducted in order to identify and study escalation of commitment in IP decision-making under laboratory circumstances. Experiments in social sciences own the distinct advantage of keeping dependent and independent variables under control and allow reliable statements regarding the causality of effects. Despite these benefits, this research method must be considered a novel approach in the field of international business.[24] With this quantitative-empirical basis, Sect. 4.3 presents two cases (the already mentioned merger of Daimler-Benz and Chrysler as well as the attempted production offshoring to China by Margarete Steiff GmbH) as illustrations of the research subject in business reality. Case study research allows the consideration of context observations, which can add further empirical evidence to the study. Chapter 5 concludes the present study with a summary of the key findings and theoretical implications, an outline of implications for business practice, as well as with a statement of research limitations and potential areas for further research.

References

Benito, G. R. G., & Welch, L. S. (1997). De-internationalization. *Management International Review, 37*(S2), 7–25.

Brockner, J., Houser, R., Birnbaum, G., Lloyd, K., Deitcher, J., Nathanson, S., et al. (1986). Escalation of commitment to an ineffective course of action: The effect of feedback having negative implications for self-identity. *Administrative Science Quarterly, 31*(1), 109–126.

Buckley, P. J., Devinney, T. M., & Louviere, J. J. (2007). Do managers behave the way theory suggests? A choice-theoretic examination of foreign direct investment location decision-making. *Journal of International Business Studies, 38*(7), 1069–1094.

Burt, S. L., et al. (2002). Retail internationalization and retail failure: Issues from the case of Marks and Spencer. *The International Review of Retail, Distribution and Consumer Research, 12*(2), 191–219.

Christopherson, S. (2007). Barriers to 'US style' lean retailing: The case of Wal-Mart's failure in Germany. *Journal of Economic Geography, 7*(4), 451–469.

Cyert, R. M., & March, J. G. (1963). *A behavioral theory of the firm*. Prentice-Hall: Englewood Cliffs.

Gandolfi, F., & Strach, P. (2009). Retail internationalization: Gaining insights from the Wal-Mart experience in South Korea. *Review of International Comparative Management, 10*(1), 187–199.

[24]Cf. Zellmer-Bruhn et al. (2016, pp. 399 ff.) and Buckley et al. (2007, p. 1069).

Hadjikhani, A., Hadjikhani, A. I., & Thilenius, P. (2014). The internationalization process model: A proposed view of firms' regular incremental and irregular non-incremetal behaviour. *International Business Review, 23*(1), 155–168.

Hutzschenreuter, T., Pedersen, T., & Volberda, H. W. (2007). The role of path dependency and managerial intentionality: A perspective on international business research. *Journal of International Business Studies, 38*(7), 1055–1068.

Kahneman, D. (2003). Maps of bounded rationality: Psychology for behavioral economics. *The American Economic Review, 93*(5), 1449–1475.

Kunz, J. (2013). Die psychologische und ökonomische Perspektive in der BWL: Eine Diskussion am Beispiel der Literatur zum Escalation of Commitment. *Die Betriebswirtschaft, 73*(3), 205–219.

Luostarinen, R. (1979). *Internationalization of the firm: An empirical study of the internationalization of firms with small and open domestic markets with special emphasis on lateral rigidity as a behavioral characteristics in strategic decision-making*. Helsinki: Helsinki School of Economics.

March, J. G., & Simon, H. A. (1958). *Organizations*. New York: Wiley.

Matthyssens, P., & Pauwels, P. (2000). Uncovering international market-exit processes: A comparative case study. *Psychology and Marketing, 17*(8), 697–719.

Mellahi, K. (2003). The de-internationalization process: A case study of Marks and Spencer. In C. Wheeler, F. McDonald, & I. Greaves (Eds.), *Internationalization – Firm strategies and management* (pp. 150–162). Basingstoke: Palgrave.

Meyer, K. E., & Thaijongrak, O. (2013). The dynamics of emerging economy MNEs: How the internationalization process model can guide future research. *Asia Pacific Journal of Management, 30*(4), 1125–1153.

Oesterle, M.-J. (1999). Fiktionen der Internationalisierungsforschung. In J. Engelhard & W. A. Oechsler (Eds.), *Internationales Management* (pp. 219–245). Wiesbaden: Gabler.

Oesterle, M.-J., Elosge, C., & Elosge, L. (2016). Me, myself and I: The role of CEO narcissism in internationalization decisions. *International Business Review, 25*(5), 1114–1123.

Oviatt, B. M., & McDougall, P. P. (1994). Toward a theory of international new ventures. *Journal of International Business Studies, 25*(1), 45–64.

Papadakis, V. M., Lioukas, S., & Chambers, D. (1998). Strategic decision-making processes: The role of management and context. *Strategic Management Journal, 19*(2), 115–147.

Schmid, S. (2002). Die Internationalisierung von Unternehmungen aus der Perspektive der Uppsala-Schule. *WiSt-Wirtschaftswissenschaftliches Studium, 31*(7), 387–392.

Schotter, A., & Beamish, P. W. (2013). The hassle factor: An explanation for managerial location shunning. *Journal of International Business Studies, 44*(5), 521–544.

Simon, H. A. (1955). A behavioral model of rational choice. *The Quarterly Journal of Economics, 69*(1), 99–118.

Van der Pligt, J. (1996). Judgement and decision making. In G. R. Semin & K. Fiedler (Eds.), *Applied social psychology* (pp. 173–197). London: Sage.

Vernon, R. (1966). International investment and international trade in the product cycle. *The Quarterly Journal of Economics, 80*(2), 190–207.

Welch, C., Nummela, N., & Liesch, P. (2016). The internationalization process model revisited: An agenda for future research. *Management International Review, 56*(6), 783–804.

Wolf, J. (2013). *Organisation, Management, Unternehmensführung: Theorien, Praxisbeispiele und Kritik* (5th ed.). Wiesbaden: Gabler.

Zellmer-Bruhn, M., Caligiuri, P., & Thomas, D. C. (2016). Experimental designs in international business research. *Journal of International Business Studies, 47*(4), 399–407.

Chapter 2
Rationality as the Basic Criterion for the Evaluation of Judgment and Decision-Making Processes

Prior to an exploration of bounded rationality in internationalization processes of companies, it is necessary to take a closer look at the general matter of rationality in judgment and decision-making processes. This is because internationalization processes are shaped by a series of consecutive decisions based on the individual and organizational expectations of decision-makers. These judgment and decision-making processes should be based on rational grounds, or in other words, on an appropriate analysis of alternatives as well as on information processing.[1] Rationality is the basic criterion for the evaluation of the plausibility of processual decisions. Yet, as already pointed out in the introduction of this dissertation, the actions of decision-makers and their expectations are not necessarily based on objective, fully justifiable grounds: Not only are managers working in difficult environments (particularly in the context of international business), in which they are confronted with imperfect situational contexts, e.g., lack of information, but they are also subjected to cognitive dispositions that trigger boundedly rational and even so-called irrational behavior. But in addition to potential limits of rationality there is furthermore the fundamental question of what rationality actually is. What defines 'objective and fully justifiable' grounds? In different contexts, the term of rationality is used by philosophers, theologians, mathematicians, sociologists, and economists.[2] A clarification of this dissertation's underlying understanding of rationality is therefore inevitable for a thorough analysis of bounded rationality in the context of internationalization processes. This clarification will be conducted in Sect. 2.1.

Over the past decades, economists have contributed to a large base of literature on judgment and decision-making theory. These theories have in common that they

[1]Cf. Bronner (2004, col. 229).

[2]Cf. Valcárcel (2004, col. 1238); see also Nida-Rümelin (1992, p. 131), for an interesting discussion about the understanding of rationality in philosophy (by tendency theoretical-Kantian and principled) as well as in economics (by tendency practical and consequential).

B. Röber, *Escalation of Commitment in Internationalization Processes*, MIR Series in International Business, https://doi.org/10.1007/978-3-319-69102-2_2

deal with decision-makers who are confronted with a set of alternatives in specific situations. As it will be shown in Sect. 2.2.1, however, they differ with regard to the underlying premises of human behavior and rationality. Some JDM theories consider decision-makers' actions to be the result of rational and economic choices. Often, they reveal a prescriptive perspective and imply neoclassical behavioral assumptions. This means that decision-makers are allegedly prospectively supported by corresponding theories and that they are factually able to draw rational conclusions. Alternatively, other JDM theories acknowledge the bounded rationality of decision-makers. These approaches tend to explain decision paths in a descriptive manner and apply rather behavior-oriented, i.e., more realistic, behavioral assumptions. In other words, decision paths are retrospectively explained and the complexity of decision-making processes in reality is recognized. Hence, decision-making theories can principally be distinguished in two dimensions: their prescriptive, or respectively, their descriptive nature; and their underlying behavioral assumptions (between neoclassical and behavior-oriented).[3] Section 2.2 will illustrate that decision-making theories can be located within a two-dimensional classification framework in this regard. However, this is not only limited to traditional decision-making theories. The highly popular and much cited U-Model could equally be located within this framework.[4] Since this dissertation presents inter alia a critical review of the U-Model, the framework development (in Sect. 2.2) constitutes an important basis for this study in order to assess the actual standpoint on bounded rationality of this central IP-theory.

2.1 Underlying Understanding of Rationality, Bounded Rationality, and Irrationality of the Present Study

Claiming to act rationally can be a decisive argumentative advantage over opponents in the dynamic decision-making process of organizations. The accusation of irrational behavior, on the other hand, equals an argumentative disqualification from the discourse. This is ever more the case in the context of complex decisions, which are marked by a high degree of uncertainty such as internationalization decisions. Labeling actions as rational, boundedly rational, or even irrational is therefore a powerful political instrument in organizations.[5] However, it is the apparent problem that different decision-makers draw different conclusions in similar situations while nobody would ever consider his/her own actions to be irrational. Administrators in decision-making processes—and quite specifically also in internationalization processes—tend to have distinct ideas of rational

[3]Cf. Laux et al. (2014, pp. 16–19), Wolf (2013, pp. 125 ff.), Walliser (2008, pp. 49 ff.), and Luce and von Winterfeldt (1994, p. 264).

[4]Cf. Johanson and Vahlne (1977, pp. 23 ff.).

[5]Cf. Scholl (1992, col. 2000), Berger (1992, p. 128), and Pfeffer (1981, p. 21).

behavior. Therefore, the question that needs to be asked is: What defines rationality?

In order to answer this question, academic publications—and those in social sciences in particular—distinguish different premises of rationality. On the one hand, rationality could be constituted by justified and economic choices. This perspective has long been predominant in business and economics and refers to rationality as to what it should be. On the other hand, the bounded rationality program refers to rationality as to what it actually is in reality. As such it acknowledges that cognitive resources of humans are limited and that managerial actions are on no account always based on perfect information.[6] In the following, essential theoretical foundations of rationality (Sect. 2.1.1) as well as of bounded rationality (Sect. 2.1.2) will be outlined and distinguished from irrationality (Sect. 2.1.3).

2.1.1 Theoretical Foundations of Rationality: What Constitutes Rationality in Business and Economics?

As mentioned above, researchers of various scientific disciplines dedicate themselves to the concept and to questions of rationality. Acting rationally applies commonly to sane and thoughtful decisions, which are the result of past, present and future information.[7] Furthermore, they are the consequence of the actor's critical thinking and common sense.[8] From a philosopher's perspective, rationality is relative and stands for actions, which optimize the degree of fulfillment of one's objectives based on given information.[9]

In social sciences, including economics, the understanding of rationality is largely shaped by the works of famous sociologist Max Weber and his typology of rational actions as well as by his concept of 'purpose-rational' behavior. He described social interaction to be defined by either 'traditional', 'affectual' (meaning emotional actions), 'value-rational' ("*wertrational*") or 'purpose-rational' ("*zweckrational*") motives. This is because decisions—and in a broader sense social actions in general—are exposed to the situational background of decision-makers. According to Weber, a decision-maker acts *zweckrational* if he/she evaluates the purpose, the means, and side effects of his/her actions and if he/she weighs rationally between purposes and means as well as between means and side effects. He/she weighs rationally if he/she acts neither traditionally nor affectually. However, there is the possibility of competing purposes and consequences. Purposes are competing if they are in conflict, i.e., that the completion of one excludes the

[6]Cf. Brühl (2015, pp. 58–60) and Simon (2000, pp. 25 ff.).

[7]Cf. Mallard (2012, p. 675).

[8]Cf. Boudon (2007, p. 26), for a broad—rather philosophical—discussion of a general theory of rationality and an understanding of 'common sense'.

[9]Cf. Hempel (1961–1962, p. 5).

completion of the other as a consequence. As an example of competing purposes in the energy sector, one could consider the economic production of energy on the one hand and environmental protection on the other. For the purpose of economic energy production, coal-fired power plants can be operated. Unfortunately, this is accompanied by the undesired consequence of pollution. In such case, a value-rational decision is guided by commands and requirements; or in other words, by ethically and morally desired standards. A purpose-rational decision, in contrast, is guided by the individual order of needs of the decision-maker. Ideally, the most necessary needs are satisfied first: either energy production or environmental protection. Weber refers to the "principle of marginal utility".[10] While traditional and affectual decisions are often beyond the understanding of rational behavior in social sciences, purpose-rational actions and the principle of marginal utility stand for the opposite. Latter are more comprehensible and verifiable for third persons due to more transparent and less subjective decision criteria. A 'bystander' of a purpose-rational decision-making process does not have to see eye to eye with the decision-maker on his/her order of needs, yet he/she can still follow the line of reasoning that led to action (much more than in the case of somewhat subjectively shaped traditional and affectual decisions).

2.1.1.1 Rationality According to Rational Choice Theory

Weber's analysis of marginal utility as well as the concept of purpose-rationality can conclusively be transferred into an economic understanding of rationality. Such an economic understanding is largely in conformity with a utilitarian understanding of social actions. However, utilitarian philosophers such as Jeremy Bentham and John Stuart Mill never established a specific set of 'rules of rationality'. According to them, people should maximize their utility, with positive utility understood as pleasure and negative utility as pain.[11] Both Weber's ideas, as well as the utilitarian perspective on human behavior, can be found in the Rational Choice Theory, which is the fundamental idea behind the traditional understanding of rationality in economics, and which still serves as a theoretical basis for subsequent decision-making models today.

The rational choice approach addresses primarily the pattern of judgment and decision-making processes rather than the specific actions of decision-makers themselves.[12] According to the theory, actors weigh out costs and benefits of any action before a final decision is taken.[13] Value-rational factors, however, play just a minor role in the framework. A decision-maker aligns his/her actions exclusively according to his/her individual utility. The 1992 Nobel Memorial Prize laureate in

[10]Weber (1972, p. 13).

[11]Cf. Read (2007, p. 46).

[12]Cf. Schumpeter (1984, p. 580).

[13]Cf. Scott (1999, p.126).

economics, Gary S. Becker, who is one of the most prominent authors of the Rational Choice Theory, argued that "individuals maximize welfare as they conceive it, whether they be selfish, altruistic, loyal, spiteful, or masochistic".[14] Therefore, a maximization of welfare must not be equated with selfish behavior. Rational Choice Theory does not come up with a universal prioritization of utilities and purposes. The approach is entirely about consistent patterns of actions in judgment and decision-making processes: A consistency between one's purpose and one's action is the most important and basic criterion for the evaluation of rational behavior. In other words, decisions must be logically deduced from the objectives of a decision-maker on a well-founded basis.[15] In order to do so, an actor must have clear preferences, which he/she can order (by preferring one alternative to another or by being indifferent) and which need to be transitive.[16] Yet, this does not mean that Rational Choice Theory implies generic answers. If a logical basis is given, individual actions possess an individual rationality due to individual purposes.[17] Therefore, the English rationalist philosopher Martin Hollis summarized that "rational action is its own explanation",[18] meaning that rationality is always the result of rational choices.

In consideration of all above, one can say that Rational Choice Theory has a certain normative function, which allows recommendations on how decision-makers should behave ideally. Such a normative function can also be found in the earlier established idea of the *homo economicus* or the 'economic man', which is one of the potentially most controversially discussed concepts in economics.

2.1.1.2 *Homo Economicus*: The Concept of Rational Economic Behavior

The *homo economicus* is a popular model, which is applied in classic and neoclassic economic theory and which is widely discussed in scientific literature as well as outside academic circles. It has a distinct explanatory character for human behavior under economic conditions. Despite the fact that John Stuart Mill is credited for bringing up the term of the economic man,[19] the cornerstone was already set in 1776 by Adam Smith, who famously identified that the best economic benefit for everybody is indeed achieved if every decision-maker acts in his/her own interest.[20] In order to avoid a common misunderstanding, it should be clarified that—analogous to the concept of the maximization of welfare in Rational Choice

[14]Becker (1993, p. 386) and see also Becker (1976, pp. 282 ff.).

[15]Cf. Sugden (1991, p. 751).

[16]Cf. Sect. 2.2.1.2 of the present study for a more detailed overview of these assumptions.

[17]Cf. Sect. 2.1.1.3 for more information on varieties of rationality.

[18]Hollis (1977, p. 21).

[19]Cf. Persky (1995, p. 222).

[20]Cf. Smith (1966, pp. 12–14).

Theory—'self-interest seeking' is not per se synonymous with 'selfish behavior'.[21] An altruistic decision-maker, for example, could also act out of self-interest (through making others' objectives his/her own). In economic sciences, the economic man has become a simplistic model of an actor upon whom new economic theories have been built. The axiom of self-interest seeking plays a pivotal role in the economic discourse with regard to the analysis of social interaction under economic conditions because of its fundamental importance to subsequent theories.[22]

Yet, the interpretation of self-interest seeking as rational behavior was exposed to a certain change over the past.[23] Neither in the time of Adam Smith (1723–1790) nor in the time of John Stuart Mill (1806–1873) was there an exact understanding of the meaning of rationality. To them, it had the "limited meaning of preferring more to less".[24] While questions of reason and reasoning were addressed by philosophers, Weber's concept of purpose-rationality was still unknown. Mill regarded an economic man as somebody who is driven by the desire to possess wealth and who is capable of a comparison between means in order to achieve his goals.[25] Despite the fact that—according to Mill—the notion of wealth is not limited to a monetary and material meaning, profit maximization became henceforth the predominant interpretation of self-interest seeking among economists. It was not until the middle of the twentieth century that theorists began to replace the predominant belief of classical economists about profit maximization as the main driver of social actions with new differentiating concepts, which highlighted the relevance of individual preferences of actors.[26] The introduction of individual preferences to the discourse of rational decision-making was an important step in the development towards today's understanding of the *homo economicus* because he is—unlike commonly believed—not only a man of profit maximization but rather a man of utility maximization, who acts in accordance with his incentives.[27] Nevertheless, still today self-interest is frequently mistaken as quasi equal to (selfish) profit maximization.

Assuming that profit maximization is without a link to self-interest seeking and rational economic behavior would be an equally wrong conclusion. Certainly, there could be a link between the two sides as long as profit maximization is a priority within the individual set of preferences of a decision-maker. In such case, however, the maximization of profits would only constitute a secondary objective because it is a derivative of a maximization of utility. As stated by Rational Choice Theory, the economic man acts consistently according to his preferences—even if these are

---

[21]Cf. Machlup (1978, p. 284) as well as Sect. 2.1.1.3 of the present study for more information on common misunderstandings about the economic man.

[22]Cf. Kremser (2013, p. 219) and Vriend (1996, p. 263).

[23]Cf. Zouboulakis (2014, pp. 3 ff.).

[24]Arrow (1986, p. S388).

[25]Cf. Ng and Tseng (2008, p. 267) and Persky (1995, p. 223).

[26]Cf. von Mises (1949, p. 241) and Robbins (1932, p. 18).

[27]Cf. Vriend (1996, p. 270).

different from the preferences of most people.[28] Hence, there is no universally valid assumption regarding a possible link between profit maximization and rational economic behavior. Ultimately, it comes down to the individual set of preferences of each individual.

In accordance with all of the above, some important characteristics of the *homo economicus* can be specified. Of course, these characteristics are not necessarily identical with the features of actual decision-makers. While this causes frequent criticism against the concept,[29] its supporters argue that the *homo economicus* is just a model and that—like all models—it is an abstraction. Above all, we can take the following characteristics into account:[30]

- Maximizing (optimizing) behavior: The *homo economicus* attempts to maximize the degree of achievement of his/her objectives under the restrictive condition of limited resources. In other words, he/she searches for the most useful or least expensive option according to present opportunities and his/her preferences.
- Individualistic behavior and independent tastes and preferences: The *homo economicus* acts according to his/her individual order of preferences.[31] The model is therefore limited to the individual rationality of a decision-maker, which means that it is essentially only himself/herself who determines the rationality of his/her actions. This could lead to the situation that a certain decision seems entirely irrational in one system of preferences while it is completely rational in another.
- Cognitive ability to exercise rational choices: Exercising rational choices—as postulated by Rational Choice Theory—is the third important characteristic of the *homo economicus*. As already mentioned above, he/she does not only follow his objectives in a maximizing manner, but his/her objectives are also in consistency with his/her preferences.[32]

In summary, it can be noted that the *homo economicus* is an actor who is aware of his/her individual preferences, which he/she tries to fulfill in a maximizing and consistent manner. It is largely for these reasons that the economic man serves commonly as the illustration of the economic principle.[33] However, this definition is not free of potential conflicts—particularly with neighboring scientific disciplines.

[28]Cf. Kirchgässner (2008, p. 15).

[29]Cf. Sect. 2.1.2 for an alternative understanding of rationality (as in bounded rationality).

[30]Cf. Doucouliagos (1994, p. 877).

[31]Cf. Zintl (1989, p. 53).

[32]Cf. Gäfgen (1974, p. 27).

[33]Cf. Tietzel (1981, p. 119).

2.1.1.3 Is the Economic Man Misunderstood? A Glance Over the Fence of Disciplines

Besides the considerations on the theoretical foundations of the *homo economicus* outlined above, much has been written about different models of man across academic research programs. These models are particularly relevant in social sciences and serve as a basis for the explanation of human behavior. With the economic man, the above section has only presented the possibly most prominent and most controversial example. Not only for the sake of completeness, but rather as a source of fruitful input, some of the non-economic alternatives deserve a closer examination. Throughout scholarly disciplines, the doubtful empirical validity of the *homo economicus* is frequently criticized.[34] This criticism can be summarized by the following question: Does the *homo economicus* offer a realistic description of human decision-making or is it purely a result of man-made fiction? Supposedly, the model is too simplistic and presents no workable basis for social studies. Corresponding critics make reference to publications that contradict the premises of the economic model and which state that humans are not necessarily self-interested and that they are not as rational in reality as economists have thought them to be.[35]

As alternatives, sociologists have introduced the *homo sociologicus* and political scientists have presented the *homo politicus* in an effort to overcome these aforementioned shortcomings. In principle, the model of the sociological man is guided by the assumption that humans act according to their role in society. In other words, against the background of societal expectations as well as sanctions and rewards, humans behave differently depending on their social positions.[36] Political scientists, on the other hand, build on Aristotle and the concept of the political man. The political man acts according to ethical principles and tries to decide what is best for society.[37] While these concepts certainly have their *raison d'être* by providing more accuracy under certain circumstances, they provide a narrow understanding of the maximization of utility principle. As outlined in Sect. 2.1.1.2, motivations and preferences of humans are multifaceted. This raises doubt about the differentiability of the different ideas of man in social sciences. If the individual set of preferences of a decision-maker is defined by societal roles or by the outcome for everybody in society, the actor could very well decide economically in order to maximize his/her utility. Thus, it could be possible that *homo sociologicus* or *homo politicus* on the one side, and *homo economicus* on the other, are quite similar. In brief, economist Fritz Machlup concluded that the history of the *homo economicus* is also a "history of misunderstandings".[38]

---

[34]Cf. Kerscher (2013, p. 15).

[35]Cf. Machlup (1978, pp. 269–273).

[36]Cf. Dahrendorf (2006, pp. 105–106).

[37]Cf. Faber et al. (2002, p. 328) and Nyborg (2000, p. 310).

[38]Machlup (1978, p. 267).

However, this does not mean that one should waive the criticism against the economic man entirely. The argument of a doubtful empirical validity remains.[39] Additionally, conflicts of interests in business reality seem to be preprogrammed as soon as individual sets of preferences clash while they are supposed to coincide. For example, what happens if the individual preferences of a decision-maker collide with the externally given targets that he/she is required to meet? With regard to the research problem of the present study, one could easily imagine a conflict in which managers prefer to adhere to a failing internationalization process (for their individual preferences)[40] while the side of the company owners prefers to withdraw from the project.

2.1.1.4 Conflicting Motives of Owners and Managers as Primary Stakeholders of the Firm: Whose Rationality Are We Discussing?

In order to address the issue of conflicting preferences in firms, one has to keep in mind that different perceptions of welfare also come along with different ideas of rational choices. While a selfish person might behave entirely differently compared to an altruistic person, both can act rationally according to their own perceptions of welfare. Likewise, there are underlying differences of rationality in companies. Management literature has long been dedicated to questions around conflicting stakeholder interests as a result of agency problems and/or opportunism.[41] Fundamental differences arise, for example, when shareholders and other stakeholders have differing ideas about social responsibilities and firm performance. Obviously, this builds on the assumption that shareholders—unlike employees and other actors of the community[42]—have a strong priority on returns.[43] Essentially, any employee might be pursuing objectives that are different from the ones given to him/her by his/her employer in order to maximize his/her own utility (e.g., safeguarding of competences, budgets, etc.). Senior managers, however, represent possibly the group that is most likely to be inclined to act contrary to the objectives of shareholders—due to their influence on corporate results.[44] This argument is largely based on the behavioral theory of the firm, which considers companies to be political coalitions in which stakeholders pursue different interests.[45] In family

[39]Cf. Sect. 2.1.2.

[40]Cf. the following section for information on individual internationalization benefits for managers.

[41]Cf. Jensen and Meckling (1976) for fundamental literature on agency theory.

[42]Cf. Freeman et al. (2004, pp. 364 ff.), Berman et al. (1999, p. 491), Harrison and Freeman (1999, pp. 479 ff.), and Hambrick (1983, p. 690).

[43]Freeman (1984, p. 9), argues that owners also seek management control besides returns. Hence, shareholders have a strong but not exclusive priority on returns.

[44]Wright and Ferris (1997, pp. 77 ff.).

[45]Cf. Cyert and March (1963, p. 31) and March (1962, pp. 662 ff.).

businesses, for example, conflicting interests between the management and the owners of the firm arise regularly. Corresponding issues surface particularly in situations that are marked by a need to accomplish the goals of the owners despite a questionable benefit for the rest of the firm (e.g., non-economic provision of jobs for clan members).[46] Such a dilemma highlights that it is possible to distinguish between a fundamental rationality of entire organizations and an individual rationality that is shaped by specific stakeholder interests.[47] Therefore, rationality is not unidimensional.[48]

Due to the fact that the present study attempts to explore bounded rationality in internationalization processes, it has to be clarified whose rationality will be discussed: the individual rationality of decision-makers or the underlying rationality for the company as an entire organization. The former is usually referred to as 'formal' or 'procedural' rationality.[49] Every actor seeks to maximize the perceived utility outcome of his/her actions according to his/her individual set of preferences. Conforming rational decision-making processes go hand in hand with the characteristics of the *homo economicus*. As long as somebody's actions are procedurally consistent and in accordance with his/her preferences, he/she chooses formally rationally. Thus, the decision-making process has to be[50]:

1. Purposeful
2. Based on objective and complete information
3. Systematic and consistent (and therefore verifiable for third persons)

Obviously, the concept of formal rationality bears the risk that virtually any action could be advocated as rational—as long as the above-mentioned criteria are met. For example, if an investment banker attempts to lose as much money as quickly as possible, he/she could always buy downgraded government bonds, which have already been defaulting. Probably, such action does not seem to be rational in the eyes of the reader, but within the set of preferences of this very particular banker, it is. The apparent problem is that an objective rationality is very hard to assess, as it has been prominently analyzed by the influential late twentieth century American philosopher Donald Davidson in "Problems of Rationality".[51] Building on the earlier mentioned concept of purpose-rationality of Max Weber, one could say that 'competing purposes' are equally valid—as long as they are formally and procedurally rational, meaning that they are based on a decision-making process

---

[46]Cf. Fernández and Nieto (2006, p. 343), Chrisman et al. (2004, p. 338), Schulze et al. (2002, p. 249), and Tagiuri and Davis (1996, p. 202).

[47]Rational actions from a company perspective, for example, should yield in long term economic success with the highest possible benefit for all stakeholders.

[48]Cf. Bartlett (1986, p. 221) and von Mises (1933, p. 32).

[49]Cf. Brühl (2015, pp. 58–59), Simon (1986, p. S211), Pfohl and Braun (1981, pp. 128–131), and Gäfgen (1974, p. 26).

[50]Cf. Grünig and Kühn (2013, p. 38).

[51]Davidson (2004, pp. 39 ff.).

that respects the subjective values and order of interests of the respective decision-makers.[52]

Despite the authors, who follow the supposition that there is not a single form of rationality, it is a common request to call upon people 'to act rationally'. This is because in many cases there seems to be a fundamental, implicit agreement about the rationality of objectives: An investment banker tries to invest his/her money as well as possible, meaning to secure a return as high as possible and to defer to as little risk as possible. Fundamental agreements, such as in the given example, caused other authors to consider another dimension of rationality; one which refers to the 'substantive' or 'objective rationality' of decisions.[53] Under a given utility function, it implies that the objectives of decision-makers themselves need to be appropriate, not just the decision-making process. Hence, substantive or objective rationality does not only evaluate the decision-making process itself but the process outcome as well.[54] According to this view, different ideas of rationality are not necessarily an issue because there is a unifying consent about the question of what rational action actually is. In terms of the behavioral theory of the firm, one could argue that there must be a *minimum consensus* between the different political coalitions in companies. Under the idea of substantive or objective rationality, owners and managers are expected to pull together in an attempt to overcome conflicting decision-motives. Business practice and theory have paid tribute to this understanding of rationality in the past. Against the background of the above mentioned agency problems, firms tend to implement target agreements for their managers in order to align goals. In addition, financial incentives such as 'pay for performance' help to secure congruence between managers' objectives and the objectives of the firm. In business theory, the Stewardship approach proposed a model of managers, in which they act in the best interest of the organization because of an assumed positive relationship between the success of the organization and managers' satisfaction.[55] These examples showcase the pertinence of the idea of a unifying consent about rationality between share- and stakeholders that is characteristic for the substantive or objective rationality perspective.

Yet for the context of internationalization processes, it could easily be supposed that senior managers pursue international expansion strategies for different goals than those of owners and other stakeholders. This is explained by the circumstance that they often own at best a smaller fraction of a company's shares, which serves as an incentive to benefit from corporate resources in addition to their salary.[56] In order to maximize their own welfare, senior managers could, for example, attempt

---

[52]Cf. Grüning and Kühn (2013, p. 37).

[53]Cf. ibid.; Dimitratos et al. (2011, p. 195), Simon (1986, p. S211), and Pfohl and Braun (1981, pp. 128–131).

[54]Yet this differs slightly from Max Weber's understanding of value-rational decisions, which are much more the consequence of social intentions.

[55]Cf. Davis et al. (1997, p. 25).

[56]Cf. Oesterle et al. (2013, p. 190).

to benefit from perquisites such as corporate airliners and corporate 'empires' as results of the international growth of their employer.[57] As long as these perquisites are a priority within their individual sets of preferences, the pursuit of an internationalization strategy would be (formally) rational from the managers' point of view even if such a strategy had an adverse effect on the rest of the firm (since it satisfies the managers' needs at least). In such a scenario, it is possible to imagine a situation in which managers are selfishly inclined to adhere to an internationalization process despite failing results.

In general however, it does not seem to be justified to assume that internationalization is primarily carried out against the objectives of the entire firm, because most decisions are likely to be taken in good faith. Furthermore, conflicts of interest between owners and managers are not necessarily preprogrammed: Despite the fact that the question of a link between internationalization and firm performance has not yet been sufficiently answered, it can be stated that successful internationalization processes hold at least the potential for high returns for shareholders.[58] Moreover, managers might profit from additional employment possibilities, high salaries, as well as other 'perks' such as international business trips. Therefore, it should be rational for owners and managers alike to pull together and to be interested in an economically successful international performance of their firm.[59] In support of this view, previous research (the stakeholder view) has shown that there is a positive link between the attention that a firm gives to its stakeholders and its performance[60]—due to the stakeholders' distinguished influence on corporate success.[61] Hence, internationalization processes are certainly—among many motives—driven by the self-interest of managers. In the majority of cases, however, this is not conflicting with the substantive rationality and objectives of the employing firm.

In summary and against the background of the differing concepts of rationality, this study recognizes that there are conditions imaginable under which managers are interested in adhering to failing internationalization processes. Under general circumstances, however, it can be assumed that managers take their internationalization decisions in good faith and not against the objectives of their corporation. This is often fostered by incentives and other target agreements in business reality, which align the formal objectives of the manager with the superordinated substantive objectives of the firm. Therefore, it is assumed that under normal circumstances there is a fit between the formal rationality of a decision-maker and the substantive rationality of their firm (i.e., managers try to take decisions that are best for the firm).

---

[57] Cf. Harris and Raviv (1991, p. 300).

[58] Cf. Oesterle et al. (2013, pp. 187 ff.).

[59] Admittedly, the presented line of argumentation concentrates on owners and managers. 'Blue-collar-employees' can very well be negatively affected by internationalization processes as internationalization can lead to production offshoring and job-losses.

[60] Cf. Magill et al. (2015, p. 1685), Berman et al. (1999, p. 501), Waddock and Graves (1997, pp. 303 ff.), Huselid (1995, pp. 635 ff.), and Pfeffer (1994, pp. 27 ff.).

[61] Cf. Strange et al. (2009, p. 396).

Lately, and particularly in the light of current research results from cognitive psychology, however, it seems to be unlikely that decision-makers are always aware of their preferences and that they constantly possess the cognitive ability to exercise rational choices.[62] Hence, the question arises whether the model of the economic man succeeds in explaining judgment and decision-making processes under complex circumstances. In reality, human behavior could rather be "intendedly rational, but only limitedly so."[63]

2.1.2 Theoretical Foundations of Bounded Rationality

At the time of the above mentioned introduction of individual preferences to the discourse of rational decision-making,[64] in the 1950s and 1960s, scholars began to turn away from an orthodox concept of rationality, which assumes that decision-makers possess unlimited cognitive capacity as well as time and knowledge, and started to consider forms of bounded rationality.[65] Against the background of an increasing and everlasting influence of psychology on economics,[66] it has been particularly due to the works of Nobel Memorial Prize laureate in economics Herbert A. Simon, who is considered to be the father of the term of bounded rationality[67] as well as the author of the above quote, that bounded rationality has left a distinguished mark on judgment and decision-making literature. The question of how to deal with limitations of social actors and—in the context of this study—decision-makers is a cornerstone in this perspective. Simon criticized the concept of the rational *homo economicus*, saying that "recent developments in economics, and particularly in the theory of the business firm, have raised great doubts as to whether this schematized model of economic man provides a suitable foundation on which to erect a theory [...]".[68]

Simon considered primarily two forms of limitations for decision-makers and referred to these, metaphorically spoken, as scissors. The first blade depicts the task environment and limited information availability, stating that decision-makers are by no means perfectly informed. The second blade represents limited computational capabilities of actors, i.e., cognitive limitations, which impair rational choices.[69] Given this metaphor, Simon's works are essentially marked by the

[62]Cf. Saßmannshausen (2009, p. 61).

[63]Simon (1976, p. xxviii).

[64]Cf. Sect. 2.1.1.2.

[65]Cf. Basel and Brühl (2013, p. 745) and Gigerenzer and Selten (2002, p. 3).

[66]For further information on the relation between these two scholarly disciplines refer to DellaVigna (2009, p. 315).

[67]Cf. Selten (2002, p. 13).

[68]Simon (1955, p. 99).

[69]Cf. Simon (1990, p. 7).

assumption that perfect decisions might exist, but—due to the bounded rationality of decision-makers—the necessary steps are not conducted.[70] First, it seems to be impossible to identify the clear likelihood of outcomes of one's actions due to limited information availability. Second, and even more critically, preferences of decision-makers do not seem to be as clear as it is foreseen by scholars with high estimation for the concept of the economic man.[71] Instead of being steady and definite, sets of preferences seem to be inconsistent and variable. Current streams of research, which follow this understanding of rationality, are often referred to as 'behavioral' (e.g., behavioral economics, behavioral finance, etc.).[72]

Management scholars—particularly in judgment and decision-making literature—have found great interest in bounded rationality and one of its most pivotal ideas: satisficing (a *portmanteau* of satisfying and sufficing).[73] According to this concept, a decision-maker does not simply have the opportunity to decide for a utility-maximizing alternative because he/she would first have to search for such an option. Unlike under the assumptions of Rational Choice Theory, decision alternatives are not transparently open to choice because of, for example, lacking abilities to compute and compare decision consequences. Under satisficing circumstances, an uninformed decision-maker would hope for an ideal option while he/she actually secures minimum requirements, which need to be met by any alternative under consideration. This means that any decision that offers a satisfactory yet minimal level of utility is worth considering. As long as such a satisficing alternative meets the marginal cost of its search, a satisfier could choose accordingly.[74] As a result, he/she deviates from the path of the *homo economicus*, reaching satisfactory but not optimal results.[75] This line of thought could additionally be supported by the 'theory of the second best'.[76] In brief, this theory could be summarized as follows: The second best alternative in a decision situation could turn out to be utility enhancing (in comparison to the first best option) if not every single precondition for the first best option is fulfilled.[77] In other words, a satisficing second best alternative could turn out to be a better choice.

---

[70]Cf. Basel and Brühl (2013, p. 747).

[71]Cf. Pomerol and Adam (2006, p. 34).

[72]Cf. Camerer et al. (2004) and their Roundtable Series in Behavioral Economics for an overview of recent studies.

[73]Cf. Bendor et al. (2009, p. 1).

[74]Cf. Simon (1979, pp. 500–503).

[75]Cf. Basel and Brühl (2013, p. 747).

[76]Cf. Rakowski (1980, p. 197), Bohm (1967, pp. 301 ff.), and Lipsey and Lancaster (1956, pp. 11 ff.).

[77]Cf. Lipsey and Lancaster (1956, p. 11), for essential literature on the 'theory of the second best'. A Paretian optimum requires the criterion that all of its preconditions must be met in order to reach the optimal state. However, if only one precondition is not met, the fulfillment of all other preconditions is not necessarily any longer desirable. On the contrary, a second best equilibrium could be rather worthwhile, as long as the preconditions for this alternative are actually entirely met. William J. Baumol (1965, p. 138) argues that in a scenario, in which 5000 supply-demand equations must be satisfied for an optimal resource allocation, the fulfillment of 3900 of these conditions is not necessarily superior to the fulfillment of only 2400.

Without a doubt, Simon's theory on bounded rationality and satisficing has been (and continues to be) pioneering. However, it lacked an empirical research foundation. As a result, the concept of bounded rationality developed henceforth in two different directions.[78] One group of scholars put the emphasis of their research on judgment under uncertainty with a critical eye on 'heuristics and biases'. In this regard, cognitive psychologists Tversky and Kahneman, who have a large impact on behavioral economics with their empirical studies, have shown that human judgment and decision-making systematically breaks the rules of rational economic behavior. As further clarified in Sect. 2.2.3.2 on Prospect Theory, decision-makers are constantly biased by their subjective perception of risks and opportunities. But furthermore, they fall into the traps of their cognitive limitations in the form of heuristics, i.e., decision patterns based on past experiences, which are applied by the human mind in order to simplify complex decision matters. Decision-makers thus replace a fact-based evaluation of the probabilities and consequences of their alternatives with heuristics. While heuristics may be useful in some situations, they can lead to severe decision errors in others.[79] Among the negative consequences are various biases, which impair judgment and decision-making. Worth mentioning are the overconfidence bias (a subjective overestimation of the objective validity as well as accuracy of ones conclusions),[80] the framing bias (a fallacy of coming to different decision conclusions based on the presentation of the decision context),[81] the base-rate fallacy (misjudged probabilities as a result of limited attention to base-rate, i.e., generic, information in comparison to specific information),[82] and bounded awareness (a limited attention to unsolicited information in comparison to the attention that is given to information that has actually been searched for).[83] Furthermore, the escalation bias must be noted (the tendency of investing further resources in a failing course of action),[84] which presents a key element of escalation of commitment that has been briefly introduced in the introduction of the present study (Sect. 1.3).[85] Due to the last bias, obviously, the heuristics and biases program is of particular importance in the context of the present study.

[78]Cf. Basel and Brühl (2013, p. 747) and Klaes and Sent (2005, p. 27).

[79]Cf. Tversky and Kahneman (1974, p. 1124).

[80]Cf. Forbes (2005, p. 624).

[81]Cf. Russo and Schoemaker (1989a, p. 16, b, p. 15) and Tversky and Kahneman (1981, pp. 453 ff.); as well as Sect. 2.2.3.2 of the present study.

[82]Cf. Ohlert and Weißenberger (2015, p. 52), Argote et al. (1990, pp. 296 ff.), and Tversky and Kahneman (1974, p. 1124).

[83]Cf. Chugh and Bazerman (2007, p. 1).

[84]Cf. Brockner (1992, pp. 39 ff.); as well as Sect. 3.3.2 of the present study.

[85]Cf. Basel and Brühl (2013, p. 748) and Bazerman and Moore (2013, p. 119).

Contradicting the scholars of the heuristics and biases group and in contrast to their negative connotation of heuristics, the second program—around psychologist Gerd Gigerenzer—argues that the first group ignores bias distinctions (e.g., singular versus repeated decision errors).[86] In reality, judgment and decision-making processes rarely follow any laws of logic at all due to decision-makers' limited time and knowledge as well as due to changing environments. Against this background, evolutionary based decision patterns are useful tools, which help to draw adaptive as well as quick, frugal, and/or accurate consequences.[87] According to Gigerenzer and his colleagues, heuristics are no source of biases but rather ecologically rational (because the rationality of a decision depends on momentary and environmental circumstances).[88]

In summary, some authors refer to heuristics and biases in a negative manner, pointing out that they impair human judgment capacities. Others refer to fast and frugal heuristics, which help to make better decisions in complex and changing environments. Thus, the bounded rationality program itself is rather heterogeneous. Yet unlike rational choice scholars, the authors of the bounded rationality program have in common that they rather describe judgment and decision-making processes as they are in reality instead of prescribing what they should be. With regard to the theoretical basis of the present study, bounded rationality represents a key element because escalation of commitment is one of its specific manifestations.[89]

2.1.3 Distinction from Irrationality

In order to fully understand bounded rationality, it is essential not to confound the concept with irrationality—a popular misinterpretation. Under bounded rationality, an actor has—at least subjectively perceived—good reason for his/her actions. The fact that a chosen decision path turned out to be wrong does not mean that the decision basis itself was irrational. The decision-maker could have simply been confronted with limited information availability, for example. Jean Tirole hit the nail on the head when he stated in this context that "we do make lots of mistakes, although I am not sure that these mistakes should necessarily be viewed as instances of irrational behaviors."[90]

A truly irrational decision-maker lacks a justifiable basis for his/her action, i.e., his/her decision is not based on reason and occurs haphazardly instead.[91] Thus, irrationality represents the opposite term of rationality, under which an action is

[86]Cf. Gigerenzer (1991, pp. 83 ff.).

[87]Cf. Gigerenzer and Gaissmaier (2011, p. 454).

[88]Cf. Gigerenzer (2008, p. 8) and Gigerenzer and Todd (1999, p. 18).

[89]Cf. Sect. 3.3.2 of the present study.

[90]Cf. Tirole (2002, p. 640).

[91]Cf. Gigerenzer and Selten (2002, p. 4).

inconclusive—meaning that it is neither purposeful nor consistent. Unlike decisions under bounded rationality, irrational behavior is therefore incomprehensible for third parties, which share the same information as the responsible decision-maker. The actor's objectives, his/her information, and his/her actions are inherently contradictory.

2.1.4 Section Conclusion

It has been the aim of this section to clarify the underlying understanding of rationality and bounded rationality for the following proceedings. On the one hand, there is the classic approach, which largely builds on Rational Choice Theory and which has presented JDM literature with the *homo economicus*, the role model of a rational actor in economics. On the other hand, the ideas of bounded rationality have changed the line of discourse and have won significant grounds over the past decades due to a growing influence of peripheral research areas such as psychology on economics. Depending on the justifiability of one's actions (i.e., the verifiability for third persons), decisions can be considered to be rational (correct justification), with bounded rationality (flawed justification), or even irrational (no justification).

Since the time of Adam Smith, the model of the economic man has provided economists with a convenient abstraction of decision-makers' behavior in economic contexts in order to hypothesize about rational choices. Nevertheless, the *homo economicus* is often at the focus of both public as well as scholarly criticism for its supposedly wrong assumptions. This could be due to the misunderstanding that self-interest seeking is often equated with profit maximization instead of maximization of utility. With good reason, however, the bounded rationality program objects that two essential assumptions of unbounded rationality are flawed. It seems to be particularly unrealistic to expect that decision-makers possess complete information availability. In addition, it is unlikely that humans have the cognitive capacity to deal with the obtainable information while they respect their specific set of preferences, i.e., decision-makers' choices may be inconsistent.[92]

Finally, this section has specified the difference between formal and substantive rationalities for the case of competing preferences. If individual preferences of decision-makers conflict, different courses of action are equally justifiable under formal rationality—as long as the decision-making process, which led to action, was procedurally consistent. In the context of the present study, this implies a possible scenario in which managers pursue internationalization processes for their individual benefit and against the objective rationality of the firm. In contrast, the objectives of a decision-maker themselves need to be appropriate (i.e., aligned with the objectives of the firm) under substantive rationality. Under normal circumstances, it can be assumed that there is a fit between the formal rationality of a

[92]Cf. Walliser (2008, p. 103).

decision-maker and the substantive rationality of the firm since there should be a unifying consent between the involved share- and stakeholders. In general, there are sufficient arguments that support the view that the internationalization decisions of managers are primarily carried out along the objectives of the entire firm and in good faith. First and foremost, this is based on the rationale that internationalization holds the potential for high yields and that it is thus equally desirable for managers as well as other stake- and shareholders of the firm.

2.2 Study-Specific, Rationality-Related Classification of Judgment and Decision-Making Approaches

Identifying and solving decision problems is an essential topic in various scientific disciplines. This includes economics, in which the academic discourse on possible patterns of decision-making behaviors is firmly anchored.[93] Decisions under uncertainty constitute one of the most important problems for business management. They are shaped by the objectives, visions and strategies of a firm, while they influence selfsame in return for the future. Today, business environments are characterized by large complexities, which complicate decision-making processes based on common sense—above all in multinational organizations such as MNEs. In response to these complexities, judgment and decision-making approaches attempt to address logical and/or empirical analyses of decision-makers.[94] Due to the enormous strategic significance of judgment and decision-making processes for companies, the scientific field around individual and organizational decision theory has great relevance.[95] JDM literature is not only manifold, but it can also be categorized by different criteria. Inter alia, this includes whether or not the identified pattern of JDM considers strategically planned or impulsive ad-hoc decision outcomes, questions of information availability, circumstantial risk complexities, etc.[96] However, these examples are only of secondary interest in the context of the present study. In the following, the prescriptive and descriptive perspectives as well as the underlying behavioral assumptions of JDM approaches will be at the center of interest. This approach allows a statement regarding the bounded rationality and rational choice contents in corresponding theories.

But why is it reasonable at all to classify different judgment and decision-making approaches at this point? Much like some of the traditional decision-making theories, the U-Model offers—at least implicitly—a certain explanatory value for decision-making in internationalization processes. With the present study, the

[93]Cf. Wolf (2013, p. 125) and Simon (1976, p. 8).

[94]Cf. Eisenführ et al. (2010, p. 3).

[95]Cf. von der Oelsnitz (1999, p. 157).

[96]Cf. Snowden and Boone (2007, pp. 68 ff.), Dean and Sharfman (1996, pp. 368 ff.), and Payne (1976, pp. 366 ff.).

U-Model is subjected to a critical review in this regard. In order to evaluate the actual standpoint on bounded rationality of this central IP-theory, its prescriptive/descriptive basis as well as its behavioral assumptions need to be assessed.[97] Therefore, a plausible general classification framework for judgment and decision-making approaches needs to be developed first. The development of such a framework presents the main purpose of the present section. In this context, the following part will cover the applied classification criteria.

2.2.1 Classification Criteria

As mentioned in the beginning of this chapter, judgment and decision-making models can fundamentally be differentiated by their prescriptive/descriptive nature and by their underlying behavioral assumptions (between neoclassical and behavior-oriented).[98] Theories, which cover a desired decision content or outcome, are associated with the prescriptive branch of decision-making theories. Corresponding approaches try to depict how decision-makers should behave in judgment and decision-making situations and serve as instruments for reasonable choices of compositional alternatives. In contrast, theories that build on empirical observations describe how decision-makers actually conduct their choices.[99] An additional differentiating criterion can be found in the postulated behavioral assumptions in judgment and decision-making processes. On the one hand, some theories assume in a neoclassical manner that decision-makers come to a result based on purposeful and consistent choices, i.e., that ideal solutions are identifiable and always adopted.[100] On the other hand, other approaches are marked by a behavior-oriented, i.e., more realistic, perspective on judgment and decision-making processes.

2.2.1.1 Prescriptive and Descriptive Perspective

Prescriptive Approaches

Prescriptive and descriptive judgment and decision-making theories constitute two different 'decision-making philosophies'.[101] The prescriptive branch, which is also referred to as decision analysis, embodies the classic approach, which has been established earlier than the descriptive side of JDM literature.

---

[97] Cf. Sect. 3.2.

[98] Cf. Laux et al. (2014, pp. 16–19), Wolf (2013, pp. 125 ff.), Walliser (2008, pp. 49 ff.), Meyer (2000, p. 7), van der Pligt (1996, p. 30), and Luce and von Winterfeldt (1994, p. 264).

[99] Cf. Osterloh (2004, col. 222).

[100] Cf. Dunning (1988, p. 14).

[101] Cf. Fox (2015, p. 85).

Decision content and corresponding predictions are at the center of analysis.

As already mentioned above, judgment and decision-making theories, which are shaped by a prescriptive element, tend to make a statement and/or a prediction on how decision-makers should act. Therefore, the decision content is central to corresponding approaches.

Formal scientific and analytical methods are applied.

Prescriptive JDM approaches are often shaped by a high degree of formality. These concepts frequently build on mathematical formulas and analytical reviews in order to predict ideal alternatives. In the eyes of some scholars, these procedures are equally plausible as basic premises of classical logic.[102]

Corresponding theories build on simplified models of reality.

In order to meet the requirements for such a formal approach, simplified and often hypothetical models of reality are introduced. These turn corresponding theories into abstracted approaches to decision-making problems.

Under these difficult restrictions, however, accurate predictions and prescriptions regarding decision-makers' behavior in judgment and decision-making processes are hardly possible. So what would be the point of prescriptive JDM concepts? Their aim is to present a plausible approach to hypothetical and idealized decision problems, which is built on logic and reasoning.[103] A decision-maker, who wishes to come to a result based on prescriptive JDM concepts, must accept these restrictions as well as the resultant ground rules, which are inevitably associated with these approaches. Not surprisingly, JDM approaches, which are marked by prescription, often tend to lack empirical observations.[104]

Descriptive Approaches

In contrast, descriptive JDM approaches attempt to describe decision-makers' actions as they actually are in reality and to explain how they are justified. Therefore, the interest is primarily focused on decision-making processes and not necessarily on the decision content.

Decision-making process is at the center of analysis.

Descriptive JDM approaches do not provide procedural input in order to solve the question of how to come to ideal decisions. Instead, they draw accurate pictures of the actual decision-making process. This means that the development of realistic decision-making premises is at the center of interest and that they are not treated as a given (as in prescriptive theories).[105]

---

[102] Cf. Kumar and Subramaniam (1997, p. 64) and Pfohl and Braun (1981, p. 74); for an example of such a formalized and mathematical JDM perspective, cf. Schneeweiß (1963, pp. 203–212).

[103] Cf. Rapoport (1989, p. vii).

[104] Cf. Simon (1959, p. 255).

[105] Cf. Langer and Rogowski (2011, p. 180).

Corresponding theories constitute conceptualizations of JDM processes, which are based on empirical insights.

Unlike their prescriptive counterparts, descriptive approaches cover actual situations or simulations of realistic scenarios.[106] Corresponding JDM concepts are often the conceptualized result of empirical observations, which attend to actually pursued objectives and conducted actions of decision-makers in an attempt to analyze and abstract underlying decision-making patterns.[107] Laboratory experiments, for example, yielded in empirical evidence that test subjects act repeatedly against the premises of prescriptive JDM approaches.[108]

Descriptive JDM theories do not build a priori on simplified models of reality.

The fact that descriptive JDM approaches build on empirical observations has the consequence that they are—when compared to their prescriptive counterparts that claim to provide a procedural decision-making input—seemingly less precise in terms of their advisory capability for decision-makers.[109] Yet at the same time, they allow more profound hypotheses regarding actual judgment and decision-making processes because they do not build on simplified models of reality a priori.[110]

By observing deviations from the postulations of prescriptive concepts and by describing as well as structuring the actual JDM process, descriptive theories help to uncover general laws of social interaction, which, in return, adjust the axioms of prescriptive theories to realistic conditions.[111]

2.2.1.2 Behavioral Assumptions

Neoclassical Behavioral Assumptions

The second criterion by which JDM theories can be differentiated is the underlying behavioral assumption about decision-makers in corresponding processes. First, theories may assume in a neoclassical manner that decision-makers come to a result based on purposeful and consistent choices:

JDM theories, which imply neoclassical behavioral assumptions, regard decision-makers as purposeful and consistent with regard to their preferences.

Corresponding theories suppose that decision-makers possess the cognitive capability to identify and adopt ideal solutions. In other words, they choose

[106]Cf. Rapoport (1989, p. vii).

[107]Cf. Pfohl and Braun (1981, p. 131) and Heinen (1976, pp. 30 ff.).

[108]Cf. Laux et al. (2014, pp. 155–157).

[109]It has been referred to 'seemingly' because the reader should recall that the advisory capability of prescriptive JDM approaches is heavily constricted by rigid assumptions.

[110]Cf. Meyer (2000, p. 2) and Pfohl and Braun (1981, p. 74).

[111]Cf. Laux et al. (2014, pp. 157–158).

systematically and base their action on objective and complete information.[112] Therefore, decision-makers execute purposeful decisions, which are consistent and in accordance with their preferences. This implies a logical axiomatic basis. For example, transitivity of preferences constitutes a ground rule. Under transitivity, it is assumed that a decision-maker, who prefers alternative A to B and who favors B over C, will consequently choose A over C.[113] Another example would be the ordering axiom, according to which decision-makers are actually capable of making comparisons, i.e., ranks, between alternatives.[114] This means that they have the option to choose alternative A over B (or vice versa) or to be indifferent between these two possibilities.

Behavior-Oriented Assumptions

Alternatively, JDM theories may be characterized by behavior-oriented assumptions regarding decision-makers' actions:

> Behavior-oriented JDM theories build on realistic assumptions as they acknowledge factual limitations for decision-makers in reality.

Corresponding theories acknowledge the factual limitations for decision-makers and are therefore principally closer to reality. Factual limitations refer, for example, to the lacking information availability in decision-making processes as well as to the impaired cognitive capability of decision-makers to process the available information.

2.2.2 *Judgment and Decision-Making Approaches Shaped by Rational Choice or Bounded Rationality*

Due to the above-outlined classification criteria (which serve the development of a plausible general classification framework for judgment and decision-making approaches), a statement regarding the rational choice and bounded rationality contents in judgment and decision-making approaches is feasible. One could certainly argue that theories, which apply a prescriptive perspective and which build on neoclassical behavioral assumptions, are unequivocally attributed to rational choice approaches, i.e., approaches that build on Rational Choice Theory. These concepts frequently build on mathematical formulas, analytical reviews, and simplified models of reality in order to reach purposeful and consistent solutions to decision problems. The described characteristics highlight that prescriptive-neoclassical JDM approaches go hand in hand with the traditional economic postulate of rationality, which aims at purposeful and consistent decisions. In contrast, JDM concepts marked by a descriptive and behavior-oriented base can

[112]Cf. Olsen (1994, p. 82) and Schwenk (1985, p. 501).

[113]Cf. Bell et al. (1988, p. 16) and Fishburn (1983, p. 293).

[114]Cf. Laux et al. (2014, p. 41).

clearly be attributed to the sphere of bounded rationality. These draw accurate pictures of the actual decision-making process in order to reach conceptualizations with respect for the factual limitations of decision-makers. Therefore, descriptive-behavior-oriented JDM approaches go along with the bounded rationality program, which intends to describe judgment and decision-making processes realistically.[115]

Some scholars even hold the belief that there is a clear dichotomy of JDM theories in this regard.[116] Despite the plausibility of this belief, a definite statement regarding such a dichotomy cannot be given as easily. This is because prescriptive approaches may also consider previously (empirically) identified decision biases. 'How to decide under given rationality limitations' would be a guiding question of such approaches.[117] In addition, early approaches of descriptive judgment and decision-making literature are often rooted in a critique of the prescriptive side. As such, they applied the postulate of rationality, identified contradictions, and ultimately modified the prescriptive element of the original idea.[118] Furthermore, concepts can very well provide a prescriptive as well as a descriptive perspective.[119] Considering these examples, it becomes clear that the proposed framework only allows for a rough classification of judgment and decision-making theories. Due to the potential multi-dimensionality of JDM approaches, a precise classification is difficult. Nevertheless, the framework allows for an assessment of rational choice and bounded rationality contents in decision-making concepts.

2.2.3 *Exemplary Classification of Specific Judgment and Decision-Making Concepts*

Decision models are of substantial importance for the economic research program, which is sometimes referred to as a decision-oriented discipline.[120] There is a multitude of different (partial-) concepts, which form a heterogeneous field.[121] In order to illustrate the scope of this field, two of the most prominent judgment and decision-making concepts will be illustrated as examples in the following, in order to point out their prescriptive and descriptive elements as well as their underlying behavioral assumptions. Despite the potential multi-dimensionality of JDM approaches, the following examples can almost be considered as textbook cases for rational choice and bounded rationality JDM approaches. Thereby, they also serve as two convenient extremes within the general classification framework for

---

[115]Cf. von Winterfeldt (1989, pp. 499 ff.).

[116]Cf. Wolf (2013, p. 125); cf. also von Winterfeldt (1989, pp. 499 ff.).

[117]Cf. Loomes and Sugden (1982, pp. 805 ff.) and their Regret Theory as an example.

[118]Cf. Bamberg et al. (2012, p. 6).

[119]Cf. Bleichrodt et al. (2001, pp. 1498 ff.) and Luce and von Winterfeldt (1994, pp. 263 ff.).

[120]Cf. Laux et al. (2014, p. 4).

[121]Cf. Wolf (2013, p. 128).

judgment and decision-making approaches, which is developed in the present section.

2.2.3.1 Expected Utility Theory

The Expected Utility Theory (EUT) is likely to be one of the best-known theoretical approaches to decision-making under risk and uncertainty. According to EUT, an ideal alternative in a decision-making process provides the maximum expected value for the decision-maker in terms of utility. Different choice alternatives are compared in couples under consideration of their probability. EUT is the standard theory of individual decision-making and as such it has a continuous, theory-building impact on economic literature.[122] It is sometimes divided in 'objective' as well as 'subjective' EUT.[123] Unlike the younger subjective EUT, the slightly older objective approach assumes specified decision probabilities. Its advancement, however, also considers a personalistic view, i.e., personal and psychological perceptions of probability.[124] Nevertheless, both have a common basis and both provide a 'consequentialist' perspective on decision-making.[125] While the objective EUT stands in the limelight of the present section, subjective EUT will be specifically covered in in the context of escalation of commitment in Sect. 3.3.3.1.

The underlying, general foundation of EUT was originally developed by Daniel Bernoulli in 1738, whereas the axiomatic (contemporary) foundation has been provided by John von Neumann and Oskar Morgenstern in the 1940s.[126] In the eighteenth century, scholars were convinced that a gambler should pay any admission fee in order to participate in a lottery as long as it is less than the expected monetary value of the game. Bernoulli, however, disagreed and argued that the personal value of a gamble does not necessarily equal its monetary value and proposed the idea that the gamble's worth is defined by the subjective benefit, i.e., utility.[127]

He gave greater substance to his argument by the provision of the St. Petersburg lottery as a paradoxical example. This hypothetical game circles around one essential question: How many Ducats should a player pay in order to enter a coin-flip game, in which he/she will win an amount of 2^n Ducats and in which n

[122] Cf. Starmer (2000, pp. 332 ff.).

[123] Cf. Savage (1972, pp. 27 ff.) for a fundamental basis of subjective EUT.

[124] Cf. Fishburn (1981, p. 139) and Savage (1972, p. 3).

[125] Cf. Hammond (1998b, p. 215); see also March and Olsen (1989, pp. 160–162), on the logic of consequentiality (against the logic of appropriateness): "In a logic of consequentiality, behaviors are driven by preferences and expectations about consequences. Behavior is willful, reflecting an attempt to make outcomes fulfill subjective desires, to the extent possible."

[126] Cf. Tversky (1975, p. 163), Bernoulli (1954, p. 24), and von Neumann and Morgenstern (1953, pp. 73–76).

[127] Cf. Bernoulli (1954, p. 24): "[. . .] the determination of the value of an item must not be based on its price, but rather on the utility it yields."

is the (uncertain) number of rounds that will be played? For example, if the player chooses heads, the game will last as many rounds as it will take for heads to occur. As the chances of heads are 50% in every round, the game will probably not take very long and the prize will be small. However, the difficulty of this lottery lies in the circumstance that it could theoretically take an infinite number of rounds for heads to occur. In this case, the lottery prize will grow with every additional round ad infinitum. At the same time, however, the likelihood for this event is decreasing with every additional round. According to the predominant belief at the time (based on the expected monetary value), the player's payment should be as high as possible because the potential payoff is theoretically infinite.[128] But as Bernoulli rightfully saw, this is only the case if the decision is taken along naive stochastic decision criteria.[129] He believed that people would only be willing to pay a fraction of their available financial resources in order to enter the lottery. Bernoulli solved this paradox with the realization that previous stochastic approaches neglected the subjective relevance of decision results for the players: Neither do they consider the risk, which is involved in the decision process, nor the specific interest of decision-makers in certain decision outcomes.[130] In short, behind the Bernoulli principle stands the recognition that an ideal choice has to maximize the expected utility of a decision problem and not necessarily the expected monetary outcome.[131]

But it was not until the middle of the twentieth century that economic scholars began to develop a renewed and increased interest in the Bernoulli principle. In 1944, John von Neumann and Oskar Morgenstern rejuvenated the expected utility hypothesis by axiomatizing it in order to use it in the context of utility functions.[132] In fact, their modern application consists of a series of axioms, which concern the relation of preferences of decision-makers in lotteries. As long as the preferences of decision-makers fulfill the axioms, there will be a utility function with a corresponding expected utility, which can be maximized.[133] This structured perspective on preferences goes largely hand in hand with the preference assumptions in Rational Choice Theory. Besides the prominent and influential axiomatic structure of von Neumann and Morgenstern, numerous additional axiomatizations have been contributed by other scholars.[134] In order to point out the prescriptive and descriptive elements as well as the underlying behavioral assumption of EUT, the

[128]Cf. Starmer (2000, p. 333).

[129]Cf. Samuelson (1977, p. 25); cf. also Casella (1985, pp. 83 ff.), for a broad review of Bayes methods; according to the Bayes estimator (μ-rule), the expected utility of the lottery is calculated as follows: $E(2^n) = \sum_{n=1}^{\infty} 2^n \left(\frac{1}{2}\right)^n = +\infty$.

[130]Cf. Starmer (2000, pp. 333–334) and Rapoport Orwant (1962, pp. 1–3).

[131]Cf. Heun (2007, p. 20).

[132]Cf. von Neumann and Morgenstern (1953, pp. 73–76).

[133]Cf. Eisenführ et al. (2010, p. 249) and Coombs et al. (1970, p. 122).

[134]Cf. inter alia Hammond (1988, pp. 25 ff.), Luce and Raiffa (1957, p. 23), and Herstein and Milnor (1953, pp. 291 ff.).

axioms need to be addressed briefly. For the present study, however, a focus on the major (i.e., original) axioms will suffice. Coombs and colleagues as well as Eisenführ and colleagues give an informative overview in this regard.[135]

'Complete ordering and transitivity', 'continuity' as well as 'independence' of preferences are the axiomatic cornerstones of EUT.[136] As in Rational Choice Theory, it is possible to compare different pairs of lotteries in order to make a preference statement according to the first axiom ($a \geq b$ or $b \geq a$). Furthermore, the order of preferences should be transitive (as long as $a \geq b$ and $b \geq c$ it follows that $a \geq c$). According to the axiom of continuity, there will be a combination of two lotteries (a compound lottery of a and c), which is at least as good as a third lottery b as long as $a \geq b \geq c$. Ultimately, the axiom of independence, which is sometimes referred to as 'substitution', states that preferences between two lotteries a and b do not change, if both lotteries intertwine with a third lottery c (they are independent from c).[137] Only if decision-makers' preferences fulfill these axioms, there will be a utility function with which different lotteries can be game-theoretically compared and with which the preferences of decision-makers can be ranked according to the possible outcomes and probabilities (the outcomes are obviously between x_{max} and x_{min}).[138] However, von Neumann and Morgenstern did not provide any information with regard to the calculus in order to determine the respective probabilities. It is simply assumed that they are either already known or calculated independently from the utility function.[139]

Considering these statements on EUT, it can easily be argued that this particular approach provides the possibility of a prescriptive reading, because it gives an indication of how people should act in judgment and decision-making processes.[140] EUT is also premised on formal scientific and analytical methods due to its applied mathematical and axiomatic approach. Furthermore, simplifying assumptions about decision-makers are made. Under these restrictions, a decision-maker should calculate the utility of his/her alternatives, make a comparison, and choose the option with the maximum utility. Besides this prescriptive content, EUT also complies with neoclassic behavioral assumptions. First, decision-makers benefit from complete information. Second, if the axiomatic system is met, a decision-maker will have the opportunity to identify and adopt an ideal alternative, i.e., the option with the maximum utility. Third, effects that limit cognitive skills are not foreseen. Furthermore, there is a lack of an empirical evidence for von Neumann's and Morgenstern's considerations. In fact, other studies showed that the axioms of EUT were regularly violated under realistic circumstances.[141] As a result, current

---

[135]Cf. Eisenführ et al. (2010, pp. 250 ff.) and Coombs et al. (1970, pp. 122–126).

[136]Cf. Hammond (1998a, pp. 152–157).

[137]Cf. Eisenführ et al. (2010, pp. 250 ff.).

[138]Cf. Coombs et al. (1970, pp. 122–126).

[139]Cf. Eisenführ et al. (2010, pp. 248–250).

[140]Cf. Starmer (2000, p. 334).

[141]Cf. Tversky (1975, p. 163).

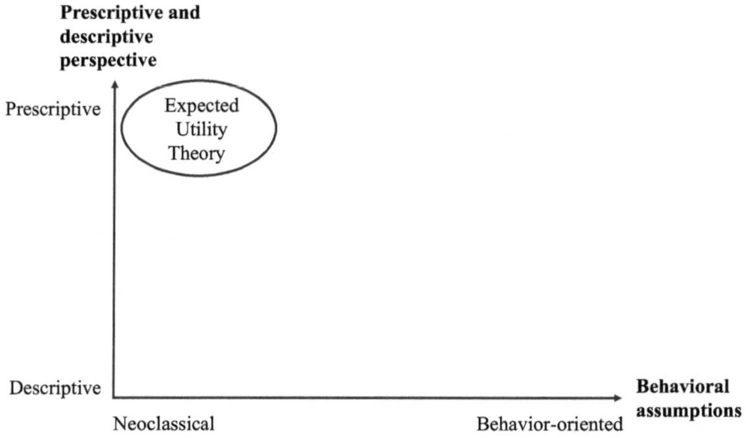

Fig. 2.1 Classification of specific judgment and decision-making concepts I (Expected Utility Theory). Source: Own figure

decision theories tend to redefine or to ignore the axiomatic system of EUT.[142] In short, this particular JDM concept serves as an ideal example to illustrate the prescriptive-neoclassical side of judgment and decision-making approaches. In this regard, Amos Tversky stated that expected utilities constitute a prescriptive theory, which determines optimal decisions under scientific conditions.[143] Figure 2.1, which will be further developed in the following,[144] provides a classifying overview.

2.2.3.2 Prospect Theory

Prospect Theory (PT) is one of the most significant contributions to judgment and decision-making literature in recent history and was established by Daniel Kahneman and Amos Tversky in the 1970s. It builds on a critique of the lacking descriptive perspective of EUT. With their criticism, the two authors also aimed at the axiomatic structure of EUT, which is regularly violated in reality.[145] According to Kahneman's and Tversky's theory, the determining factors for economic decisions do not lie in final assets but rather in the potential gains and losses for decision-makers and the question of how they are perceived. The authors continued to develop their theory in the past.[146] The current approach of cumulative PT is the

[142]Cf. Dubra et al. (2004, pp. 118 ff.), Dekel (1986, pp. 304 ff.), and Machina (1982, pp. 277 ff.).

[143]Cf. Tversky (1975, p. 163).

[144]Figure 2.1 serves as a graphic illustration of the classification framework for JDM approaches, which is applied in the present study. It will be readopted in Sect. 3.2 for the classification of the U-Model.

[145]Cf. Kahneman and Tversky (1979, p. 263).

[146]Cf. Tversky and Kahneman (1992, pp. 297 ff.); for a comparison between the variations of Prospect Theory cf. Fennema and Wakker (1997, pp. 53 ff.).

most prominent concept in its field.[147] In 2002, Daniel Kahneman received the Nobel Memorial Prize in economics for his works.[148]

PT is the result of empirical observations.[149] Therefore, it serves well in order to describe deviations from the behaviors foreseen by theories, which build on rational choice literature. Kahneman and Tversky presented five phenomena (nonlinear preferences, framing effects, loss aversion, risk-seeking, as well as source dependence), which have been observed in various experiments and which contradict the axiomatic foundation of EUT.[150] Partially, these phenomena can develop a significant importance in the context of escalation of commitment[151] and will be further referred to in Sects. 3.3.3 and 3.3.4.

The first phenomenon, nonlinear preferences, is caused by the so-called 'certainty effect'.[152] In short, this bias describes the tendency of decision-makers to overrate events that are completely certain against events that are only probable. Economist Maurice Allais, who presented the Allais Paradox, has already foreseen this in the 1950s as a violation of the independence axiom of EUT.[153] In 1979, Kahneman and Tversky designed an experimental study based on his idea (cf. Fig. 2.2).[154] In this experiment, 72 participants were confronted with two decision problems. For each decision problem there were two options to choose from (Problem 1: Options A and B; Problem 2: Options C and D).[155] The options of the first decision problem offered a greater opportunity of winning a certain amount of Israeli Shekels (ILS) in comparison to the options of the second problem. At the same time, the options of the second decision problem were direct derivatives of the options of the first decision problem: Option C equaled Option A minus a 66% chance of winning 2400 ILS and, likewise, Option D equaled Option B minus a 66% chance of winning 2400 ILS. Thus, Options A and C as well as Options B and D were equivalent. In Kahneman's and Tversky's experiment, Option A provided a higher expected payout than Option B (at a slightly higher risk of not winning anything). The exact same was true for Options C and D (at generally lower expected payouts). Due to the equivalency of options, a consistent decision-maker should always prefer either the riskier and more profitable options (A and C) or the safer yet less profitable options (B and D). In reality, however, decision-makers chose inconsistently.

For the first decision problem, 82% of participants preferred the 'safe bet' B, with which they would have won 2400 ILS with complete certainty. At the same

[147]Cf. Eisenführ et al. (2010, p. 423) and Shimizu (2007, p. 1495).

[148]Amos Tversky deceased in 1996.

[149]Cf. Levy (1997, pp. 89–93).

[150]Cf. Tversky and Kahneman (1992, p. 298).

[151]Cf. Sharp and Salter (1997, pp. 103–104).

[152]Cf. Tversky and Kahneman (1992, p. 298) and Kahneman and Tversky (1979, p. 265).

[153]Cf. Allais (1953, p. 505).

[154]Unlike Allais's original consideration, their variation of the experiment referred to moderate instead of very large gains.

[155]Kahneman and Tversky (1979, pp. 265–266).

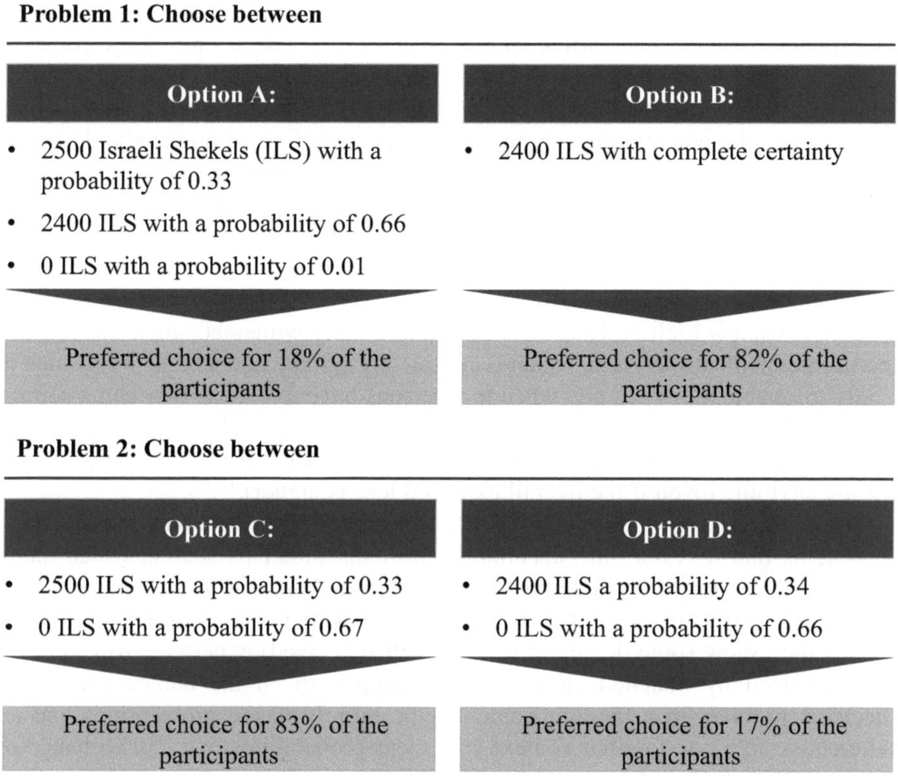

Fig. 2.2 Kahneman's and Tversky's variation of the Allais Paradox. Source: Own figure, based on Kahneman and Tversky (1979, pp. 265–266)

time, only 18% of participants chose Alternative A with a higher expected payout and a 1% risk of not winning anything. For the second decision problem, however, only 17% selected the 'safe bet', whereas 83% of test persons chose the riskier yet more profitable Option C. This inconsistency is a clear violation of the independence axiom of EUT. Under independence, there should not be a change of preferences between a and b, if any probability mixture intertwines equally with both options (if $a \geq b$ holds, then $p \cdot a + (1-p) \cdot c \geq p \cdot b + (1-p) \cdot c$ must hold as well).[156] The Allais Paradox, however, provides evidence that a significant majority of participants violates this axiom by combining Options B and C. Apparently, the majority of test persons selected a mixed strategy between risk-taking and risk-avoiding.[157] Tversky and Kahneman summarized that the difference between the probabilities of 0.99 and 1.00 (as in the first decision problem) "has more impact on preferences" than the difference between the probabilities of 0.33 and 0.34 (as in the second decision problem).[158]

[156]Cf. the previous section on EUT and its axiomatic foundation.

[157]Cf. Fiegenbaum and Thomas (1988, p. 88).

[158]Tversky and Kahneman (1992, p. 298).

Another contradictory example against the axiomatic basis of EUT can be found in 'framing effects'. According to this specific bias, decision-makers come to different conclusions based on the presentation of the decision problem context. When an option is framed negatively, decision-makers tend to incur higher risks in order to avoid a potential loss. When an alternative is framed positively, decision-makers tend to be more defensive.[159] This is supported by Kahneman's and Tversky's observations of 'loss aversion' and 'risk-seeking'. Loss aversion describes the phenomenon that test persons usually overstate the avoidance of losses relative to the acquisition of gains. For example, the gain of 50 € does not result in the same amount of satisfaction as the loss of 50 € results in dissatisfaction (which is usually higher). Risk-seeking is particularly witnessed when subjects are confronted with a small loss, which is completely certain, and a large loss, which is 'only' probable. For example, when test persons have to choose between a certain loss of 100 € ($p = 1.00$) and a probable loss of 200 € ($p = 0.75$), most decision-makers will opt for the second alternative because it holds a 25% chance of not losing anything (even if the overall expected loss is higher).[160]

The last phenomenon, which has been presented by Kahneman and Tversky, highlights that it is not only uncertainty itself but rather its source, which has a distinguishable impact on judgment and decision-making behaviors (source dependence).[161] Experiments yielded in the insight that participants prefer lotteries in which they show some degree of (at least self-perceived) expertise, over lotteries characterized by matched chances. For example, given the choice between a decision problem in a familiar context with entirely vague probabilities and an alternative in a non-familiar context with clear probabilities (e.g., 50% chance of failure, 50% chance of success in a coin toss) most subjects will opt for the first decision problem regardless of the lacking probability information. Thus, when it comes to decisions under uncertainty, subjects prefer a familiar decision context.[162]

As a result of these empirically diagnosed phenomena, Kahneman and Tversky developed PT in order to describe the actual decision-making process of test persons.[163] Their theory differentiates between two different phases in JDM processes. First, there is the editing phase and, second, there is the evaluation phase. The former organizes and reformulates the choice alternatives as a step of simplification in order to prepare the latter. These redefined alternatives are the prospects to which Kahneman and Tversky refer with their theory.[164] The editing phase itself consists of six major operations, with which test persons transform the decision

[159]Cf. Bazerman (1984, p. 333).

[160]Cf. Kahneman and Tversky (1979, pp. 268–269); Kahneman and Tversky label this observation as a 'reflection effect'.

[161]Cf. Loewenstein and Issacharoff (1994, pp. 157 ff.).

[162]Cf. Certo et al. (2008, p. 116) and Tversky and Kahneman (1992, p. 298); much literature on source dependence is furthermore rooted in the empirical (experimental) observations of Ellsberg (1961, p. 650).

[163]Cf. Tversky and Kahneman (1992, pp. 297–298).

[164]Cf. Laux et al. (2014, p. 174) and Kahneman and Tversky (1979, pp. 274–280).

alternatives and their perceived probabilities. Essentially, these operations can be summarized as follows[165]:

1. 'Coding' describes the identification of a reference point, which allows the assessing of decision outcomes in terms of gains and losses (i.e., the deviations from the reference point).
2. 'Combination' allows the accumulation of probabilities of prospects with identical outcomes.
3. 'Segregation' serves as an instrument to separate the riskless elements of prospects in order to evaluate assured minimal outcomes across different alternatives.
4. Components that are common to all available prospects may be treated with 'cancellation'.
5. 'Simplification' describes the rounding of probability and outcome values (i.e., highly unlikely events can be left aside).
6. 'Detection of dominance' involves the search and elimination of dominated alternatives.

The operations in the editing phase support the execution of the following evaluation phase. Kahneman and Tversky argue that the overall value V of an edited prospect is defined by two scales: π and v. The first scale π links every outcome probability with a subjective decision weight $\pi(p)$. It is necessary to state that π is not a probability measure itself.[166] Much rather, it is a statement about the impact of the perceived probability of an event on the desirability of selfsame (recall that test persons favor certain events over uncertain events).[167] The second scale v links every outcome with a subjective value of that outcome $v(x)$. Considering all of the above, the basic value equation of Prospect Theory, which includes π and v, takes the following form[168]:

$$V\ (x, p; y, q) = \pi(p)\ v(x) + \pi(q)\ v(y)$$

Building on their empirical observations, Kahneman and Tversky identified three main characteristics of their value function, which is sketched below. First, the function could be shifting because the reference point for gains and losses is not fixed. Second, the value function should be convex for losses (below the reference point) and concave for gains (above the reference point) because of the changing risk attitude of decision-makers. Third, the value function should be steeper for losses than for gains, as decision-makers overrate losses (cf. Fig. 2.3).[169]

In conclusion, Prospect Theory presents a prime example of a descriptive-behavior-oriented JDM approach. First, it can very well be attributed to theories

[165]For further information on the components of the editing phase cf. Kahneman and Tversky (1979, pp. 274–275) or the introduction to Prospect Theory of Levy (1992, pp. 171 ff.).

[166]Cf. Schaub (1997, p. 171).

[167]Cf. Levy (1992, p. 181).

[168]Cf. Kahneman and Tversky (1979, pp. 275–276).

[169]Cf. Levy (1992, p. 181) and Kahneman and Tversky (1979, p. 278).

Fig. 2.3 Value function of Prospect Theory. Source: Kahneman and Tversky (1979, p. 279)

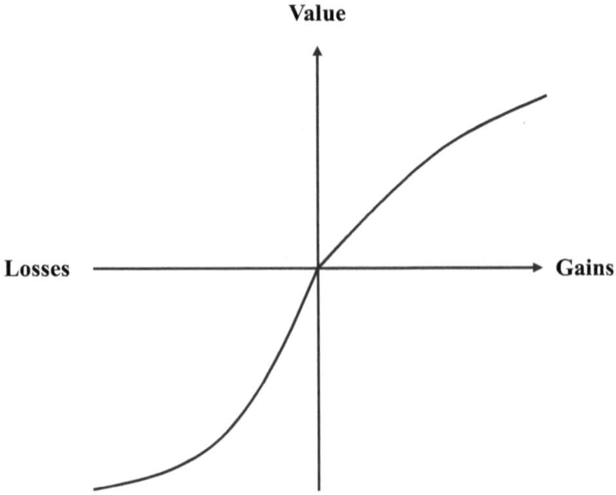

that apply a descriptive perspective. PT is the result of empirical insights, which contradict EUT and its axiomatic structure. It describes what the actions of decision-makers look like in reality and not necessarily what they should look like. Furthermore, PT aims primarily at a conceptualization of the empirically observed decision-making processes. Second, PT is shaped by realistic behavior-oriented assumptions about decision-makers. This is reflected in multiple examples of behavioral biases, which Kahneman and Tvesky presented. These biases are triggered by lacking information availability as well as by lacking cognitive capabilities of decision-makers.[170] Prospect Theory presents, furthermore, a contradiction to EUT because decision-makers are not considered to be utility-maximizing actors, who decide on the premises of scientific preconditions.[171] Therefore, Fig. 2.4 locates Prospect Theory at the opposite end of Expected Utility Theory.

2.2.4 Section Conclusion

Theories for judgment and decision-making are manifold and non-uniform in several dimensions. Against this background, it has been the aim of Sect. 2.2 to develop a suitable classification framework in order to allow a statement regarding the bounded rationality and rational choice contents in corresponding theories. Decision-making theories can, on the one hand, be distinguished by their prescriptive or respectively by their descriptive nature. On the other hand, the underlying

[170]Cf. Levy (1997, p. 105).

[171]Cf. Shimizu (2007, p. 1496).

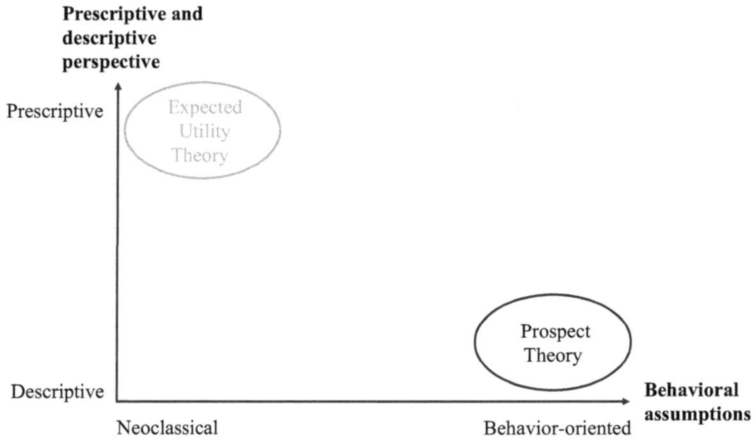

Fig. 2.4 Classification of specific judgment and decision-making concepts II (Prospect Theory). Source: Own figure

behavioral assumption (between neoclassical and behavior-oriented) serves as an additional criterion. Figure 2.5 summarizes the classification criteria.

Despite the fact that JDM theories may be multi-dimensional with regard to these classification criteria, academic literature fundamentally considers first and foremost two opposite end positions. First, prescriptive-neoclassical JDM approaches can be attributed to rational choice theories. Second, descriptive-behavior-oriented JDM approaches can be seen as theories under bounded rationality. In an attempt to give a content-related overview of these two extreme positions, the structures and elements of Expected Utility Theory as well as of Prospect Theory have been pointed out in the present section.

2.3 Chapter Conclusion

In conclusion of this chapter, one can state that JDM theories differ at least as much as the underlying interpretations of rational behavior. Fundamentally, one can distinguish between the classic concept of (unbounded) rationality, which largely builds upon Rational Choice Theory, and the idea of bounded rationality, which respects both information as well as cognitive limitations of decision-makers. The latter has gained increased significance over the past decades along with a higher estimation of psychological insights in economics. These two interpretations of rationality are reflected in JDM approaches. Despite a potential multi-dimensionality, prescriptive-neoclassical JDM approaches seem to go hand in hand with the traditional economic postulate of rationality. In contrast, JDM concepts marked by a descriptive and behavior-oriented base can be connected with bounded rationality. Due to the circumstance that the different ideas of rational

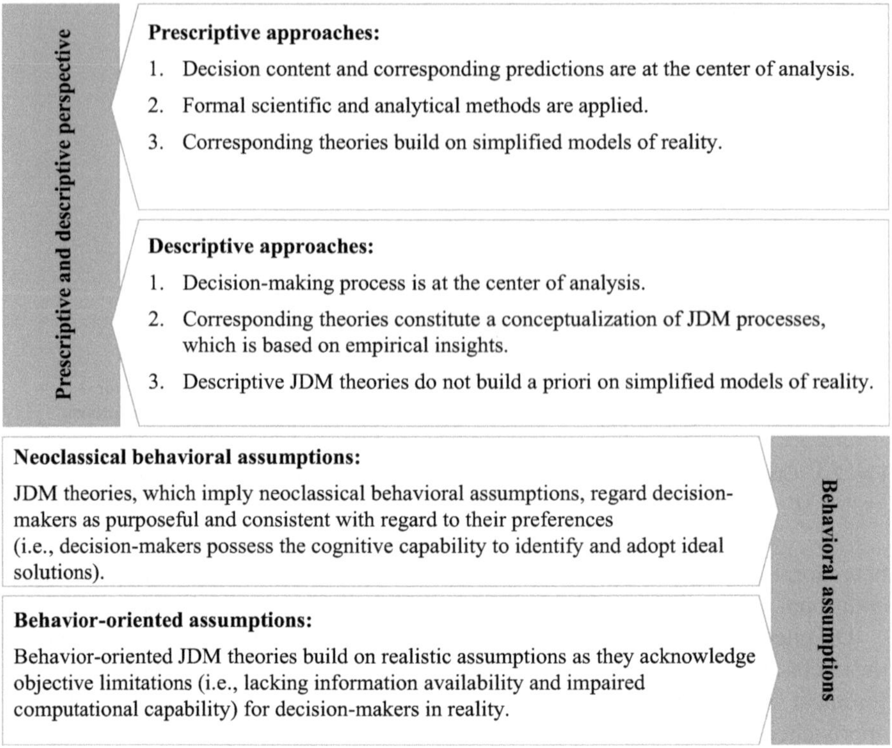

Fig. 2.5 Classification criteria. Source: Own figure

behavior are reflected in JDM approaches, it is also possible to classify such concepts in this regard.

References

Allais, M. (1953). Le comportement de l'homme rationnel devant le risque: Critique des postulats et axiomes de l'école américaine. *Econometrica, 21*(4), 503–546.

Argote, L., Devadas, R., & Melone, N. (1990). The base-rate fallacy: Contrasting processes and outcomes of group and individual judgment. *Organizational Behavior and Human Decision Processes, 46*(2), 296–310.

Arrow, K. J. (1986). Rationality of self and others in an economic system. *Journal of Business, 59*(4), 385–399.

Bamberg, G., Coenenberg, A. G., & Krapp, M. (2012). *Betriebswirtschaftliche Entscheidungslehre* (15th ed.). Munich: Franz Vahlen.

Bartlett, R. V. (1986). Ecological rationality: Reason and environmental policy. *Environmental Ethics, 8*(3), 221–239.

Basel, J. S., & Brühl, R. (2013). Rationality and dual process models of reasoning in managerial cognition and decision making. *European Management Journal, 31*(6), 745–754.

Baumol, W. J. (1965). Informed judgment, rigorous theory and public policy. *Southern Economic Journal, 23*(2), 137–145.
Bazerman, M. H. (1984). The relevance of Kahneman and Tversky's concept of framing to organizational behavior. *Journal of Management, 10*(3), 333–343.
Bazerman, M. H., & Moore, D. A. (2013). *Judgement in managerial decision making* (8th ed.). Hoboken: Wiley.
Becker, G. S. (1976). *The economic approach to human behavior*. Chicago: University of Chicago Press.
Becker, G. S. (1993). Nobel lecture: The economic way of looking at behavior. *Journal of Political Economy, 10*(3), 385–409.
Bell, D. E., Raiffa, H., & Tversky, A. (1988). Descriptive, normative, and prescriptive interactions in decision making. In D. E. Bell, H. Raiffa, & A. Tversky (Eds.), *Decision making: Descriptive, normative, and prescriptive interactions* (pp. 9–30). Cambridge: Cambridge University Press.
Bendor, J. B., Kumar, S., & Siegel, D. A. (2009). Satisficing: A 'pretty good' heuristic. *The BE Journal of Theoretical Economics, 9*(1), 1935–1704.
Berger, U. (1992). Rationalität, Macht und Mythen. In W. Küpper & G. Ortmann (Eds.), *Mikropolitik – Rationalität, Macht und Spiele in Organisationen* (2nd ed., pp. 115–130). Opladen: Westdeutscher Verl.
Berman, S. L., Wicks, A. C., Kotha, S., & Jones, T. M. (1999). Does stakeholder orientation matter? The relationship between stakeholder management models and firm financial performance. *Academy of Management Journal, 42*(5), 488–506.
Bernoulli, D. (1954). Exposition of a new theory on the measurement of risk. *Econometrica, 22*(1), 23–36.
Bleichrodt, H., Pinto, J. L., & Wakker, P. P. (2001). Making descriptive use of prospect theory to improve the prescriptive use of expected utility. *Management Science, 47*(11), 1498–1514.
Bohm, P. (1967). On the theory of "second best". *The Review of Economic Studies, 34*(3), 301–314.
Boudon, R. (2007). *Essais sur la théorie générale de la rationalité*. Paris.
Brockner, J. (1992). The escalation of commitment to a failing course of action: Toward theoretical progress. *Academy of Management Review, 17*(1), 39–61.
Bronner, R. (2004). Entscheidungsprozesse in Organisationen. In G. Schreyögg, A. von Werder (Eds.), *Handwörterbuch Unternehmensführung und Organisation* (col. 229–239). Stuttgart: Schäffer-Poeschel.
Brühl, R. (2015). *Wie Wissenschaft Wissen schafft*. Konstanz: UVK Verlagsgesellschaft mbH.
Camerer, C. F., Loewenstein, G., & Rabin, M. (2004). *Advances in behavioral economics*. Princeton: Princeton University Press.
Casella, G. (1985). An introduction to empirical Bayes data analysis. *The American Statistician, 39*(2), 83–87.
Certo, S. T., Connelly, B. L., & Tihanyi, L. (2008). Managers and their not-so rational decisions. *Business Horizons, 51*(2), 113–119.
Chrisman, J. J., Chua, J. H., & Litz, R. A. (2004). Comparing the agency costs of family and non-family firms: Conceptual issues and exploratory evidence. *Entrepreneurship Theory and Practice, 28*(4), 335–354.
Chugh, D., & Bazerman, M. H. (2007). Bounded awareness: What you fail to see can hurt you. *Mind and Society, 6*(1), 1–18.
Coombs, C. H., Dawes, R. M., & Tversky, A. (1970). *Mathematical psychology: An elementary introduction*. Englewood Cliffs: Prentice Hall.
Cyert, R. M., & March, J. G. (1963). *A behavioral theory of the firm*. Prentice-Hall: Englewood Cliffs.
Dahrendorf, R. (2006). *Homo Sociologicus* (16th ed.). Wiesbaden: VS Verlag für Sozialwissenschaften.
Davidson, D. (2004). *Problems of rationality*. Oxford: Oxford University Press.

Davis, J. H., Schoorman, F. D., & Donaldson, L. (1997). Toward a stewardship theory of management. *Academy of Management Review, 22*(1), 20–47.

Dean, J. W., & Sharfman, M. P. (1996). Does decision process matter? A study of strategic decision-making effectiveness. *Academy of Management Journal, 39*(2), 368–392.

Dekel, E. (1986). An axiomatic characterization of preferences under uncertainty: Weakening the independence axiom. *Journal of Economic Theory, 40*(2), 304–318.

DellaVigna, S. (2009). Psychology and economics: Evidence from the field. *Journal of Economic Literature, 47*(2), 315–372.

Dimitratos, P., Petrou, A., Plakoyiannaki, E., & Johnson, J. E. (2011). Strategic decision-making processes in internationalization: Does national culture of the focal firm matter? *Journal of World Business, 46*(2), 194–204.

Doucouliagos, C. (1994). A note on the evolution of homo economicus. *Journal of Economic Issues, 28*(3), 877–883.

Dubra, J., Maccheroni, F., & Ok, E. A. (2004). Expected Utility Theory without the completeness axiom. *Journal of Economic Theory, 115*(1), 118–133.

Dunning, J. H. (1988). The eclectic paradigm of international production: A restatement and some possible extensions. *Journal of International Business Studies, 19*(1), 1–31.

Eisenführ, F., Weber, M., & Langer, T. (2010). *Rationales Entscheiden* (5th ed.). Berlin: Springer.

Ellsberg, D. (1961). Risk, ambiguity, and the savage axioms. *The Quarterly Journal of Economics, 75*(4), 643–669.

Faber, M., Petersen, T., & Schiller, J. (2002). Homo oeconomicus and homo politicus in ecological economics. *Ecological Economics, 40*(3), 323–333.

Fennema, H., & Wakker, P. (1997). Original and cumulative Prospect Theory: A discussion of empirical differences. *Journal of Behavioral Decision Making, 10*(1), 53–64.

Fernández, Z., & Nieto, M. J. (2006). Impact of ownership on the international involvement of SMEs. *Journal of International Business Studies, 37*(3), 340–351.

Fiegenbaum, A., & Thomas, H. (1988). Attitudes toward risk and the risk-return paradox: Prospect theory explanations. *Academy of Management Journal, 31*(1), 85–106.

Fishburn, P. C. (1981). Subjective expected utility: A review of normative theories. *Theory and Decision, 13*(2), 139–199.

Fishburn, P. C. (1983). Transitive measurable utility. *Journal of Economic Theory, 31*(2), 293–317.

Forbes, D. P. (2005). Are some entrepreneurs more overconfident than others? *Journal of Business Venturing, 20*(5), 623–640.

Fox, J. (2015). From "economic man" to behavioral economics. *Harvard Business Review, 93*(5), 78–85.

Freeman, R. E. (1984). *Strategic management: A stakeholder approach*. Cambridge: Cambridge University Press.

Freeman, R. E., Wicks, A. C., & Parmar, B. (2004). Stakeholder theory and "the corporate objective revisited". *Organization Science, 15*(3), 364–369.

Gäfgen, G. (1974). *Theorie der wirtschaftlichen Entscheidung* (3rd ed.). Tübingen: Mohr (Siebeck).

Gigerenzer, G. (1991). How to make cognitive illusions disappear: Beyond "Heuristics and Biases". *European Review of Social Psychology, 2*(1), 83–115.

Gigerenzer, G. (2008). *Rationality for mortals: How people cope with uncertainty*. Oxford: Oxford University Press.

Gigerenzer, G., & Gaissmaier, W. (2011). Heuristic decision making. *Annual Review of Psychology, 62*, 451–482.

Gigerenzer, G., & Selten, R. (2002). *Bounded rationality – The adaptive toolbox*. Cambridge: MIT Press.

Gigerenzer, G., & Todd, P. M. (1999). Fast and frugal heuristics: The adaptive toolbox. In G. Gigerenzer, P. M. Todd, & ABC Research Group (Eds.), *Simple heuristics that make us smart* (pp. 3–34). New York: Oxford University Press.

Grünig, R., & Kühn, R. (2013). *Entscheidungsverfahren für komplexe Probleme* (4th ed.). Berlin: Heidelberg.

Hambrick, D. C. (1983). High profit strategies in mature capital goods industries: A contingency approach. *Academy of Management Journal, 26*(4), 687–707.

Hammond, P. J. (1988). Consequentialist foundations for expected utility. *Theory and Decision, 25*(1), 25–78.

Hammond, P. J. (1998a). Objective expected utility: A consequentialist perspective. In S. Barberà, P. J. Hammond, & C. Seidl (Eds.), *Handbook of utility theory* (pp. 143–211). Dordrecht: Kluwer.

Hammond, P. J. (1998b). Subjective expected utility. In S. Barberà, P. J. Hammond, & C. Seidl (Eds.), *Handbook of utility theory* (pp. 213–271). Dordrecht: Kluwer.

Harris, M., & Raviv, A. (1991). The theory of capital structure. *The Journal of Finance, 46*(1), 297–355.

Harrison, J. S., & Freeman, R. E. (1999). Stakeholders, social responsibility, and performance: Empirical evidence and theoretical perspectives. *Academy of Management Journal, 42*(5), 479–485.

Heinen, E. (1976). *Grundlagen betriebswirtschaftlicher Entscheidungen* (3rd ed.). Wiesbaden: Gabler.

Hempel, C. G. (1961–1962). Rational action. *Proceedings and Addresses of the American Philosophical Association, 35*, 5–23.

Herstein, I. N., & Milnor, J. (1953). An axiomatic approach to measurable utility. *Econometrica, 21*(2), 291–297.

Heun, M. (2007). *Finanzmarktsimulation mit Multiagentensystemen: Entwicklung eines methodischen Frameworks*. Wiesbaden: Gabler.

Hollis, M. (1977). *Models of man: Philosophical thoughts on social action*. London: Cambridge University Press.

Huselid, M. A. (1995). The impact of human resource management practices on turnover, productivity, and corporate financial performance. *Academy of Management Journal, 38*(3), 635–672.

Jensen, M. C., & Meckling, W. H. (1976). Theory of the firm: Managerial behavior, agency costs and ownership structure. *Journal of Financial Economics, 3*(4), 305–360.

Johanson, J., & Vahlne, J.-E. (1977). The internationalization process of the firm – A model of knowledge development and increasing foreign market commitments. *Journal of International Business Studies, 8*(1), 23–32.

Kahneman, D., & Tversky, A. (1979). Prospect Theory: An analysis of decision under risk. *Econometrica, 47*(2), 263–291.

Kerscher, K.-J. (2013). *Homo Oeconomicus und Menschenbild: Form und Wesen einer beachtenswerten Spannung*. Marburg: Metropolis-Verlag.

Kirchgässner, G. (2008). *Homo Oeconomicus: The economic model of behaviour and its applications in economics and other social sciences*. New York: Springer.

Klaes, M., & Sent, E. M. (2005). A conceptual history of the emergence of bounded rationality. *History of Political Economy, 37*(1), 27–59.

Kremser, C. E. W. (2013). Die Historizität des Homo Oeconomicus. *Zeitschrift für Wirtschafts- und Unternehmensethik, 14*(2), 218–236.

Kumar, V., & Subramanian, V. (1997). A contingency framework for the mode of entry decision. *Journal of World Business, 32*(1), 53–72.

Langer, A., & Rogowski, W. (2011). Deskriptive Entscheidungstheorie. In M. Schwaiger & A. Meyer (Eds.), *Theorien und Methoden der Betriebswirtschaft. Handbuch für Wissenschaftler und Studierende* (pp. 179–191).

Laux, H., Gillenkirch, R. M., & Schenk-Mathes, H. (2014). *Entscheidungstheorie*. Berlin: Springer.

Levy, J. S. (1992). An introduction to Prospect Theory. *Political Psychology, 13*(2), 171–186.

Levy, J. S. (1997). Prospect Theory, rational choice, and international relations. *International Studies Quarterly, 41*(1), 87–112.
Lipsey, R. G., & Lancaster, K. (1956). The general theory of second best. *The Review of Economic Studies, 24*(1), 11–32.
Loewenstein, G., & Issacharoff, S. (1994). Source dependence in the valuation of objects. *Journal of Behavioral Decision Making, 7*, 157–168.
Loomes, G., & Sugden, R. (1982). Regret theory: An alternative theory of rational choice under uncertainty. *The Economic Journal, 92*(368), 805–824.
Luce, R. D., & Raiffa, H. (1957). *Games and decisions: Introduction and critical survey*. New York: Wiley.
Luce, R. D., & von Winterfeldt, D. (1994). What common ground exists for descriptive, prescriptive, and normative utility theories? *Management Science, 40*(2), 263–279.
Machina, M. J. (1982). "Expected utility" analysis without the independence Axiom. *Econometrica, 50*(2), 277–323.
Machlup, F. (1978). *Methodology of economics and other social sciences*. New York: Academic Press.
Magill, M., Quinzii, M., & Rochet, J. C. (2015). A theory of the stakeholder corporation. *Econometrica, 83*(5), 1685–1725.
Mallard, G. (2012). Modelling cognitively bounded rationality: An evaluative taxonomy. *Journal of Economic Surveys, 26*(4), 675–704.
March, J. G. (1962). The business firm as a political coalition. *The Journal of Politics, 24*(4), 662–678.
March, J. G., & Olsen, J. P. (1989). *Rediscovering institutions*. New York: The Free Press.
Meyer, R. (2000). *Entscheidungstheorie* (2nd ed.). Wiesbaden: Gabler.
Ng, I. C. L., & Tseng, L.-M. (2008). Learning to be sociable: The evolution of homo economicus. *American Journal of Economics and Sociology, 67*(2), 265–286.
Nida-Rümelin, J. (1992). Ökonomische Rationalität und praktische Vernunft. In M. Hollis & W. Vossenkuhl (Eds.), *Moralische Entscheidung und rationale Wahl*. Munich: Oldenbourg.
Nyborg, K. (2000). Homo economicus and homo politicus: Interpretation and aggregation of environmental values. *Journal of Economic Behavior and Organization, 42*(3), 305–322.
Oesterle, M.-J., Richta, H. N., & Fisch, J. H. (2013). The influence of ownership structure on internationalization. *International Business Review, 22*(1), 187–201.
Ohlert, C. R., & Weißenberger, B. E. (2015). Beating the base-rate fallacy: An experimental approach on the effectiveness of different information presentation formats. *Journal of Management Control, 26*(1), 51–80.
Olsen, J. P. (1994). Choice in an organized Anarchy. In J. G. March & J. P. Olsen (Eds.), *Ambiguity and choice in organizations* (2nd ed.). Olso: Universitetsforlaget.
Osterloh, M. (2004). Entscheidungsorientierte Organisationstheorie. In G. Schreyögg, A. von Werder (Eds.), *Handwörterbuch Unternehmensführung und Organisation* (col. 222–229). Stuttgart: Schäffer-Poeschel.
Payne, J. W. (1976). Task complexity and contingent processing in decision making: An information search and protocol analysis. *Organizational Behavior and Human Performance, 16*(2), 366–387.
Persky, J. (1995). Retrospectives: The ethology of homo economicus. *The Journal of Economic Perspectives, 9*(2), 221–231.
Pfeffer, J. (1981). *Power in organizations*. Marshfield: Pitman.
Pfeffer, J. (1994). *Competitive advantage through people*. Boston: Harvard Business School Press.
Pfohl, H.-C., & Braun, G. E. (1981). *Entscheidungstheorie*. Munich: Verlag Moderne Industrie.
Pomerol, J. C., & Adam, F. (2006). On the legacy of Herbert Simon and his contribution to decision-making support systems and artificial intelligence. In J. N. D. Gupta, G. A. Forgionne,

& T. M. Mora (Eds.), *Intelligent decision-making support systems* (pp. 25–43). London: Springer.
Rakowski, J. (1980). The theory of the second best and the competitive equilibrium model. *Journal of Economic Issues, 14*(1), 197–207.
Rapoport, A. (1989). *Decision theory and decision behaviour – Normative and descriptive approaches*. Dordrecht: Kluwer Academic Publishers.
Rapoport, A., & Orwant, C. (1962). Experimental games: A review. *Behavioral Science, 7*(1), 1–37.
Read, D. (2007). Experienced utility: Utility theory from Jeremy Bentham to Daniel Kahneman. *Thinking and Reasoning, 13*(1), 45–61.
Robbins, L. (1932). *An essay on the nature and significance of economic science*. Auburn. Reprinted 2007.
Russo, J. E., & Schoemaker, P. J. H. (1989a). *Confident decision making: How to make the right decision every time*. London: Piatkus.
Russo, J. E., & Schoemaker, P. J. H. (1989b). *Decision traps*. New York: Doubleday.
Samuelson, P. A. (1977). St. Petersburg paradoxes: Defanged, dissected, and historically described. *Journal of Economic Literature, 15*(1), 24–55.
Saßmannshausen, S. P. (2009). Der Homo Oeconomicus im Spiegel kognitions- und biopsychologischer Erkenntnisse. In N. Goldschmidt & H. G. Nutzinger (Eds.), *Vom Homo Oeconomicus zum Homo Culturalis* (pp. 61–86). Berlin: LIT Verlag.
Savage, L. J. (1972). *The foundations of statistics* (2nd ed.). New York: Dover.
Schaub, H. (1997). *Sunk Costs, Rationalität und ökonomische Theorie*. Stuttgart: Schäffer-Poeschel.
Schneeweiß, H. (1963). Nutzenaxiomatik und Theorie des Messens. *Statistische Hefte, 4*(1), 178–220.
Scholl, W. (1992). Politische Prozesse in Organisationen. In E. Frese (Ed.), *Handwörterbuch der Organisation* (col. 1993–2004). Stuttgart: Schäffer-Poeschel.
Schulze, W. S., Lubatkin, M. H., & Dino, R. N. (2002). Altruism, agency, and the competitiveness of family firms. *Managerial and Decision Economics, 23*(4–5), 247–259.
Schumpeter, J. A. (1984). The meaning of rationality in the social sciences. *Journal of Institutional and Theoretical Economics, 140*(4), 577–593. Zeitschrift für die gesamte Staatswissenschaft.
Schwenk, C. R. (1985). The use of participant recollection in the modeling of organizational decision process. *Academy of Management Review, 10*(3), 496–503.
Scott, J. (1999). Rational choice theory. In G. Browning, A. Halcli, & F. Webster (Eds.), *Understanding contemporary society: Theories of the present* (pp. 126–138). Thousand Oaks: Sage.
Selten, R. (2002). What is bounded rationality? In G. Gigerenzer & R. Selten (Eds.), *Bounded rationality – The adaptive toolbox* (pp. 13–36). Cambridge: MIT Press.
Sharp, D. J., & Salter, S. B. (1997). Project escalation and sunk costs: A test of the international generalizability of agency and prospect theories. *Journal of International Business Studies, 28*(1), 101–121.
Shimizu, K. (2007). Prospect Theory, behavioral theory, and the threat-rigidity thesis: Combinative effects on organizational decisions to divest formerly acquired units. *Academy of Management Journal, 50*(6), 1495–1514.
Simon, H. A. (1955). A behavioral model of rational choice. *The Quarterly Journal of Economics, 69*(1), 99–118.
Simon, H. A. (1959). Theories of decision-making in economics and behavioral science. *The American Economic Review, 49*(3), 253–283.
Simon, H. A. (1976). *Administrative behavior* (3rd ed.). New York: Macmillan.
Simon, H. A. (1979). Rational decision making in business organizations. *The American Economic Review, 69*(4), 493–513.
Simon, H. A. (1986). Rationality in psychology and economics. *Journal of Business, 59*(4), 209–224.

Simon, H. A. (1990). Invariants of human behavior. *Annual Review of Psychology, 41*(1), 1–20.
Simon, H. A. (2000). Bounded rationality in social science: Today and tomorrow. *Mind and Society, 1*(1), 25–39.
Smith, A. (1966). *An inquiry into the nature and causes of the wealth of nations* (Vol. 1). New Rochelle: Arlington House.
Snowden, D. J., & Boone, M. E. (2007). A leader's framework for decision making. *Harvard Business Review, 85*(11), 68–76.
Starmer, C. (2000). Developments in non-expected utility theory: The hunt for a descriptive theory of choice under risk. *Journal of Economic Literature, 38*(2), 332–382.
Strange, R., Filatotchev, I., Buck, T., & Wright, M. (2009). Corporate governance and international business. *Management International Review, 49*(4), 395–407.
Sugden, R. (1991). Rational choice: A survey of contributions from economics and philosophy. *The Economic Journal, 101*(407), 751–785.
Tagiuri, R. & Davis, J. (1996). Bivalent attributes of the family firm. *Family Business Review, 9*(2), 199–208.
Tietzel, M. (1981). Die Rationalitätsannahme in den Wirtschaftswissenschaften oder Der Homo Oeconomicus und seine Verwandten. *Jahrbuch für Sozialwissenschaft, 32*(2), 115–138.
Tirole, J. (2002). Rational irrationality: Some economics of self-management. *European Economic Review, 46*(4), 633–655.
Tversky, A. (1975). A critique of Expected Utility Theory: Descriptive and normative considerations. *Erkenntnis, 9*(2), 163–173.
Tversky, A., & Kahneman, D. (1974). Judgment under uncertainty: Heuristics and biases. *Science, 185*(4157), 1124–1131.
Tversky, A., & Kahneman, D. (1981). The framing of decisions and the psychology of choice. *Science, 211*(4481), 453–458.
Tversky, A., & Kahneman, D. (1992). Advances in Prospect Theory: Cumulative representation of uncertainty. *Journal of Risk and Uncertainty, 5*(4), 297–323.
Valcárcel, S. (2004). Rationalität. In G. Schreyögg & A. von Werder (Eds.), *Handwörterbuch Unternehmensführung und Organisation* (col. 1236–1244). Stuttgart: Schäffer-Poeschel.
Van der Pligt, J. (1996). Judgement and decision making. In G. R. Semin & K. Fiedler (Eds.), *Applied social psychology* (pp. 173–197). London: Sage.
Von der Oelsnitz, D. (1999). Stand und Entwicklungsperspektiven der betriebswirtschaftlichen Entscheidungsforschung. *Zeitschrift für Planung, 10*(2), 157–176.
Von Mises, L. (1933). *Grundprobleme der Nationalökonomie*. Jena: Gustav Fischer.
Von Mises, L. (1949). *Human action: A treatise on economics*. New Haven: Yale University Press.
Von Neumann, J., & Morgenstern, O. (1953). *Theory of games and economic behavior* (3rd ed.). Princeton: Princeton University Press.
Von Winterfeldt, D. (1989). A re-examination of the normative-descriptive distinction in decision analysis. *Annals of Operations Research, 19*(1), 499–502.
Vriend, N. J. (1996). Rational behavior and economic theory. *Journal of Economic Behavior and Organization, 29*(2), 263–285.
Waddock, S. A., & Graves, S. B. (1997). The corporate social performance-financial performance link. *Strategic Management Journal, 18*(4), 303–319.
Walliser, B. (2008). *Cognitive economics*. Berlin: Springer.
Weber, M. (1972). *Wirtschaft und Gesellschaft* (5th ed.). Tübingen: Mohr Siebeck.
Wolf, J. (2013). *Organisation, Management, Unternehmensführung: Theorien, Praxisbeispiele und Kritik* (5th ed.). Wiesbaden: Gabler.
Wright, P., & Ferris, S. P. (1997). Agency conflict and corporate strategy: The effect of divestment on corporate value. *Strategic Management Journal, 18*(1), 77–83.
Zintl, R. (1989). Der Homo Oeconomicus: Ausnahmeerscheinung in jeder Situation oder Jedermann in Ausnahmesituationen. *Analyse und Kritik, 11*(1), 52–69.
Zouboulakis, M. S. (2014). *The varieties of economic rationality: From Adam Smith to contemporary behavioural and evolutionary economics*. Milton Park: Routledge.

Chapter 3
Escalation of Commitment in Internationalization Processes

Judgment and decision-making plays a significant role for the internationalization of firms. This concerns—first and foremost—two issues, which have been fittingly summarized by Peter Buckley and colleagues: Where should the international activity be located and how should it be controlled?[1] Decisions concerning location choice as well as market entry mode have a defining influence on the success or the failure of the international venture. Hence, it is no exaggeration to argue that judgment and decision-making processes play a vital role in the context of the internationalization of firms.

3.1 Overview of Internationalization Research and Identification of the Importance of the Uppsala Internationalization Process Model

Over the past few decades, scholars in the field of international business have dedicated themselves to the subject of internationalization decisions. In doing so, two fundamentally different views turned out to be dominant.[2] One stream of literature offers a rather traditional economic point of view on the internationalization of firms. This perspective draws on economic theories in order to explain foreign direct investment decisions.[3] Beyond the research object of the firm, it considers the wider functioning and the structure of the economic system as parts of internationalization decisions.[4] In this regard, the transaction cost approach,[5] the

[1]Cf. Buckley et al. (2004, p. 4, 2007, p. 1069).

[2]Cf. Andersson (2000, p. 63).

[3]Cf. Forsgren and Johanson (2010, p. 283) and Björkman and Forsgren (2000, p. 10).

[4]Cf. Vahlne and Johanson (2013, p. 190).

[5]Cf. Hennart (1982, p. 166).

B. Röber, *Escalation of Commitment in Internationalization Processes*, MIR Series in International Business, https://doi.org/10.1007/978-3-319-69102-2_3

internalization theory,[6] and the eclectic paradigm[7] can be seen as prominent exponents. This stream of literature is sometimes even called the "rational choice view" in internationalization research because decision-makers are assumed to be well informed and not impaired by their cognitive limitations.[8] According to this view, firms can base their internationalization decisions on an analysis of market characteristics as well as on respective challenges and opportunities.[9] Dunning's eclectic paradigm, for example, foresees an (equity based) internationalization to be suitable if ownership-specific, internalization, and locational advantages can be identified by a firm.[10] While Dunning offers a finer distinction, these advantages can be summarized as follows: The first refers to—broadly speaking—competitive advantages in a market, the second describes the benefit of an incorporation of up- and/or downstream activities in a firm across borders, and the third refers to a high location attractiveness of a specific (foreign) market. With regard to its economic-theoretical foundations, the eclectic paradigm is built on theories of monopolistic competition and location choice as well as on a transaction cost perspective.[11] While the traditional economic stream of internationalization research has its strengths—namely, the consideration of firm specifics (e.g., the size of the business or firm-specific knowledge) as well as of its environment—it also tends to exclude open questions around the change of these parameters over time.

These open questions are addressed by a second stream in internationalization research, which could be considered as the answer to the above-described traditional economic approach. This stream of literature is not exclusively interested in single internationalization decisions. Much rather it covers the questions of 'how', 'when', and 'where' to internationalize in a sequence of decision periods. Hence, it aims at shedding light on to the development process of international businesses over time.[12] While the second stream of literature is mainly influenced by the studies of Penrose,[13] Cyert and March,[14] as well as Aharoni,[15] it is primarily connected with the names of a group of Scandinavian researchers, who shaped the Uppsala School of Thought.[16] The joint works of Jan Johanson and Jan-Erik Vahlne stand out as the most prominent publications of this group.[17] Starting in

[6]Cf. Buckley and Casson (1991, p. 45, 2009, pp. 1563 ff.) and Teece (1986, pp. 21 ff.).

[7]Cf. Dunning (1980, pp. 9 ff., 1988, pp. 1 ff., 2000, pp. 163 ff.).

[8]Andersson (2000, p. 64).

[9]Cf. Johanson and Vahlne (2009, p. 1426).

[10]Cf. Dunning (1979, p. 272).

[11]Cf. Johanson and Vahlne (1990, p. 11).

[12]Cf. Schmid (2002, p. 387).

[13]Cf. Penrose (2009, p. 8).

[14]Cf. Cyert and March (1963, p. 31).

[15]Cf. Aharoni (1966, pp. 14 ff.).

[16]Cf. Forsgren and Johanson (2010, pp. 283 ff.), Johanson and Vahlne (1977, pp. 23 ff.), Johanson and Wiedersheim-Paul (1975, pp. 305 ff.), and Carlson (1966, pp. 5 ff.).

[17]Cf. Andersen (1993, p. 210).

1977, they began to develop a processual theory on internationalization: the Uppsala Internationalization Process Model.[18] In the 1970s, the predominant IB perspective was US-centric. Against this background, the motivation behind the development of the U-Model was the possible finding of an explication about the internationalization behavior of firms from small market economies.[19] Johanson and Vahlne observed that internationalization happens incrementally as managers continuously acquire knowledge about foreign markets.[20] With this insight, they developed the U-Model, which acknowledges that decision-makers are confronted with different information contexts during the internationalization process and that they come to different decisions, depending on their current state of knowledge.

Due to its processual perspective on the internationalization of firms as well as due to its respect for limited information availability for decision-makers, the U-Model is considered to be a realistic abstraction,[21] which defines the currently prevailing perspective within the field of internationalization research and which enjoys immense popularity in international business literature.[22] As it takes the behavioral theory of the firm[23] into account, and as it emphasizes the role of knowledge in the internationalization process, the U-Model was and still is leading the way for subsequent, rather behaviorist, studies. Hutzschenreuter and colleagues, who conducted a bibliometric analysis of contemporary internationalization research, argue that the U-Model "set the stage [...] for the study of internationalization positions, paths, and processes, and much of the subsequent literature on internationalization."[24] As of 2017, a short search with Google Scholar revealed that a total of 10,246 publications cited Johanson's and Vahlne's initial study—many of which from the current year. This highlights the continued interest in the U-Model by academia. Furthermore, the (relatively)[25] recent review of the U-Model by Johanson and Vahlne themselves, published in the pages of Journal of International Business Studies, illustrates the continued relevance of their approach despite its initial publication in 1977.[26]

It is noteworthy that the U-Model is commonly associated with behaviorist theories, which build on bounded rationality. Indeed, it does consider Cyert's and March's theory of the firm,[27] and it does account for limited information availability. Yet as outlined in Sect. 2.1.2 of the present study, rational action of decision-makers is not only impaired by limited information availability but also by a limited

[18]Cf. Johanson and Vahlne (1977, pp. 23 ff., 1990, pp. 11 ff., 2009, pp. 1411 ff.).

[19]Cf. Forsgren and Johanson (2010, p. 284).

[20]Cf. Sullivan and Bauerschmidt (1990, p. 19).

[21]Cf. Schmid (2002, p. 390).

[22]Cf. Hutzschenreuter et al. (2007, pp. 1055–1056) and Sullivan and Bauerschmidt (1990, p. 20).

[23]Cf. Cyert and March (1963, pp. 114 ff.) and Aharoni (1966, p. 17).

[24]Hutzschenreuter et al. (2007, p. 1056).

[25]In comparison to the date of publication of the initial study (1977).

[26]Cf. Johanson and Vahlne (2009, pp. 1411 ff.).

[27]Cf. Sect. 2.1.1.4 for a short insight into the significance of the theory of the firm.

cognitive capability of decision-makers to process the given information. Despite its path-breaking processual perspective, this aspect is possibly neglected by the U-Model and allows the assumption that the seemingly realistic foundations of the theory present an argumentative gap. As cognitive biases have a distinct influence on judgment and decision-making processes of managers in a general context, it is likely that they also have an influence on the decisions within the internationalization process of firms.

Against this potential shortcoming, the present study attempts to explore whether or not there is substantial evidence for the display of bounded rationality in the form of escalation of commitment in internationalization processes. Escalation of commitment presents a behavioral bias, which misleads a decision-maker into continued investments in a failing course of action.[28] As such, it could be an example for the cognitive limitations that influence internationalization process decision-making in a contradicting manner to the U-Model. In order to discuss this assumption, the actual rational choice and bounded rationality contents of Johanson's and Vahlne's approach need to be critically classified first. For this purpose, the following Sect. 3.2 is dedicated to the classification of the U-Model within the two-dimensional framework, which has been introduced in Sect. 2.2 of the present study.[29] Thereafter, Sect. 3.3 will outline the specifics of escalation of commitment and present its potential impact on internationalization process decision-making.

3.2 Study-Specific, Rationality-Related Classification of the Uppsala Internationalization Process Model

Whether or not the display of escalation of commitment in internationalization process decision-making contradicts the U-Model depends first and foremost on the theory's prescriptive and descriptive perspective as well as on its behavioral assumptions. The following section will therefore attempt to clarify this matter by introducing the U-Model in depth and by classifying selfsame with regard to the above mentioned criteria. The applied taxonomy will be similar to the line of thought of the exemplary classification of judgment and decision-making concepts in Sect. 2.2.3.

---

[28]Cf. Brockner et al. (1986, p. 122).

[29]Cf. Sect. 2.2.1 for the previously outlined classification criteria.

3.2.1 Internationalization Processes According to the U-Model

Essentially, the U-Model consists of two different parts. On the one hand, it is built on an empirical basis (Johanson's and Wiedersheim-Paul's study of four Swedish companies), which is reflected in the identified pattern of internationalization (Sect. 3.2.1.1). On the other hand, it presents a theoretical model of internationalization (Sect. 3.2.1.2). Both parts will be outlined in the following.

3.2.1.1 Pattern of Internationalization

Against the background of Johanson's and Wiedersheim-Paul's study of four Swedish companies, Johanson and Vahlne identified a recurring pattern of internationalization.[30] This pattern is shaped by the so-called 'establishment chain' of internationalization, which—in return—is related to the 'psychic distance' to targeted markets.[31]

It is the principal insight of the establishment chain that the internationalization of a firm in a specific country develops in four successive stages. With each stage there comes a different market entry mode[32] as well as—at least implicitly—a higher degree of international involvement in the form of an increased commitment of resources to the market under consideration.[33] The firms, which have been reviewed by Johanson and Vahlne, showed no international activities initially. Over time, they began the internationalization process with exports via independent representatives (export agents). Later on, sales subsidiaries and finally manufacturing facilities were put into operation (cf. Fig. 3.1).

Occasionally, the establishment chain is criticized as a non-representative simplification since it does not consider neither advances in entry mode literature, e.g., studies on licensing and joint ventures, nor the multifaceted drivers of entry mode choices, e.g., firm resources.[34] Johanson and Vahlne partially responded to this criticism that the lacking consideration of respective market entry modes is not problematic as they were not common (at that time) for the Swedish firms, which were under review.[35]

The other observation of the internationalization pattern is related to a successively growing psychic distance to targeted markets. The original publication of the U-Model defines psychic distance as "the sum of factors preventing the flow of

[30]Cf. Johanson and Wiedersheim-Paul (1975, pp. 305 ff.).

[31]Cf. Johanson and Vahlne (1977, p. 24).

[32]Stage 3 and Stage 4 are in fact both foreign direct investments, yet, they fulfill very different tasks in the foreign market.

[33]Cf. Andersen (1993, p. 210) and Johanson and Vahlne (1990, p. 13).

[34]Cf. Andersen (1993, p. 222).

[35]Cf. Johanson and Vahlne (2009, p. 1422).

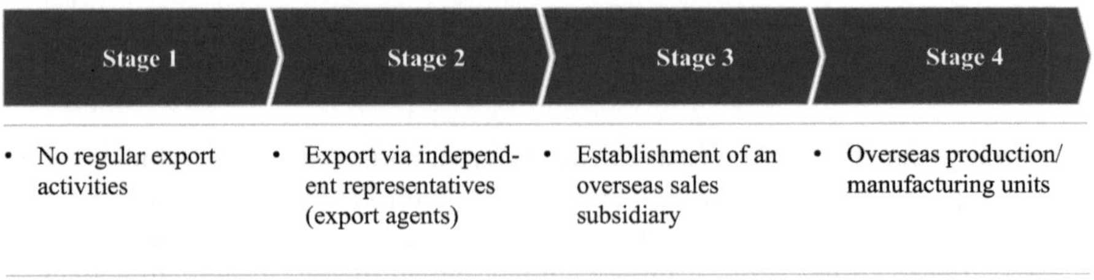

Fig. 3.1 Establishment chain of internationalization. Source: Own figure, based on Andersen (1993, p. 210) and Johanson and Vahlne (1977, p. 24)

information from and to the market."[36] Specifically, it is about, for example, differences in language, education, business practices, culture, and industrial development.[37] It is argued that firms begin to internationalize in markets that they understand best, as this reduces market risks and uncertainties.[38] With increasing internationalization knowledge, markets characterized by more psychic distance come into question for further internationalization steps. The reasoning behind this argument is, inter alia, associated with the liability of foreignness for international ventures, i.e., the cost associated with an unfamiliarity with the foreign market environment.[39] As a result, firms show a progressive expansion pattern towards less similar and more complex markets (cf. Fig. 3.2).[40]

With their latest update, Johanson and Vahlne pointed out that the domestic market may not necessarily be "the most relevant unit in terms of psychic distance" because factors preventing the flow of information can eventually even be found at home (i.e., within the domestic market).[41] Therefore, the authors refined their psychic distance argument and concluded that problems of firms arise with network structures and a "liability of outsidership",[42] which could surface in specific markets as well as in broader regions (irrespective of the corresponding foreignness).[43] In summary, the internationalization pattern of firms is shaped by steadily increasing internationalization knowledge as well as by a continuous progressive expansion towards high psychic distance markets over time.[44]

[36] Johanson and Vahlne (1977, p. 24).
[37] Cf. Johnston et al. (2012, p. 38).
[38] Cf. Johanson and Vahlne (1990, p. 13).
[39] Cf. Johanson and Vahlne (2009, p. 1412) and Zaheer (1995, p. 341).
[40] Cf. Sullivan and Bauerschmidt (1990, p. 20).
[41] Johanson and Vahlne (2009, p. 1421).
[42] Johanson and Vahlne (2009, p. 1411) and see also Johanson and Vahlne (2003, pp. 83 ff.).
[43] Cf. Rugman and Verbeke (2007, pp. 200 ff.).
[44] Cf. Petersen et al. (2003, pp. 39 ff.).

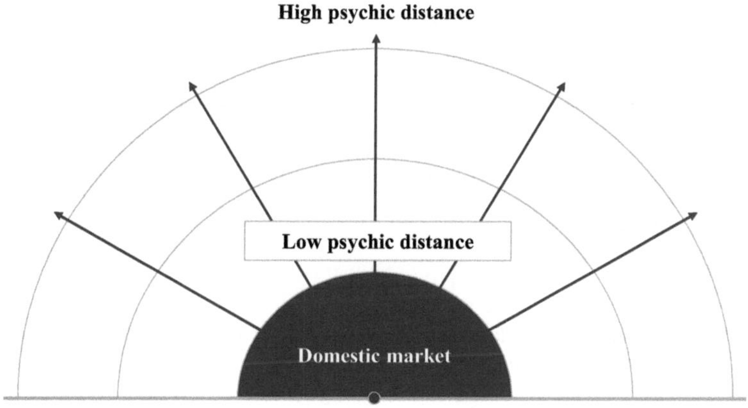

Fig. 3.2 Progressive expansion pattern towards higher psychic distance. Source: Own figure

3.2.1.2 Model of Internationalization

Based on the empirical insights, Johanson and Vahlne developed a dynamic model according to which a firm's progressive expansion and increasing foreign market involvement are rooted in the gradual accumulation of knowledge (i.e., organizational learning).[45] The authors consider their model as an abstraction of "an interplay" between knowledge development and increasing foreign market commitments in reality.[46] The fundamental logic behind the model is based on the high degree of uncertainty with which managers are frequently confronted prior to internationalization decisions and which entails a reluctance towards doing business abroad. During the early stages of an internationalization process—and due to first experiences—decision-makers are additionally facing hard facts, which hold the potential to increase the reluctance towards further, immediate internationalization steps as a result of a confrontation with one's own overoptimistic expectations. Only with increasing internationalization knowledge over time as well as with a growing self-confidence of decision-makers is this reluctance eventually reduced and further internationalization steps become initiated.[47] The U-Model depicts this process with a differentiation between 'state' and 'change' aspects of internationalization. The former consist of 'market commitment' as well as 'market knowledge' and the latter of 'commitment decisions' as well as 'current (business) activities'. Due to an assumed reciprocal and repeated affecting between state and change aspects (e.g., high market knowledge is followed by new commitment decisions, which increase market commitments in return), it can be regarded as a dynamic model (cf. Fig. 3.3).[48]

---

[45]Cf. Sullivan and Bauerschmidt (1990, p. 29).

[46]Johanson and Vahlne (2006, p. 166).

[47]Cf. Petersen et al. (2003, p. 42).

[48]Cf. Andersen (1993, p. 211) and Johanson and Vahlne (1977, pp. 26–27).

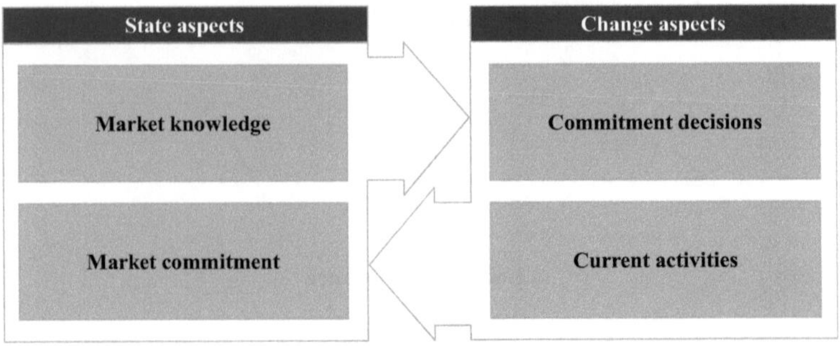

Fig. 3.3 Interplay between the state and change aspects of internationalization. Source: Own figure, modeled after Johanson and Vahlne (1977, p. 26)

'Market commitment' is put together from the amount of resources committed to the foreign market as well as from the degree of commitment. These inputs are not identical: While the first could be operationalized best by the size of an investment, the second refers primarily to the (lack of) transferability of an investment, i.e., the permanence of the commitment.[49] Johanson and Vahlne do not assume a general analogousness between market commitment and market investment. As companies interact in multiple ways with other market participants in a foreign country, a variety of other factors, which result in dependence as well as decision irreversibility, determine the commitment to a foreign market (e.g., long term agency contracts, deployment of human resources, etc.).[50] In a broad sense, intangible commitments matter as much as (plain monetary) investments.[51] It must also be mentioned that the later stages of the establishment chain imply a high market commitment because foreign direct investments (i.e., Stages 3 and 4) are difficult to reverse (in comparison to the export-based internationalization in Stage 2) and require the binding of resources. While the model predicts that an initial commitment—and the resultant dependence for the firm—will lead to further ones, an escalation of selfsame is not foreseen. Only in Mats Forsgren's and Jan Johanson's discussion of the U-Model, the reader's awareness is briefly turned to the possibility of an escalation of commitment as well as to the resultant dependencies for future decisions. This line of thought, however, is not further pursued in their publication.[52]

In addition to the buildup of commitment, firms acquire important 'market knowledge' due to their involvement in foreign markets. To a certain extent, market knowledge enables decision-makers to perceive risks and opportunities correctly. On the one hand, objective knowledge may be bought from outside partners while, on the other hand, experiential knowledge must be developed with one's own

[49] Cf. Andersen (1993, p. 211) and Johanson and Vahlne (1977, p. 27).

[50] Cf. Forsgren and Johanson (2010, p. 300) and Johanson and Vahlne (2006, pp. 168–169).

[51] Cf. Forsgren (2002, p. 263) and Hadjikhani (1997, pp. 50–52).

[52] Cf. Forsgren and Johanson (2010, p. 300).

international business activities. In both cases, the knowledge factor is related to the psychic distance of targeted foreign markets because internationalization to countries marked by high psychic distance requires previously accumulated objective and experiential knowledge in closer markets. The interpretation of knowledge as a resource builds a bridge between market commitment and market knowledge. From this perspective, a large knowledge regarding a specific country stands for a valuable (intangible) resource commitment to the respective market.[53]

Change aspects ('commitment decisions' and 'current activities') constitute the second important building block of the dynamic U-Model. The previously outlined state aspects are exposed to a continuous advancement as decisions about future projects as well as about ongoing activities are permanent drivers of a firm's international development. In this process, commitment decisions can be viewed as the reaction to the perceived risks and opportunities of current activities. In summary, the above mentioned reciprocal and repeated affecting between state and change aspects illustrates that even very small internationalization steps are part of a learning process, which increases the internationalization knowledge of a firm. Thus, every internationalization decision changes the current internationalization state of the firm. Likewise, a new state, better market knowledge for example, presents an incentive for further internationalization steps. Therefore, an internationalization process according to the U-Model is marked by permanent changes, with which a firm will always advance its international involvement over time.[54]

3.2.2 *Classification of the U-Model's Descriptive and Prescriptive Perspective*

In Sect. 2.2, it has been indicated that the U-Model offers at least potentially an explanatory value for decision-making in internationalization processes and that it is subjected to a critical review with the present study. In order to substantiate this statement, the U-Model's prescriptive and descriptive perspective will be critically discussed in the following. This classification is built on the same criteria, which have been in introduced in Sect. 2.2.1.[55] The reader should recall that a specific approach is usually considered to be descriptive, if it puts primarily the decision-making process at the center of analysis, if it conceptualizes the actual JDM process based on empirical insights, and if it does not build a priori on simplified models of reality. In contrast, a prescriptive approach puts the decision content and corresponding predictions at the center of analysis, applies formal scientific and analytical methods, and builds on simplified models of reality.[56]

---

[53]Cf. Forsgren (2002, p. 263), Schmid (2002, p. 388), and Johanson and Vahlne (1977, p. 28).

[54]Cf. Schmid (2002, p. 389).

[55]Cf. Sect. 2.2.4 of the present study for a summarizing overview of the mentioned criteria.

[56]Cf. Sect. 2.2.1 of the present study.

Johanson and Vahlne award their theory only a "limited predictive value".[57] According to the opinion of the authors, the U-Model's focus is set on the explanation of the "characteristics of the internationalization process of the firm".[58] As outlined before, such a processual understanding of judgment and decision-making problems is indicative for a descriptive approach. This is furthermore supported with a statement by the authors, in which they express their hope "that the model will contribute to conceptualization in the field of internationalization" (ergo, it is about the contribution to and not about the application of a conceptualization).[59] The empirical insight gained from the four Swedish cases is the basis of this conceptualization. This represents a proceeding that is, again, quite typical for descriptive approaches to JDM. Yet most importantly, Johanson and Vahlne themselves offer an interpretation as they characterize their model to be descriptive due to its argumentative basis, which builds on Cyert's and March's behavioral theory of the firm, which questions classic economic beliefs.[60] Figure 3.4 provides an overview of selected quotes of Johanson's and Vahlne's works, which support an interpretation of the U-Model as a descriptive approach. Other scholars as well tend to consider the U-Model as a (rather) realistic, that is to say descriptive, approach.[61] Mainly, this thinking is justified with the U-Model's empirical basis in the form of the establishment chain and the psychic distance to targeted markets.

In contrast to this descriptive reading of the U-Model, Johanson's and Vahlne's theory is also criticized as exceedingly deterministic and unidirectional.[62] A critique, which has been—at least implicitly—nurtured when the authors argued that an initiated internationalization process will proceed "regardless" of whether or not strategic decisions are made in this direction.[63] The U-Model implies that there is a predefined internationalization path, which determines the choice of foreign markets as well as the foreign market entry mode.[64] In this context, Forsgren points out that there is a significant similarity between the U-Model and an economic life cycle process.[65] Firstly, this is justified by the U-Model's prediction that each phase of the internationalization process is linked to the previous one, and because the outcome of the former constitutes the input for the latter. Secondly, the sequence of the process follows a certain formal logic, which is defined by the market risk as well as by a firm's knowledge and organizational learning. According to the U-Model, a firm will incrementally extend its internationalization until the existing

---

[57] Johanson and Vahlne (1977, p. 23).

[58] Johanson and Vahlne (2009, p. 1411).

[59] Johanson and Vahlne (1977, p. 23).

[60] Cf. Cyert and March (1963, pp. 114 ff.).

[61] Cf. Schmid (2002, p. 390).

[62] Cf. Perks and Hughes (2008, p. 312), Melin (1992, p. 104), Turnbull (1987, pp. 23–26), Reid and Rosson (1987, pp. 7–8), and Reid (1983, pp. 44–45).

[63] Johanson and Vahlne (1990, p. 12).

[64] Cf. Schmid (2002, p. 390).

[65] Cf. Forsgren (2002, p. 267).

Descriptive content

»

"We hope that the model will contribute to conceptualization in the field of internationalization of the firm [...]"

(Johanson, J., Vahlne, J.-E. (1977), p. 23)

"The model is based on empircal [sic] observations from our studies in international business at the University of Uppsala [...]"

(Johanson, J., Vahlne, J.-E. (1977), p. 24)

"The Uppsala model explains the characteristics of the internationalization process of the firm."

(Johanson, J., Vahlne, J.-E. (2009), p. 1411)

"We considered the model to be descriptive, largely because we based it on Cyert and March (1963)."

(Johanson, J., Vahlne, J.-E. (2009), p. 1412) «

Fig. 3.4 Exemplary descriptive content of Johanson's and Vahlne's writings. Source: Own figure

market risk (R_i) reaches the firm's maximum tolerable market risk (R^*_i). With increasing market knowledge, the maximum tolerable market risk is increasing as well, and further internationalization efforts are made. While this logic seems to reveal a deterministic procedure indeed, Johanson and Vahlne defend their model with the note that internationalization may proceed regardless of strategic decisions but not regardless of firm performance.[66] They foresee uncertainty-reducing commitment decisions if the existing market risk (R_i) exceeds the maximum tolerable market risk (R^*_i). The nature of uncertainty-reducing commitment decisions, however, remained vague with the 1977 publication. In 2009, Johanson and Vahlne refined their argument and stated that internationalization might decline or even cease in unfavorable circumstances. While this answers the determinism reproach to a certain extent, the authors' statement remains ambiguous because they also repeat their (still relatively deterministic) argument that internationalization "will continue as long as the performance and prospects are favorable."[67]

Furthermore, business reality is simplified in the U-Model. "Solutions to market operations problems", for example, "are searched for in the neighborhood of the problem".[68] While this is plausible reasoning, it demonstrates that the U-Model

[66]Cf. Johanson and Vahlne (2009, p. 1412).

[67]Johanson and Vahlne (2009, p. 1412).

[68]Johanson and Vahlne (1977, p. 29).

Prescriptive Content

"In such a model [n.b., the U-Model] the outcome of one decision [...] constitutes the input of the next."

(Johanson, J., Vahlne, J.-E. (1977), p. 26)

"[...] we say that scale-increasing decisions will be taken when $R_i < R^*_i$. [n.b., R_i = existing market risk situation; R^*_i = maximum tolerable market risk]. The firm will incrementally extend its scale of existing operations [...] until its tolerable risk frontier (R^*_i) is met."

(Johanson, J., Vahlne, J.-E. (1977), p. 30)

"We also think that the model can be useful in planning and decision making in the firm [...] thus giving a better base for planning and executing the internationalization process."

(Johanson, J., Vahlne, J.-E. (1977), p. 31)

"More recent empirical studies have indicated that the internationalization process as explained by our model has a positive impact on performance. Our model can therefore [...] be used for prescriptive purposes."

(Johanson, J., Vahlne, J.-E. (2009), p. 1413)

Fig. 3.5 Exemplary prescriptive content of Johanson's and Vahlne's writings. Source: Own figure

does—in fact—make simplifying assumptions a priori.[69] Johanson and Vahlne also imply a certain instrumental understanding of their model, when they argue that it could be a useful application for "planning and decision making".[70] In 2009, they argued additionally that their theory could be used for prescriptive purposes. Overall, the U-Model remains a theory, which interprets internationalization primarily as an ongoing, forward moving process towards international expansion. With its predefined internationalization path, the U-Model possesses a significant predictive capacity and could thus also be interpreted as a prescriptive approach to JDM in internationalization processes (cf. Fig. 3.5).

In summary, the U-Model and its processual understanding as well as its empirical foundation show clear attributes of descriptive JDM approaches. Likewise, however, it presents an instrumental basis in order to deal with the pitfalls of internationalization due to its prescriptive and predictive statements. Thus, the U-Model is ambiguous and allows a descriptive as well as a prescriptive interpretation. This conclusion is not only demonstrated with Johanson's and Vahlne's somewhat contradictory statements (cf. Figs. 3.4 and 3.5), but it is furthermore

[69]Cf. Forsgren (2002, p. 269).

[70]Johanson and Vahlne (1977, p. 31).

supported by Forsgren and Johanson, who argued that "some researchers have been interested in the normative, rather than descriptive, implementations of the model."[71]

3.2.3 *Classification of the U-Model's Behavioral Assumptions*

Besides the prescriptive and descriptive perspective, the second differentiating criterion for judgment and decision-making models is the underlying behavioral assumption. On the one hand, JDM theories may build on behavior-oriented assumptions. This means that a respective JDM approach takes into consideration that decision-makers are confronted with limited environmental information availability and that they also have to deal with the problem of their own limited cognitive capability to process the given information (due to behavioral biases, e.g., escalation of commitment). On the other hand, the postulate could build on neoclassical behavioral assumptions: This means that decision-makers actually possess the ability to identify and adopt ideal solutions and that they act consistently and purposefully in accordance with their own preferences in a maximizing manner.

Not only because of the U-Model's proximity to the behavioral theory of the firm, it offers a realistic idea of what decision-makers' behavior in internationalization processes may actually look like. Internationalization decisions according to the U-Model are not necessarily considered to be the result of a strictly rational JDM process because they are assumed to be "in response to perceived" risks and opportunities.[72] Since risks and opportunities can be perceived differently, corresponding JDM processes may vary as well. The U-Model's specific consideration of managerial perceptions clarifies that decision-makers' knowledge is restricted. Complete information for decision-makers, however, constitutes a key element of neoclassical behavioral assumptions. Thus, the U-Model and its consideration of incomplete knowledge disqualifies as a clear-cut example of a neoclassical JDM approach. Behavior-oriented JDM theories, on the other hand, take the limited information availability for decision-makers into account. Furthermore, Johanson and Vahlne highlight the uncertainty, with which decision-makers are confronted in internationalization processes. This uncertainty is reflected in the difficulty of an assessment of the tolerable and existing market risk situations. Due to these aspects, the authors consider uncertainty and bounded rationality to be the "underlying assumptions"[73] of their model (cf. Fig. 3.6).

---

[71]Forsgren and Johanson (2010, p. 284).

[72]Johanson and Vahlne (1977, p. 29); cf. also Schmid (2002, p. 389).

[73]Johanson and Vahlne (2009, p. 1412).

Behavior-oriented content

»

"Another constraint on the problem solution is the lack of, and difficulty of obtaining market knowledge in international operations"

(Johanson, J., Vahlne, J.-E. (1977), p. 26)

"We assume [...] that the uncertainty effect concerns the market uncertainty, that is the decision-makers' perceived lack of ability to estimate the present and future market and market-influencing factors."

(Johanson, J., Vahlne, J.-E. (1977), p. 29)

"The underlying assumptions of our 1977 model are uncertainty and bounded rationality."

(Johanson, J., Vahlne, J.-E. (2009), p. 1412) «

Fig. 3.6 Exemplary behavior-oriented content of Johanson's and Vahlne's writings. Source: Own figure

Their evaluation, however, tends to be premature because the U-Model does not consider the second relevant element of behavior-oriented JDM approaches: Often, limited cognitive capabilities of decision-makers hamper their ability to actually process the available decision-making information. In this context, it is worthwhile to recall Herbert A. Simon's understanding of bounded rationality, to which he referred—metaphorically spoken—as a pair of scissors. While the first blade represents the limited information availability for decision-makers, the second depicts their limited computational capability to process the available information. Especially, cognitive limitations and behavioral biases (such as overconfidence) belong into the sphere of the latter and present significant decision-making issues for decision-makers in reality.[74] Yet, neither cognitive limitations nor respective behavioral biases are subjects of discussion within the U-Model (which shows that uncertainty and bounded rationality are not fully reflected—contrary to the above cited quote of Johanson and Vahlne). Considering the previously outlined importance of heuristics and biases for managerial judgment and decision-making processes,[75] this seems to be a considerable shortcoming of the U-Model. It could be the case that decision-makers in internationalization processes are not only confronted with lacking knowledge and high uncertainty, but that they also have difficulties to deal cognitively with the limited information that they possess. Furthermore, one could argue that the U-Model considers decision-makers at least implicitly to be rational actors in a neoclassical sense. First and foremost, this is supported with the U-Model's assumption that they weight purposefully

[74]Cf. Sect. 2.1.2.

[75]Cf. Sect. 2.1.2 for more information on the heuristics and biases program of bounded rationality.

Neoclassical content

»

"Using this framework we say that scale-increasing decisions will be taken when $R_i < R^*_i$. [...] Uncertainty-reducing commitments on the other hand will be made when $R_i > R^*_i$."

(Johanson, J., Vahlne, J.-E. (1977), p. 30)

"[...] given the circumstances, the decision makers in our model are rational. Clearly, knowledge is never complete."

(Johanson, J., Vahlne, J.-E. (2009), p. 1418) «

Fig. 3.7 Exemplary neoclassical content of Johanson's and Vahlne's writings. Source: Own figure

between existing (R_i) as well as tolerable market risks (R^*_i). According to the theory, new commitment decisions are consistently taken on the basis of existing market knowledge and market commitments. This implies the ability of an evaluation regarding the internal and external environment of the firm. Even if this happens under the restriction of incomplete knowledge, consistent and purposeful decisions are typical neoclassical behavioral assumptions. Furthermore, experience plays a major role in the U-Model because it can increase the rational decision-making ability of decision-makers.[76] According to the U-Model, experienced decision-makers possess the cognitive capability to identify and adopt ideal solutions.[77] This happens—in a maximizing manner—either with further commitment decisions or with uncertainty-reducing actions. Johanson and Vahlne consider decision-makers in their model to be rational actors—under the limiting restriction of incomplete knowledge (cf. Fig. 3.7).

In summary, the U-Model does not apply neoclassical assumptions about decision-makers as they usually do not possess complete information in the theoretical construct. Therefore, it is no orthodox JDM approach in the sense of Rational Choice Theory. Behavior-oriented assumptions, however, are limited to lacking information availability and high uncertainty in international markets. Cognitive dispositions are not taken into consideration. Thus, decision-makers in internationalization processes have 'a limited horizon', but within this limitation they are expected to act purposefully and consistently with regard to their preferences.

[76]Cf. Buckley et al. (2007, p. 1072).

[77]Cf. Johanson and Vahlne (1977, p. 29).

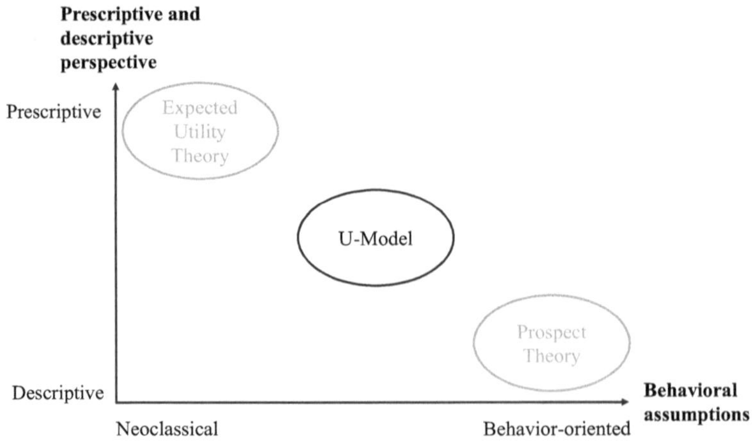

Fig. 3.8 Classification of the U-Model as a JDM concept. Source: Own figure

3.2.4 Section Conclusion

As the present study presents inter alia a critical review of the U-Model, it was the aim of this section "to clarify whether or not the U-Model is actually as realistic as supposed, to discuss its stance with regard to bounded rationality contents, and to highlight its implicit assumption of rationally proceeding decision-makers".[78] For this purpose, the classification framework, which was introduced in Sect. 2.2, has here been applied. As it was mentioned before, JDM theories in general are potentially multi-dimensional with regard to their prescriptive and descriptive perspective as well as to their behavioral assumptions.[79] In this respect, the U-Model is no exception because it is shaped by prescriptive as well as by descriptive elements. This conclusion is not only documented by contrasting statements of the authors but also by Forsgren and Johanson, who highlighted different interpretation possibilities of the model.[80] On a scale between unidimensional prescriptive and descriptive JDM approaches (such as EUT and Prospect Theory) it should therefore be located in the middle (cf. Fig. 3.8).

Furthermore, it is recorded that the U-Model cannot be considered a JDM approach, which is built on neoclassical or behavior-oriented premises alone. Due to its consideration of incomplete information in internationalization processes, fully rational choices—as foreseen by EUT for example—cannot be executed. At the same time, however, it is not possible to attribute the U-Model to JDM approaches, which apply behavior-oriented assumptions. In this regard, Johanson's and Vahlne's theory is limited by the lacking consideration of cognitive

[78] As stated in Sect. 1.4 of the present study.

[79] Cf. Sect. 2.2.2 for more information on the multi-dimensionality of JDM approaches.

[80] Cf. Forsgren and Johanson (2010, p. 284).

dispositions and behavioral biases. Due to its ambiguousness with regard to neo-classical and behavior-oriented contents, the U-Model is located between Expected Utility Theory and Prospect Theory in the previously developed classification framework, which is depicted in Fig. 3.8.[81]

In conclusion of this classification of the U-Model, one must say that the theory cannot be considered a JDM approach based on rational choices. Yet, it is certainly neither a completely realistic model of bounded rationality. In a way, decision-makers are—at least implicitly—expected to act rationally, i.e., consistently and purposefully (with regard to their preferences), under the restriction of incomplete information. Against this insight, it is safe to say that the U-Model implies at least inter alia rationally proceeding managers. Thus, it must also allow for a critical review in this regard.

3.3 Escalation of Commitment as a Contradiction to the Anticipated Internationalization Process According to the U-Model

In the field of international business, scholarly articles, which address market exits in internationalization processes, are underrepresented compared to studies that cover the international growth of firms.[82] In 2005, Gabriel Benito pointed appropriately out, that it is "suggestive" that international market exit decisions do not appear in the "anthology on the state-of-the-art in international business research",[83] the Oxford Handbook of International Business.[84] From the representatives of the Uppsala School of Thought, only Welch and Wiedersheim-Paul have undertaken a critical review of failures in (export-staged) internationalization processes.[85] Furthermore, an interesting study has been presented by Matthyssens and Pauwels, who studied internal and external drivers of internationalization exits and corresponding behavioral processes with a comparative case study design in a marketing-psychological related context.[86] Besides a change-accelerating effect of a firm's strategic flexibility on internationalization exits, they noticed a gap between the scholastically identified (supposed beneficial) accumulation of

[81]Certainly, Expected Utility Theory and Prospect Theory present a different category of JDM approaches than the U-Model, which is not a typical JDM approach (despite providing certain decision-making information). Nevertheless, all three are depicted in Fig. 3.8 in order to give the reader a better chance of comparison.

[82]Cf. Matthyssens and Pauwels (2000, p. 698); exceptions include Oesterle (1999, pp. 225–229), Benito and Welch (1997, pp. 7 ff.), Fletcher (2001, pp. 25 ff.), Barkema et al. (1996, pp. 151 ff.), Li (1995, pp. 333 ff.), and Bonaccorsi (1992, pp. 605 ff.).

[83]Benito (2005, p. 236).

[84]Cf. Rugman (2009).

[85]Cf. Welch and Wiedersheim-Paul (1980, p. 22).

[86]Cf. Matthyssens and Pauwels (2000, p. 699).

commitment in international marketing and an actually occurring escalation situation, which leads to a strategic drift and failure of the firm. While the authors highlighted an additional need for further empirical observations in this regard, they referred to escalation of commitment as a possible gap-determining factor. The fact that their study has been published in the pages of 'Psychology and Marketing' could explain why it has gone—unfortunately—rather unnoticed in the world of international business (given its relatively low count of citations).[87]

Also with Matthyssen's and Pauwel's call for further empirical research in mind, the present study aims at a demonstration of a display of escalation of commitment in IP decision-making. It considers this particular behavioral bias as a representative of bounded rationality and as a possible contradiction to the implicit assumption of rationally proceeding managers of the U-Model. Thus, it presents an IB-relevant advancement compared to the study of Matthyssens and Pauwels, which looks—in a broader sense—at escalation of commitment as one critical factor among others in the context of internationalization exits.

Escalation of commitment has been empirically documented in different contexts and refers—generally spoken—to the tendency of decision-makers to escalate an "ineffective course of action".[88] Frequently, it is also associated with the terms 'sunk cost effect', 'entrapment' or 'too much invested to quit'.[89] As managers should usually try to perform well and in the best interest of their organization,[90] they could unconsciously escalate their decisions in a previously chosen path once they are confronted with negative results.[91] Multiple theoretical explanations have been presented for this phenomenon and different determining factors have been identified. Following Festinger's dissonance theory, for example, escalation of commitment could be caused by a cognitive incompatibility between, on the one hand, the decision-maker's knowledge and, on the other hand, his/her initial attitudes and motivations.[92]

3.3.1 Questioned Empirical Validity of the U-Model Against Business Reality and Bounded Rationality

Before the phenomenon of escalation of commitment will be thoroughly introduced in the following, a statement regarding the U-Model's empirical validity is purposeful as it could be questioned for a number of arguments. The internationalization

[87]As of 2017, a short search with Google Scholar revealed 49 citations of which only an insignificant number appeared in IB related scientific journals.

[88]Brockner et al. (1986, p. 109).

[89]Cf. Ibid.; Teger (1980, pp. 10–11) and Staw (1976, p. 27).

[90]Cf. the remarks on the Stewardship approach in Sect. 2.1.1.4.

[91]Cf. Sleesman et al. (2012, p. 547).

[92]Cf. Beauvois et al. (1993, p. 2) and Festinger (1957, pp. 260 ff.).

process of firms has often been analyzed.[93] A number of studies support the foreseen incremental internationalization path of the U-Model, thus confirming that international experiences as well as organizational learning have a significant (positive) impact on the international growth of firms.[94] Likewise, however, there are research results that indicate that not all businesses approach the internationalization process as it is predicted by the U-Model's stages theory.[95] Possible deviations have been studied in different contexts. The observation that new business ventures make right away use of global demand structures is often the common denominator of these critical approaches. Such businesses leapfrog over the stages of the establishment chain of internationalization (this could mean that wholly owned subsidiaries are established in a foreign market, even if no export activities have preceded). 'International New Ventures' or 'Born Globals', as these firms are called, have not only stirred up certain business branches (e.g., the retail industry due to new technologies) but have also left their mark in international business literature.[96] Whether or not one could consider this approach to be a processual model of internationalization is disputed because corresponding—rather entrepreneurial—companies move along unexpected and not necessarily processual lines of global expansion.[97]

In recent statements in response to their critics, Johanson and Vahlne do not dispute a declining validity of the establishment chain.[98] They agree that the context of internationalization has changed drastically over the past few decades due to lower transportation and communication costs. However, they defend the establishment chain altogether because the building of a firm "from scratch" and the corresponding "process of learning and building commitment will take time" today as much as yesterday.[99] Similarly, the authors justify the unaltered validity of the psychic distance dimension of their observations. Psychic distance seems to contradict the International New Venture research program, which highlights that Born Globals enter markets with a rather general, globally valid knowledge. According to this perspective, corresponding businesses benefit from an increased confidence (due to their globally valid knowledge) with which they target attractive markets regardless of their psychic proximity—thus contradicting the predicted internationalization path of the original version of the U-Model. Yet, according to Johanson and Vahlne, this does not imply a lack of importance of psychic distance altogether, as it has an unchanged effect on various factors for firms abroad (such as

[93]Cf. Barkema et al. (1996, p. 153).

[94]Cf. Luo and Peng (1999, pp. 287–289), Cavusgil (1984, pp. 195 ff.), and Luostarinen (1979, pp. 196 ff.).

[95]Cf. Nordström (1991, p. 24), Sullivan and Bauerschmidt (1990, p. 19), and Papadopoulos and Denis (1988, pp. 38 ff.).

[96]Cf. Oviatt and McDougall (2005, p. 537), Rialp et al. (2005, p. 147), and Oviatt and McDougall (1994, p. 45).

[97]Cf. Kalinic et al. (2014, p. 635).

[98]Cf. Johanson and Vahlne (2009, pp. 1421 ff.).

[99]Johanson and Vahlne (2009, p. 1421).

relationship building with local partners). At the same time, however, they acknowledge that the link between targeted markets and psychic distance has weakened in the past.[100] In summary of the above arguments, it can be stated that the U-Model has been subjected to critical reviews with mixed results in the past.[101]

Despite Johanson's and Vahlne's response to their critics, it cannot be overlooked that the U-Model is marked by certain inconsistencies with regard to its validity in behavioral decision-making realities. In the introduction of this study it has been referred to the North-American activity of the British retailer Marks & Spencer as well as to the international experiences of Wal-Mart in South Korea and Germany.[102] These particular cases can be considered as representative examples of numerous failed internationalization projects in corporate reality, which are—at least in this severity—unforeseen in the U-Model. According to Johanson's and Vahlne's theory, any firm would react with a careful, step by step internationalization to the limited information availability, with which it is confronted abroad. 'Step by step' means that additional internationalization investments are only carried out if the existing market risk (R_i) is lower than the tolerable market risk (R^*_i). Thereby, a firm would engage in organizational learning and overcome its information deficit, and it should not come to failed internationalization results. Yet apparently, the actual decision-making procedure in internationalization process reality can—quite factually—contradict this postulate given the above examples. Decision-makers have either consciously not kept a balance between existing and tolerable market risks, or they were subjected to a misperception of the involved risks. This raises the suspicion that there is a gap between the rational decision-making mechanism according to the U-Model and its empirical validity in business reality, which is possibly shaped much more by bounded rationality. With regard to this disparity between theory and practice, Forsgren and Johanson speculate that it could be related to a tension between the "locus of learning" and the "locus of decision making", which has been overlooked in the U-Model.[103] In smaller companies, it is usually the decision-maker himself (or the decision-making unit), who acquires new market knowledge. In bigger firms, this congruence can probably not be witnessed. Yet, if these two structural units are separate, a scenario, in which firms gain foreign market knowledge in the field (e.g., in the targeted markets) while further internationalization decisions are taken by different structural units elsewhere (e.g., the headquarters), is plausible. As interesting as this speculation is, the potential tension between the locus of learning and the locus of decision-making illustrates first and foremost a bigger, underlying issue of the U-Model for the context of the present study: Insights about the actual behavior and rationality of decision-making managers in internationalization processes are still underdeveloped.[104]

---

[100] Cf. Johanson and Vahlne (2009, p. 1420).

[101] Cf. Andersen (1993, p. 222).

[102] Cf. Sect. 1.3.

[103] Forsgren and Johanson (2010, p. 294).

[104] Cf. Hutzschenreuter et al. (2007, p. 1056).

3.3.2 Escalation of Commitment as a Form of Bounded Rationality

In consideration of the aforementioned research of Matthyssens and Pauwels on internationalization exits and corresponding psychological behaviors, one could also look at escalation of commitment as another plausible explanation for failing internationalization processes. Yet, what is meant with escalation of commitment precisely? As explained before, behavioral research streams in business and economics question orthodox judgment and decision-making approaches against the background of current psychological research insights. Very much in this regard, escalation of commitment could be seen as a representative of bounded rationality as it presents a deviation from classical, rational-choice based decision-making literature.[105] It consists, broadly speaking, of decision-makers who refuse to acknowledge negative feedback that they have received in response to (usually their own) initial actions. Quite the contrary, they do not quit the decision process. Instead, responsible decision-makers even reinforce the "failing course of action"[106] with further commitments, i.e., resource allocations of time and capital, despite more than questionable prospects.[107] One could say that escalation of commitment is a behavioral bias, which misleads decision-makers to consider previous decision outcomes for current decision problems—while they should only consider the costs and benefits at the respective decision period. As they include the consideration of previously invested resources in their current decision problem, they act contrary to JDM approaches based on Rational Choice Theory.[108] In an economic context, escalation of commitment implies unjustified investments that are made in order to balance previous investment failures, thus "throwing good money after bad".[109] There are numerous examples of escalation of commitment in business practices, in which managers adhere to their failing decisions. Most illustrative is probably the example of stock traders, who can easily get locked-in with previous decisions once they incurred losses (due to an avoidance of the realization of selfsame losses). Unforgotten are the examples of criminally charged traders such as Jérôme Kerviel or Howie Hubler, who were responsible for multi-billion losses of their financial institutions (Société Générale and Morgan Stanley) during the financial crisis of 2007–2008. However, this is not exclusively a

[105]Cf. Donthu and Unal (2014, p. 210).

[106]Brockner et al. (1986, p. 122).

[107]Cf. Kunz (2013, pp. 209–210), Moser et al. (2013, pp. 363 ff.), Denison (2009, pp. 135–136), Sivanathan et al. (2008, pp. 1 ff.), Wong et al. (2008, pp. 248–249), Moon (2001a, pp. 104 ff., b, pp. 534–535), Rao and Monk (1999, p. 496 ff.), Ghosh (1997, p. 88), and Chenhall and Morris (1991, p. 32).

[108]Cf. Ku (2008, p. 222), Whyte (1993, p. 431), Garland and Newport (1991, pp. 55–56), and Singer and Singer (1986, p. 197).

[109]Brockner et al. (1986, p. 110).

(monetary) economic phenomenon.[110] For instance, in the past as much as today, governments tend to escalate their commitment to ineffective policies.[111]

In its current sense, escalation of commitment has initially been described by Barry M. Staw in 1976.[112] According to the structured experiments, which he conducted with his students as test persons, a typical escalation situation consists, firstly, of large amounts of resources, which need to be invested in a specific course of action. Secondly, decision-makers must receive a negative feedback to their chosen course of action sometime later. Lastly, decision-makers need to have the choice to either withdraw from the course of action or to continue investments. Staw supplied a test group with funds ('high responsibility'), which were at the disposal of the respective test persons. The students had the choice between two different research and development projects. Later on, however, they received a negative feedback to their project—regardless of their choice. Against this background the students had to decide between project withdrawal and continued investments. Meanwhile, a different test group for control purposes had to decide whether or not to continue investments in a failing research and development project, which they took over from a colleague ('low responsibility'). It turned out that the low responsibility group decided significantly more often to reverse the investment and to discontinue the allocation of further funds under failing circumstances (cf. Fig. 3.9).[113] As the degree of commitment was the only altered variable in this experiment, the different decision patterns were traced back to the effect of escalation of commitment.

This escalation phenomenon is also known under different terms such as 'entrapment problems'.[114] However, the differences between the corresponding concepts are not always clear, as the terms are not uniformly applied in scientific publications. As a result, they are difficult to distinguish.[115] Authors who attempt to define a distinction argue that entrapment problems are shaped by accumulated 'waiting costs', which are higher than the expected utility of the result of the wait. Unlike in escalation situations (in which previous losses can hypothetically still be balanced by future gains), this is supposedly always the case, when decision-makers face small (irretrievable) losses, which are nevertheless significant as they incur over longer periods of time (e.g., the wait for a bus). Despite these—somewhat marginal—distinguishing points, the corresponding concepts share a bottom line: Previous decision outcomes impact current decision-making problems.

---

[110]Cf. Wong et al. (2006, p. 283).

[111]While examples for this matter are naturally controversial, one could count the Vietnam War as a manifestation of escalation of commitment (cf. Brockner (1992, p. 39), Staw (1981, p. 577), and Brockner et al. (1979, p. 494).

[112]Cf. Staw (1976, pp. 27 ff.).

[113]Cf. Wong et al. (2006, p. 283), Bazerman et al. (1984, p. 142), and Staw (1976, p. 27).

[114]Cf. Brockner et al. (1981, pp. 68 ff., 1982, pp. 247 ff.), Nathanson et al. (1982, pp. 193 ff.), and Rubin and Brockner (1975, pp. 1054 ff.).

[115]Cf. Kunz (2013, p. 209).

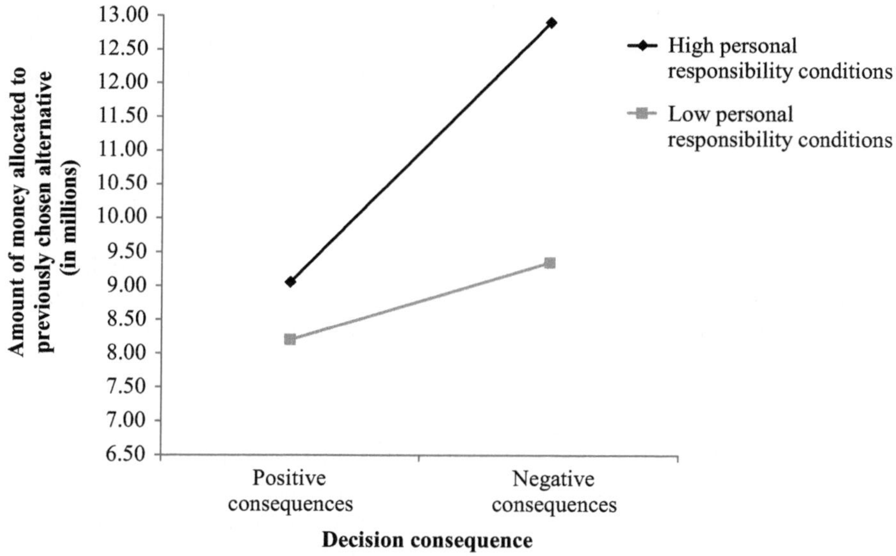

Fig. 3.9 Results of Staw's experimental study on escalation of commitment. Source: Staw (1976, p. 38)

Furthermore, they consider escalating behavior as a decision error and refer inter alia to psychological mechanisms as a possible answer to the question of why decision-makers adhere to a previously chosen path in spite of a negative decision feedback.[116]

In contrast to this critical perspective, there are also some scientific studies that attempt to justify escalation of commitment game-theoretically and economically. According to these publications, escalation to a course of action could be the appropriate answer to decision dilemmas and the consequence of incomplete information. For example, incentives to escalate can be found in scenarios in which several firms bid for a single contract (game-theoretic argument) or when new information is revealed during the decision-making process (information argument).[117] Other authors claim to show mathematical justifications for escalation of commitment.[118] However, what these authors oversee has been summarized best by Staw. He argued that "there should be no effects of justification or norms for consistency on commitment" if escalation of commitment was a phenomenon that only surfaced when it is factually justifiable.[119] In other words, if escalation of commitment was not a behavioral bias, only objectively verifiable decision

[116]Cf. Kunz (2013, p. 206).

[117]Cf. Chulkov (2007, p. 29).

[118]Cf. Tang (1988, p. 79).

[119]Staw (1981, p. 584).

arguments—such as probabilities—should decide over the decision outcome. Yet, this contradicts empirical insights entirely, which indicate that "observers of a commitment situation do not generally reach the same decisions as [...] actors who have experienced losses"[120]—despite the fact that both have been presented with identical objective decision arguments.

Certainly, there is only a fine line between escalation of commitment and the simple acknowledgement of changed decision circumstances. In many cases it is hard to tell whether or not one is still in a phase of patiently holding out with a previously chosen course of action (which could present the possibility of a turnaround of negative results) or whether one is already in a cycle of escalation of commitment. Therefore, one might ask at what point it is justified to speak of escalation of commitment. According to Staw, it is justified to speak of escalation if a decision-maker's commitment to his/her actions is "beyond what would be warranted by the 'objective' facts of the situation".[121] Naturally, scholars disagree about what constitutes the 'objective' facts of the situation. Some authors argue that it is justified to speak of escalation of commitment if the original decision criteria are violated on a regular basis.[122] This means, a course of action is continued (even with small resource allocations) in spite of regularly failing outcomes. Other scholars apply further requirements that need to be fulfilled first in order to speak of escalation of commitment.[123] For example, continued resource allocations need to be bigger in failing courses of action in comparison to allocations under succeeding circumstances. For the present study, escalation of commitment is defined as the neglect of previously non-achieved (predefined) objectives for current and subsequent decision problems.

3.3.3 Theory-Driven Explanations of Escalation of Commitment

After the seminal study by Staw, a number of publications have been dedicated to the abstraction of the escalation problem by identifying and developing escalation-explaining theories.[124] Sleesman and colleagues, who have quite recently studied the escalation of commitment research program meta-analytically, identified inter alia four predominant perspectives that are regularly applied as theory-driven

---

[120]Staw (1981, p. 584).

[121]Staw (1981, p. 584).

[122]Cf. Denison (2009, p. 133), Schulz-Hardt et al. (2009, p. 175), and Schmidt and Calantone (2002, pp. 104–105).

[123]Cf. Ku (2008, p. 222), Ross and Staw (1986, p. 287, 1993, p. 708), Walsh and Henderson (1989, p. 534), Singer and Singer (1986, p. 197), Staw (1981, p. 579), and Conlon and Wolf (1980, p. 172).

[124]Cf. Brockner (1992, p. 41).

explanations of escalation of commitment: subjective Expected Utility Theory (Sect. 3.3.3.1), Prospect Theory (Sect. 3.3.3.2), Self-Justification Theory (Sect. 3.3.3.3), and Self-Presentation Theory (Sect. 3.3.3.4).[125]

3.3.3.1 Subjective Expected Utility Theory

Subjective Expected Utility Theory, developed by Leonard J. Savage, is closely related to the classic understanding of 'objective' EUT, which has been presented in Sect. 2.2.3.1 of the present study.[126] The following remarks will refrain from a repetition of the in-depth presentation of this particular JDM approach and, instead, highlight the additional content of subjective EUT with direct relevance for the subject of escalation of commitment. Subjective EUT has much in common with its classic objective counterpart because it is still based on the same axiomatic foundation as well as on consistency requirements. Furthermore, it considers decision-makers to be prospectively rational actors, who "maximize future utility".[127] In other words, decision-makers act according to their preferences in a maximizing manner. At the same time and as a distinction from the classic approach, however, subjective EUT also considers differing perceptions of probability due to personal and psychological factors.[128] This reasoning is based on the recognition that not every decision problem, which is marked by uncertainty, can also be captured with a specific probability distribution.[129]

In a situation of escalation of commitment, for example, it is clear that different decision outcomes are possible (e.g., success or failure of an investment). However, a clear specification in the form of reliable outcome probabilities is often not feasible (e.g., defining the exact chances of an investment success or failure)—not least because of the influence of individual probability perceptions. Fairly regularly, managers assess crucial decision problems quite differently with regard to corresponding outcome probabilities in business reality. It is needless to say that this is a particular issue in international business, which provides substantial levels of complexity, making it even harder to identify reliable outcome probabilities. A reading of escalation of commitment through the lens of subjective EUT yields the insight that decision-makers may escalate their chosen course of action if they compare the perceived benefits of adhering to previous decisions with the perceived disadvantages of a change of mind. Thus, a decision-maker would choose the alternative that yields the bigger—subjectively perceived—utility from his/her point of view. He/she acts accordingly even if his/her perspective is biased.

[125]Cf. Sleesman et al. (2012, p. 542).

[126]Cf. Savage (1972, p. 3).

[127]Staw (1981, p. 583).

[128]Cf. Fishburn (1981, p. 139) and Savage (1972, pp. 27 ff.).

[129]Cf. Hammond (1998, p. 215).

3.3.3.2 Prospect Theory

Kahneman's and Tversky's Prospect Theory (PT) is another approach that is regularly consulted as a theory-driven explanation for escalation of commitment.[130] Since its theoretical basis has already been thoroughly presented in Sect. 2.2.3.2, the following remarks—analogous to above comments on subjective EUT—refer only to PT content, which is directly relevant to the understanding of escalation of commitment. Fundamentally, the underlying model considers two important observations: First, decision-makers over-weight losses, i.e., they become more risk-seeking after incurring losses. Second, the way, in which the decision-making context is framed, influences the actual decision. For example, decision-makers tend to be more risk-seeking if a decision outcome is framed negatively.[131]

Escalation of commitment—as it could be understood by Prospect Theory—implies that decision-makers are "in the domain of losses".[132] Due to these losses, the escalating behavior is generally seen "as an artifact of [...] framing".[133] Therefore, decision-makers will show a disposition to take high risks and to allocate further resources to previous, unsuccessful courses of action.[134] Hence, following the logic of Prospect Theory, decision-makers will prefer a small chance of success (at the risk of even higher potential losses) over a moderate yet certain loss. As a consequence, they will adhere to their previous choices—despite an ongoing negative feedback—as this is the only possibility of a future success.[135] On the contrary, abandoning a failing course of action signifies a negative decision outcome with complete certainty. As a result of this dilemma, decision-makers cling to previous decisions and escalate their commitment in an attempt to minimize decision damages.

3.3.3.3 Self-Justification Theory

Another very dominant theory-based explanation for escalation of commitment aims at the cognitive dimension of the behavioral bias and has been presented by Staw in his study of 1976.[136] He built his idea of Self-Justification Theory on Leon Festinger's Cognitive Dissonance Theory, according to which decision-makers are strongly inclined to align their—usually positive—self-image with the interpretation of their own behavior.[137] Against this background, Staw argues that the negative feedback to a chosen course of action constitutes a contradiction to the

[130] Cf. Sharp and Salter (1997, p. 102).

[131] Cf. Sect. 2.2.3.2 for a thorough presentation of 'framing effects'.

[132] Brockner (1992, p. 51).

[133] Whyte (1986, p. 311).

[134] Cf. Brockner (1992, p. 51).

[135] Cf. Kunz (2013, p. 210).

[136] Cf. Wong et al. (2006, p. 285) and Staw (1976, p. 27, 1981, pp. 578–580).

[137] Cf. Wong et al. (2006, p. 285), Aronson (1969, pp. 2–3), and Festinger (1957, p. 260).

positive self-image of personally responsible decision-makers and that it is therefore a source of cognitive dissonance.[138] As a result, decision-makers attempt to resolve the dissonance with further commitments, which seem to justify previous choices in front of themselves and/or others.[139]

As a consequence, escalation of commitment should surface when decision-makers are personally responsible for a failing decision path and when they sense a need for justification of their actions. This perspective is not only supported by Staw's experiment (because the 'high responsibility group' allocated more funds than the 'low responsibility group' in subsequent decision rounds),[140] but it has also been tested with empirical success on a regular basis in the past.[141] Escalation of commitment can thus be explained by the unwillingness of decision-makers "to admit—to themselves and/or others—that prior resources were allocated in vain".[142] With greater unwillingness there will also be a greater disposition to escalate the decision-making process.[143] By building-up further commitment in the form of additional resource allocations, a decision-maker hopes to reach the targeted objectives and to justify the chosen decision path retroactively—regardless of the likelihood of his/her success.[144]

3.3.3.4 Self-Presentation Theory

Similar to Self-Justification Theory, Self-Presentation Theory deals with cognitive issues of decision-makers and serves as an additional theory-based explanation for escalation of commitment. The latter, however, focuses on emotional aspects of decision-making as it recognizes the fact that the social anxiety of decision-makers may play a crucial role for a decision outcome.[145] This argument builds on Erving Goffman's writings on self-presentation, who highlighted that individuals have generally reason to convey an impression of themselves to others, which is in the interest of those selfsame individuals.[146] The rationale for this fairly opportunistic assumption lies in the opportunistic nature of humans as well as in the motive of a potential power augmentation in groups for decision-makers. Such power

[138]Cf. Sivanathan et al. (2008, p. 2), Wong et al. (2008, pp. 249–251), and Staw (1976, p. 40).

[139]Cf. Bazerman et al. (1984, p. 141).

[140]Cf. the comments on Staw's experiment in Sect. 3.3.2 of the present study.

[141]Cf. Wolff and Moser (2008, p. 241), Bobocel and Meyer (1994, pp. 362–363), Brockner (1992, pp. 43–49), Barton et al. (1989, pp. 541–543), Ross and Staw (1986, pp. 274 ff.), Bazerman et al. (1984, p. 150), and Caldwell and O'Reilly (1982, pp. 121 ff.)

[142]Brockner (1992, p. 40).

[143]Cf. Brockner (1992, p. 43).

[144]Cf. Sivanathan et al. (2008, p. 2), Ku (2008, p. 222), Schulz and Cheng (2002, p. 82), Rao and Monk (1999, p. 498), and Staw (1981, p. 579).

[145]Cf. Brockner et al. (1981, pp. 69–70) and Turner (1977, p. 438).

[146]Cf. Goffman (1959, pp. 3–4).

augmentations may arise due to positively perceived behaviors in social contexts.[147] As a result, decision-makers attempt to portray themselves in a positive light.

In the context of escalation of commitment, self-presentation plays a defining role. The degree of escalation may depend on the kind of social attention that decision-makers receive when they continue or end an escalation process. If ending such a process implies negative attention, the decision-maker could be inclined to do the opposite: to escalate his/her actions even further. Thus, if quitting is socially considered to be inappropriate, managers will act accordingly and present themselves as positively as possible by continuing investments, because doing so will portray them in a favorable light.[148] Such adverse social incentives, however, require a specific culture of the organization, which favors decision-makers who do not accept failure, and which overvalues managerial consistency. Thus, scholars, who apply Self-Presentation Theory as an explanation for escalation of commitment, emphasize that it is not just the self-presentation motive of managers but, furthermore, the organizational culture of a firm that causes escalation of commitment.[149]

3.3.4 *Escalation of Commitment as a Multi-determined Phenomenon*

Besides the above outlined theoretical approaches for the explanation of escalation of commitment, a rather practical taxonomy of influencing factors on escalation behavior has been developed by Barry M. Staw and Jerry Ross.[150] These factors have been derived from the state of research of the 1980s,[151] but their relevancy has recently been confirmed by Sleesman and colleagues with their previously mentioned meta-analytical study on escalation of commitment.[152] The influencing factors can be summarized in four different classes under the labels of project, psychological, social, and structural determinants. Staw and Ross considered the identified determinants to be a descriptive rather than theoretical approach to the escalation problem. As specified in the following, however, the previously outlined theory-driven explanations can be "logically positioned" within this set of determinants.[153]

---

[147]Cf. Jones and Pittman (1982, p. 233).

[148]Cf. Wong et al. (2006, p. 292).

[149]Cf. Brockner (1992, p. 56).

[150]Cf. Ross and Staw (1993, pp. 715–718) and Staw and Ross (1987, p. 43, 1989, pp. 216–218).

[151]Cf. Staw and Ross (1987, pp. 39 ff.), Ross and Staw (1986, p. 275), and Brockner and Rubin (1985, pp. 101 ff.)

[152]Cf. Sleesman et al. (2012, p. 542).

[153]Sleesman et al. (2012, p. 542).

3.3.4.1 Project Determinants

According to Ross and Staw, project determinants constitute the first factor with an important impact on escalation of commitment.[154] But what are they precisely, and how do they have a fostering influence on escalation of commitment? Project determinants are the objective characteristics of a project. The question of whether or not one withdraws from a failing course of action depends largely on objective features associated with a decision problem and on the related objective utilities of persistence and withdrawal. For example, in the case of profit-seeking companies the financial value of persisting or withdrawing will be assessed in order to determine the decision value. Similarly in the case of non-profit organizations, the utility of nonfinancial values will be pondered.[155] In a way, project determinants can explain why a certain decision path was taken in the first place.[156] Unsurprisingly, project determinants play a particularly important role during the initial stages of a decision path as it would be non-logical to "pursue a project that did not, at least on the surface, have potential merit" in the beginning.[157] The fact that the amount of available objective information changes throughout project stages could influence escalation of commitment.[158] Relevant project factors, which have the potential to determine whether or not a manager withdraws from a project, include inter alia the following:[159]

- Size of the project goal and eventual payoff[160]
- Future expenditures in order to secure the payoff[161]
- Availability of feasible project alternatives
- Number of negative feedbacks[162]
- Salvage value and closing costs of the project[163]

Yet, how do the above factors relate to the tendency of managers to escalate their decisions? First, as they ponder between persistence and withdrawal, decision-makers are confronted with decision uncertainty. This decision uncertainty involves the open questions of whether a negative feedback constitutes a temporary or a permanent problem, of the size of the potential payoff (as a result of continued investments), and of the cost of necessary future expenditures. In the light of decision uncertainty, project determinants are plausible causes of persistence.[164]

---

[154]Cf. Staw and Ross (1987, pp. 44–48) and Ross and Staw (1986, p. 275).

[155]Cf. Staw and Ross (1987, pp. 44–48).

[156]Cf. Sleesman et al. (2012, p. 542).

[157]Staw and Ross (1987, p. 45).

[158]Cf. He and Mittal (2007, p. 226).

[159]Cf. Ross and Staw (1986, pp. 275–276).

[160]Rubin and Brockner (1975, pp. 1054 ff.).

[161]Brockner et al. (1981, pp. 68 ff.).

[162]McCain (1986, pp. 280 ff.).

[163]Northcraft and Wolf (1984, pp. 233–234).

[164]Cf. Staw and Ross (1989, pp. 216–217).

Second, with the above factors in mind, decision-makers may overvalue positive trends and take them as the basis for an exclusive focus on best-case scenarios, while worst-case outcomes are discounted.[165] Lastly, once decision-makers have begun a course of action, they may simply show preferences for their initial choices throughout a project. Especially if the salvage value of a project is low and if closing costs are high, managers may feel inclined to persist with their initial decision.[166] Altogether, project determinants share the characteristic that they allow for an economic—yet possibly biased—pondering between decision-path-persistence and decision-path-withdrawal. Therefore, they fit well with the theory-driven explanation of escalation of commitment as proposed by subjective Expected Utility Theory.

3.3.4.2 Psychological Determinants

The escalation bias implies that decision-makers do not only have to deal with objective project factors, but that they also have to struggle with the pitfalls of their own psychological mind.[167] Unlike objective project determinants, psychological determinants are marked by the insight that judgment and decision-making processes on a personal level are easily flawed by erroneous assessments. These erroneous assessments are the result of the challenge that decision-makers have to process project information cognitively in order to determine whether or not to withdraw from or to persist with a project.[168] Due to the circumstance that managerial decisions are often taken on the grounds of 'gut feel' and that they are frequently contradicting the ideas of classic economic models, it turns out that decision-makers do not only persist in projects when the marginal utility is higher than the marginal cost.[169] Psychological determinants—which interfere with an accurate 'gut feel'—constitute "the most frequently studied determinant category"[170] and will probably also present the reader with a certain familiarity from day-to-day life as escalation situations are not limited to strict economic (e.g., monetary) contexts.[171] This category includes specific examples, such as the 'misperception of sunk costs', the 'focus on project completion', 'personal responsibility and 'ego threat'' of managers, as well as 'decision-maker experience and over-confidence'.

---

165 Cf. Sleesman et al. (2012, p. 542) and Moon and Conlon (2002, pp. 33 ff.).

166 Cf. Sleesman et al. (2012, p. 542) and Staw and Ross (1989, p. 217).

167 Cf. McCarthy et al. (1993, p. 22) and Staw and Ross (1987, p. 48).

168 Cf. Sleesman et al. (2012, p. 544) and Street and Anthony (1997, pp. 274–275).

169 Cf. McCarthy et al. (1993, p. 15) and Staw and Ross (1989, p. 217).

170 Sleesman et al. (2012, p. 544).

171 A popular example in this regard is the waiting time for a bus that is not on time. Once somebody has begun to wait, it becomes increasingly harder abandon the bus station with every further minute invested.

1. Misperception of sunk costs

Among the most discussed psychological drivers of escalation of commitment is the so-called sunk cost effect.[172] Sunk costs are resources—money, time, and effort—that have been spent in a certain course of action and which are non-recoverable. From a rational choice perspective, past investment results should not matter for current investment decisions and should not be taken in consideration. Arkes and Blumer, who studied the sunk cost effect most prominently, go as far as to say that "sunk costs are irrelevant to current decisions"—from a strict rational choice point of view of course.[173] In reality, however, sunk costs are "not sunk psychologically".[174] Under the sunk cost effect, decision-makers show the tendency to give 'non-rational' attention to past expenditures in the context of current decision-making problems.[175] Usually, the sunk cost effect presents itself in the inclination of administrators to allocate further resources to a project in an attempt to balance and justify prior investment losses.[176] Research has shown that decision-makers fail to recognize sunk costs for what they are, and that they appear to lack the necessary cognitive grasp in order to uncover the sunk cost effect. Therefore, it constitutes a "robust judgment error".[177] On the grounds of theory, it can be explained in two ways. First, as decision-makers seem to be under self-justification pressure after incurring losses (as they do not want to admit their decision failure), Self-Justification Theory—as presented in Sect. 3.3.3.3—helps to explain their actions.[178] Second, a sunk cost situation often implies a negative decision frame as described by Prospect Theory.[179] Therefore, one could argue that decision-makers tend to be more risk-seeking in sunk cost situations, and that they are thus escalating their investments.

2. Focus on project completion

While the sunk cost effect enjoys popularity as an explanation for escalation behavior, some scholars remark that it could be easily confounded with a focus on project completion by decision-makers.[180] In particular, Conlon and Garland have found evidence that the degree of project completion has the potential to "dominate any sunk cost effect".[181] In such cases, objective project information is not taken sufficiently into account by decision-makers because a project goal is proximal.[182]

---

[172]Cf. Arkes and Blumer (1985, pp. 124 ff.) and Thaler (1980, pp. 47–50).

[173]Arkes and Blumer (1985, p. 126).

[174]Staw and Ross (1989, p. 217).

[175]Cf. Soman (2001, p. 169).

[176]Cf. Duxbury (2012, p. 145) and Brockner et al. (1981, pp. 68 ff.).

[177]Arkes and Blumer (1985, p. 139).

[178]Cf. Sleesman et al. (2012, p. 543).

[179]Cf. Staw and Ross (1989, p. 217).

[180]Cf. Sleesman et al. (2012, p. 546).

[181]Conlon and Garland (1993, p. 402).

[182]Cf. Ting (2011, pp. 93 ff.).

Due to high levels of anticipatory emotions, decision-makers usually show a stronger desire to bring closure to current tasks in the final stage of projects. Thus, they persist with their course of action until closure; this contributes to escalation of commitment.[183]

3. Personal responsibility and 'ego threat'

An essential component of the psychological determinants of escalation of commitment is the felt responsibility of decision-makers as well as an 'ego threat'. Once managers independently initiate a certain course of action, they are also more prone to advocate their decision in the future by allocating further funds to this specific cause.[184] In fact, Staw's initial experiment on escalation of commitment of 1976 (cf. Fig. 3.9) specifically reviewed the effect of different degrees of responsibility on test groups. In his experiment, test subjects were more likely to stand by their decision path in future decision rounds when they received a negative feedback on decisions that they had to take responsibility for.[185] Usually, this is connected to a perceived need of justification for one's actions after self-inflicted decision failures. As erroneous judgments raise concerns about the qualification and reputation of a responsible decision-maker, they can present an 'ego threat' to managers (i.e., a threat to their self-image).[186] Therefore, Self-Justification Theory is commonly considered to be the underlying theoretical approach in this regard.[187]

4. Decision-maker experience and over-confidence

Finally, the degree of decision-maker experience as well as a potential affinity to over-confidence can account for psychological factors contributing to escalation of commitment. A high level of experience could establish an unrealistic self-image of a decision-maker and thus negatively affect his/her reaction in failing situations. As a result, the manager's persistence to a certain decision path could be increased and a negative project feedback could be discounted. In a way, managers may fall for the idea that they are able to 'overcome' a failing situation with further investments, allied to their self-perceived competence.[188]

3.3.4.3 Social Determinants

Decision-making processes in a group context differ significantly from similar processes executed by individuals alone as they are shaped by a different

[183]Cf. Harvey and Victoravich (2009, pp. 759 ff.) and He and Mittal (2007, p. 227).

[184]Cf. Brockner et al. (1986, p. 111).

[185]Cf. Staw and Ross (1989, p. 217) and Staw (1976, p. 38).

[186]Cf. Zhang and Baumeister (2006, pp. 881 ff.) and Sleesman et al. (2012, p. 543).

[187]Cf. Street and Anthony (1997, pp. 274–275) and Bazerman et al. (1984, p. 141).

[188]Cf. Sleesman et al. (2012, p. 543), Bragger et al. (2003, pp. 10–12), and Judge et al. (1998, pp. 167 ff.).

decision-making dynamic. Unlike psychological determinants of escalation of commitment, social determinants recognize this difference on the interpersonal level. While erroneous—yet sincere—individual convictions of decision-makers were paramount for psychological determinants, social determinants focus on factors that increase decision-makers' persistence regardless of their individual beliefs as a result of the above mentioned group dynamic.[189] For example, in competitive environments in which a management team has to decide for further project directions, managers tend to feel the need to defeat their 'argumentative competitors' and, thus, to stick with their previous arguments regardless of their convictions. As another example for group dynamics, decision-makers can align their decision path with previous courses of action, which dealt with similar decision problems—thus shaping their decision process according to the previous social context (so-called 'modeling').[190]

From a general point of view, an escalation bias is intensified in a social context (in comparison to individual contexts) because decision-makers do not merely justify their decision in front of themselves but also vis-à-vis other group members to whom they do not want to expose any faulty judgment. Therefore, the involvement of other parties in the decision-making process constitutes the necessary prerequisite for social determinants. While these other parties may surface in the form of evaluators, commentators, rivals, or simple observers of decision issues, it is the feeling of public evaluation and observation that increases decision-makers' need to justify themselves in front of others.[191] As the internal need for justification of psychological determinants has shifted to an external need for justification, it seems logical that the persistence of decision-makers is the highest in circumstances under large audiences and in situations of high social anxiety.[192]

Two observable behavioral patterns in the context of social determinants of escalation of commitment have been frequently identified in the past. First, 'face-saving' refers to the desire of decision-makers not to lose credibility with others and to appear in a favorable light.[193] The wish of not exposing erroneous decisions is well embedded in the context of Self-Presentation Theory—as explained in Sect. 3.3.3.4. Second, 'external binding' plays an equally important role for social determinants of escalation of commitment. As managerial decisions are often evaluated by other parties, decision-makers are exposed to a certain peer-pressure for consistency as well as conformity with previous courses of action.[194] Caving in to these pressures holds the potential of social recognition for decision-makers as

---

[189]Cf. Ross and Staw (1993, p. 702), Whyte (1993, pp. 430 ff.), Staw and Ross (1987, p. 55, 1989, p. 217f.), and Bazerman et al. (1984, p. 141).

[190]Cf. Staw and Ross (1987, p. 58).

[191]Cf. Sleesman et al. (2012, pp. 543–544).

[192]Cf. Brockner et al. (1981, p. 68) and Fox and Staw (1979, pp. 449 ff.).

[193]Cf. Street and Anthony (1997, p. 275), Staw and Ross (1987, p. 55), Ross and Staw (1986, p. 277), and Brockner et al. (1981; pp. 68 ff.).

[194]Cf. Chong and Syarifuddin (2010, p. 4).

they gain social approval for their firm stance (the so-called 'hero effect'). On the other hand, decision-makers, who change their positions frequently, face greater opposition.[195] Quite obviously, this requires a certain organizational setting, in which decisiveness is valued as much as the tendency of decision-makers to bind their decision-reasoning externally.

3.3.4.4 Structural Determinants

While the previous three categories of determinants focus on an individual decision-maker as the starting point for escalation of commitment, the last factor addresses the structural level of decision-making processes. Against the background of decision-making realities, which take place in groups and organizations and not at the individual level alone, additional interacting organizational elements come into play in escalation situations. In comparison to the factors taking place at the individual level, these structural determinants have been treated with limited interest in literature.[196] However, the relative lack of scholarly attention does not reflect the importance of organizational forces in decision-making reality. Once a course of action has been established at the organizational level, a withdrawal is very complicated as it could possibly involve changes within the organization itself as well as interfering political interests.

These two manifestations are part of the institutionalization of the escalation problem. In general, it is possible that a certain course of action becomes associated with the values as well as with the purposes of an organization and that it is thus considered to be a core element of the organization itself.[197] For some companies, for example, a certain product constitutes the focal piece of the company's entire product portfolio. Holding on to this product—regardless of its economic performance—could therefore present the company with an escalation situation (e.g., print-media for publishers). Likewise, for international businesses the market presence in some countries is considered to be a core element of the company's self-image and would never be put into question (e.g., McDonald's in the USA). In these cases, a change to the course of action is commonly considered to be "unthinkable" as it could shift the external perception of the company as well as its internal values.[198] Thus, institutionalized courses of action may present hived-off escalation situations as decision-making groups are not willing to adopt changes within the organization itself.

[195] Cf. Ross and Staw (1986, p. 277).

[196] Cf. Sleesman et al. (2012, p. 545), Ross and Staw (1993, p. 701), and Staw and Ross (1987, pp. 59 ff.).

[197] Cf. Goodman et al. (1980, pp. 215 ff.).

[198] Staw and Ross (1989, p. 218).

Furthermore, the institutionalization of the escalation problem is often manifested in organizational structures and policy systems.[199] This presents the second example of escalation of commitment at the structural level. Interfering political interests are not exclusive for decision-makers who are directly involved with a certain course of action and who have direct responsibility for selfsame. Very similarly, independent organizational units can also become associated with a certain decision path and are thus inclined to maintain it. Particularly in situations in which a course of action is highly important for the success of an organization, governing as well as controlling bodies tend to be affected by the escalation situation. Corresponding behavioral patterns can occasionally be witnessed in large infrastructure projects, in which the project completion becomes vital to the organization (as a current example in Germany, the failed construction process of the Berlin-Brandenburg capital airport could be considered as an example of escalation of commitment at the structural level with significantly interfering independent organizational units at work). Yet, this is also highly relevant in a context of international business. As important decisions in international management are often taken by top management groups, an unfavorable structural group dynamic could be further aggravated by an upper-echelons-perspective of decision-makers.[200] One could argue that specifically the linkages between top managers—mainly executive values and preferences—form coalitions in firms that contribute to self-enforcing escalation situations and thus influence organizational outcomes.[201]

These manifestations have consequences for firms and can contribute to non-economic decision paths. They add to an institutional inertia of organizations, meaning a lack of readiness to change organizational preferences and actions.[202] As organizations are rather slow with regard to their learning and adjusting capabilities to changing environments, they are potentially as affected as individuals by erroneous judgments in escalation situations. Therefore, as the last of the four determinants, structural factors of escalation of commitment can develop an intensifying influence in escalation scenarios.

3.3.5 *Escalation of Commitment as a Dynamic Process: The Three-Stage Model of Escalation*

A particularity of escalation of commitment is the circumstance that it is not only a multi-determined behavioral bias in judgment and decision-making processes. Moreover, the different influencing factors unfold their effect with temporal dependence.[203]

---

[199]Cf. Staw and Ross (1987, p. 60).

[200]Cf. Hambrick (2007, pp. 334 ff.) and Hambrick and Mason (1984, pp. 193 ff.).

[201]Cf. Kish-Gephart and Campbell (2015, p. 1615).

[202]Cf. Kelly and Amburgey (1991, pp. 592–595) and Hannan and Freeman (1984, p. 151).

[203]Cf. Staw and Ross (1989, p. 218).

This is very much in line with Teger, who established that escalation motives differ in temporal stages.[204] The different determinants, which have been introduced in the previous section, contribute in a self-perpetuating manner to an aggravating cycle of the behavioral bias because a little bit of escalation—induced by one factor—leads to further escalation judgments in the future, induced by other factors.[205] Thus, from a processual perspective, the different determinants of escalation of commitment should accumulate over a series of periods. In order to better understand the phenomenon and in order to answer the critical question of how escalation of commitment develops over time exactly, Barry M. Staw and Jerry Ross conceptualized a three-stage model of an escalation process (cf. Fig. 3.10).[206] While the authors introduced smaller alterations to their model in previous and later publications, the model can overall be summarized by its understanding of escalation of commitment as a dynamic process.[207] In this context, commitment is viewed as a product of costs and benefits of choice alternatives in different stages of a decision-making process. Decision-makers are confronted with an examination and reexamination of the costs and benefits of their decision path in different points in time.[208] During the reexamination, some factors pull a decision-maker towards withdrawal while others push him/her towards continued investments. The reassessment, however, tends to be flawed by the escalation bias, which is in dependence of the decision-making stage and which maintains the commitment even under questionable circumstances. In the following, the different phases of the three-stage model will be briefly outlined.

1. First stage

During the initial stage, decision-makers are confronted with decision-making economics in the form of 'perceived project economics'. Primarily, these consist of the previously introduced project determinants[209] and allow for a critical analysis of perceived costs and benefits from a rather objective stance. In other words, in this stage, the decision is defined by the anticipated perceived benefit of the decision-making outcome. Provided that an overall benefit has been identified (indicated by the symbol '+' in Fig. 3.10), 'a decision to begin a course of action' is taken and corresponding 'action' is initiated as a consequence. Subconsciously, the initial decision and the resultant action contribute to an initial buildup of commitment of decision-makers.[210]

---

[204]Cf. Teger (1980, pp. 107 ff.).

[205]Cf. Brockner et al. (1979, p. 493).

[206]Cf. Staw and Ross (1989, pp. 216 ff.).

[207]Cf. Ross and Staw (1993, pp. 701 ff.), Staw and Ross (1987, pp. 39 ff.), and Staw (1981, pp. 577 ff.).

[208]Staw and Ross (1987, p. 43).

[209]Cf. Sect. 3.3.4.1.

[210]Cf. Staw and Ross (1989, p. 218) and Ross and Staw (1986, p. 293).

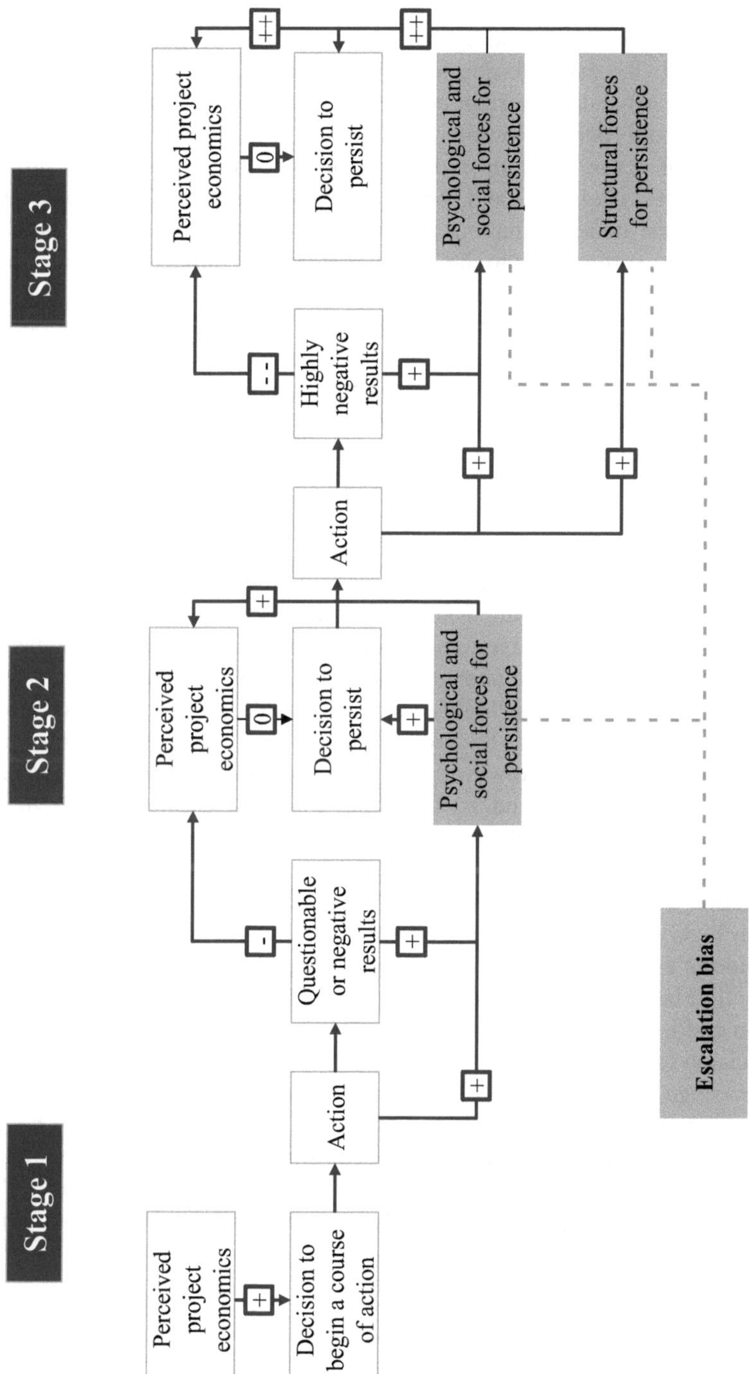

(The +, -, and 0 show positive, negative, and neutral influences respectively)

Fig. 3.10 Three-stage model of the escalation process. Source: Staw (1997, p. 207) and Staw and Ross (1989, p. 219) (modified)

2. Second stage

With the beginning of the second stage, the previously assessed economic benefit may have declined (for example due to a clear project setback or due to newly available information) and the current course of action has led to 'questionable or negative' results. In this period, however, the decision to withdraw from or to persist with the course of action no longer depends on (objectively negative) project economics alone. 'Psychological and social forces for persistence' come into play and contribute to the decision-making process. Self-justification as well as face-saving motives, for example, add to the denial of erroneous judgments by decision-makers and contribute to the maintenance of the decision-making path. Even in cases of a very clear negative feedback, responsible persons may be prone to continue with the already chosen course of action because the escalation bias, shaped by psychological and social factors, outweighs purely economic arguments. Hence, the overall situation is reassessed and the objectively bleak economic outlook is balanced by the escalation of commitment of administrators and a 'decision to persist' is taken.[211]

3. Third stage

Based on the premise of an aggravating escalation process in different periods, a favorable turn-around of a failing course of action between Stages 2 and 3 is unlikely. On the contrary, the economic outcome in business reality frequently tends to worsen over time in escalation situations.[212] Therefore, decision-makers in Stage 3 will be confronted with 'highly negative results' and not just with questionable project economics (as in the previous stage) as a result of the decision to persist in the second phase. However, this does not necessarily mean that the escalation cycle comes to an end at this point. First, the escalation bias in the form of psychological and social forces is still in effect. Second, it is additionally fostered by emerging 'structural forces for persistence', which change the character of the escalation bias. As it is possibly not a bias at the individual level alone any longer, even highly negative project economics can now be balanced by an institutionalization of escalation of commitment at the organizational level. The current course of action becomes associated with the general values and purposes of the organization and is therefore advocated by multiple decision-making bodies. As a result, a decision to persist with the course of action is taken once more.[213]

The three-stage model illustrates how escalation of commitment worsens over time and how the manifestation of the escalation bias gains complexity. It begins with the analysis of rather objective project determinants, involves psychological and social factors, and ultimately includes structural forces for persistence. Certainly—and as acknowledged by Staw and Ross—it is controversial whether or not

[211]Cf. Staw and Ross (1989, p. 218) and Ross and Staw (1986, p. 293).

[212]Cf. Staw and Ross (1989, p. 218).

[213]Cf. Ross and Staw (1986, p. 293) and Staw and Ross (1989, p. 218).

the different phases can unambiguously be identified in business reality.[214] Furthermore, additional circumstantial factors, such as decision-makers who try to disassociate themselves from failing courses of action, are not considered in the three-stage model. Therefore, the concept should not necessarily be treated as an empirically tested theory but rather as a heuristic. Nevertheless, the processual understanding of escalation of commitment does not only present a realistic idea of how escalation of commitment is constituted over time, but it also allows for an application in the context of internationalization processes. Against the background of the present study's research objective, one could argue that internationalization process decision-making is probably not immune to an escalation bias and that a testing for escalation in this specific context—building on the three-stage model—is in order.

3.3.6 *Statement of the Research Framework Under Consideration of the Theoretical and Conceptual Foundations*

With the theoretical and conceptual foundations outlined so far, it is possible to draw a research framework that puts the different building blocks of the present study in context, and which clarifies how they interact. Oesterle presented a thorough and informative overview of the potential benefits of such a theoretical-conceptual framework for scientific studies.[215] Following his statements, one can state—in a general context—that it enables authors and readers to identify the connection between the different fundamental elements within the mesh of a research study. Without such a framework, the different theoretical and conceptual building blocks would remain fragmented and without a logical interconnection. Thus, the research framework presents somewhat of a synthesis, which provides a structure and orientation for the coverage of a specific research question as it organizes the different fundamental theoretical and conceptual elements. Furthermore, it can provide an explorative perspective upon the research matter as it helps to identify a research gap, for example. The research framework could be considered as a 'building plan' for a scientific study since it provides a schematic diagram of the theoretical and conceptual foundations of the attended research problem. As such, it is a preliminary step prior to the development of a research model and the formulation of hypotheses. With the research framework as a basis, plausible hypotheses can be noted, which—in return—can be subsequently tested empirically. At the same time, however, it is distinguishable from a profound research model, which would require a less tentative statement of the underlying research problem. In short, the research framework presents a fundamental overview of the theoretical and conceptual foundations of a scientific study.

[214]Cf. Staw and Ross (1989, p. 219).

[215]Cf. Oesterle (1993, pp. 81–101).

For the present study, the research framework contributes to the exploration of bounded rationality in internationalization processes by clarifying the relation between the different theoretical aspects that have been presented thus far (cf. Fig. 3.11). In this regard, it is purposeful to consider the second chapter as the point of departure of the argumentative line that has been here applied. Rationality has been introduced as the basic criterion for the evaluation of JDM approaches. In this context, the study-underlying understanding of rationality has been clarified and a corresponding classification framework for JDM approaches has been developed. Essentially, one can distinguish between two fundamentally different theoretical perspectives. On the one hand, there is the notion of rationality, which is largely built upon Rational Choice Theory. It implies a traditional economic—and often unrealistically axiomatized—idea of human decision-making.

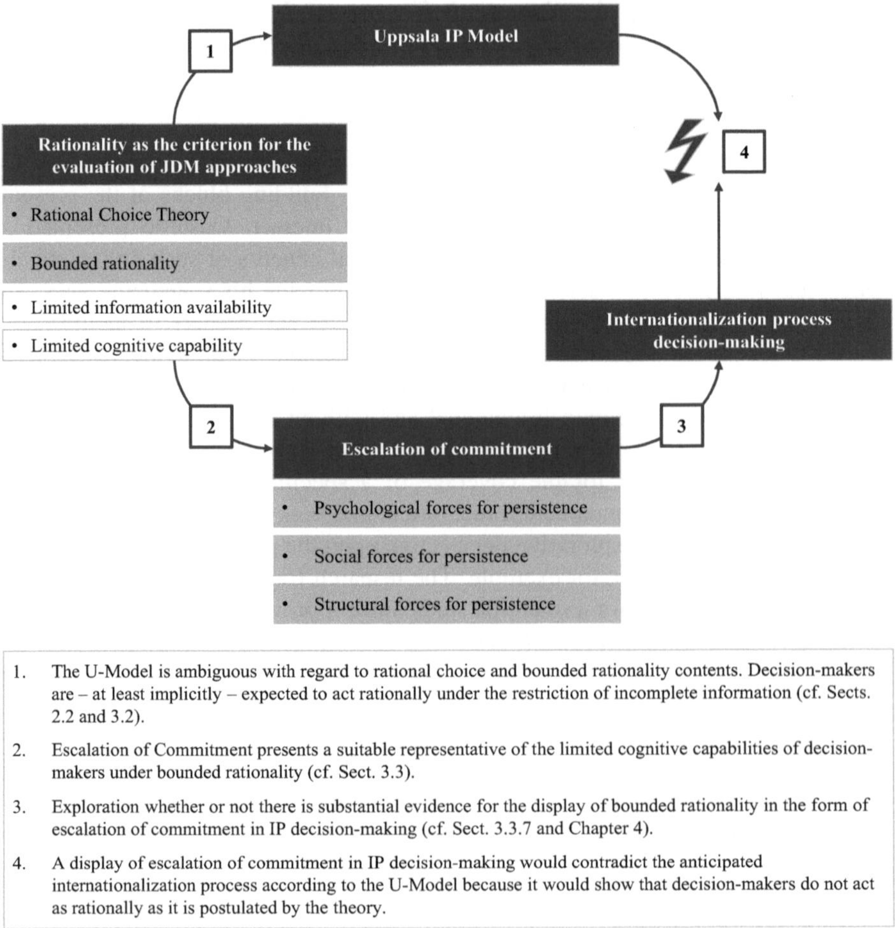

Fig. 3.11 Framework of the theoretical and conceptual foundations of the present study. Source: Own figure

On the other hand, the notion of bounded rationality serves as an alternative. This perspective on rationality acknowledges that decision-makers have no access to complete information and that they tend to lack the necessary cognitive capability to process the limited information that they have at their disposal. With rationality as the basic criterion, the Uppsala IP Model has been classified (cf. Link 1 in Fig. 3.11). The classification yielded in the insight that the theory is ambiguous with regard to its rational choice and bounded rationality contents. While the restriction of incomplete information is acknowledged by the U-Model, behavioral biases or cognitive limitations are not considered. Under the restriction of limited information availability, it expects decision-makers—at least implicitly—to act rationally, i.e., consistently and purposefully (with regard to their preferences). Against the background of this classification, the decision-making assumptions of the U-Model are questioned by the present study. In order to test these assumptions, the cognitive bias 'escalation of commitment' (primarily its psychological, social, and structural forces for persistence) has been introduced as a representative of the limited cognitive capabilities of decision-makers under bounded rationality (cf. Link 2 in Fig. 3.11). Against the background of the underlying research question (whether there is evidence for the display of bounded rationality in the form of escalation of commitment in IP decision-making), the present study aims at an empirical demonstration of this cognitive bias (cf. Link 3 in Fig. 3.11). The finding of such a display would constitute a contradiction to the decision-making assumptions of the U-Model because it would show that decision-makers do not act as rationally as it is expected by this central internationalization process approach (cf. Link 4 in Fig. 3.11).

3.3.7 Development of Hypotheses: Impact of Escalation of Commitment on Internationalization Process Decision-Making

In an attempt to analyze the above-described potential contradiction between the decision-making assumptions of the U-Model and the actual behaviors of decision-makers in reality, the present study is taking a closer look at three hypotheses. First, it is investigating whether or not there is a general impact of the previously introduced psychological, social, and structural forces for persistence of escalation of commitment on internationalization process decision-making (Sect. 3.3.7.1). Second and third, particular attention is paid to the psychic distance (Sect. 3.3.7.2) as well as to the establishment chain progress (Sect. 3.3.7.3), which present two key concepts of internationalization process literature and which can develop a moderating influence in the context of the here proposed research model (cf. Fig. 3.12).

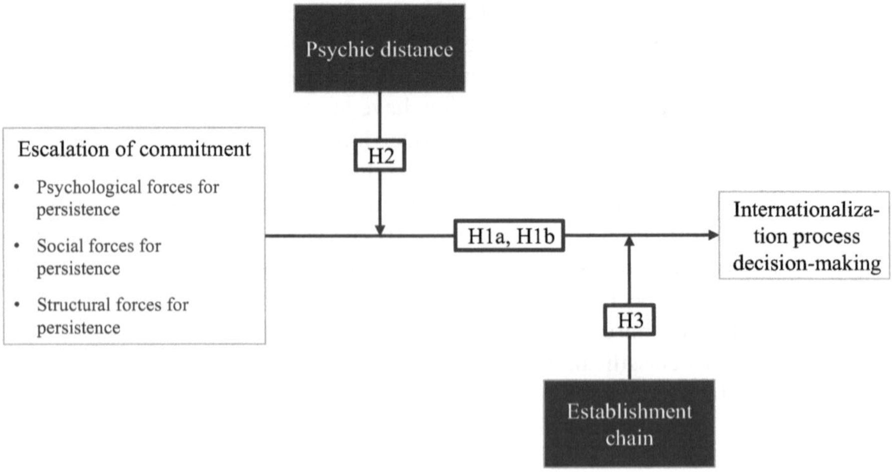

Fig. 3.12 Research model. Source: Own figure

3.3.7.1 General Impact of Escalation of Commitment on Internationalization Process Decision-Making (H1a and H1b)

As the present study is guided by the research objective of shedding light on to the matter of bounded rationality in internationalization processes of firms, the question is whether there is substantial evidence for the display of bounded rationality in the form of escalation of commitment in IP decision-making. Contrary to the implicit postulate of the U-Model, the research problem is built on the consideration that internationalization processes are not necessarily shaped by consistently and purposefully proceeding decision-makers. In Johanson's and Vahlne's theory, decision-makers are conceded the cognitive capability to limit their market commitment to a tolerable market risk. Yet, this could present an overestimation of decision-makers' rationality and of their respective cognitive capabilities in internationalization process decision-making. In reality, the actions of decision-makers in internationalization processes are not necessarily limited to a tolerable market risk. Instead, they could much rather be shaped by an 'escalation of market commitment' (cf. Fig. 3.13). By investigating the suspicion that there is an impact of bounded rationality in the form of escalation of commitment in internationalization process decision-making the present study could present somewhat of a falsification of the U-Model's implicit postulate of rationally, i.e., consistently and purposefully, acting decision-makers.

Based on the hitherto outlined explanations on internationalization processes according to the U-Model as well as on escalation of commitment, some hypotheses can be noted for the present study. Yet, in order to hypothesize about the impact of escalation of commitment in an internationalization process, first, one has to

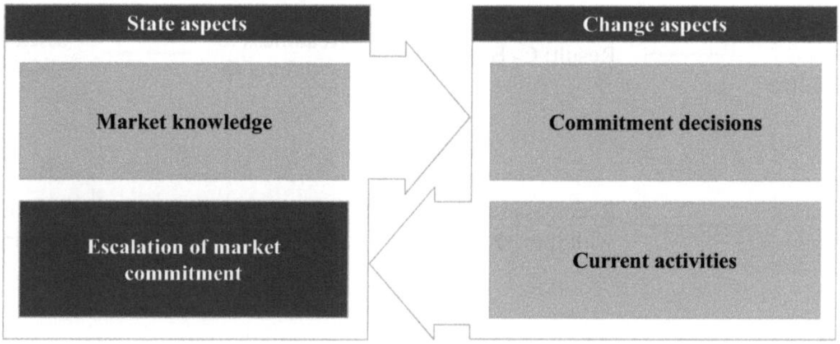

Fig. 3.13 Escalation of commitment and the U-Model. Source: Own figure

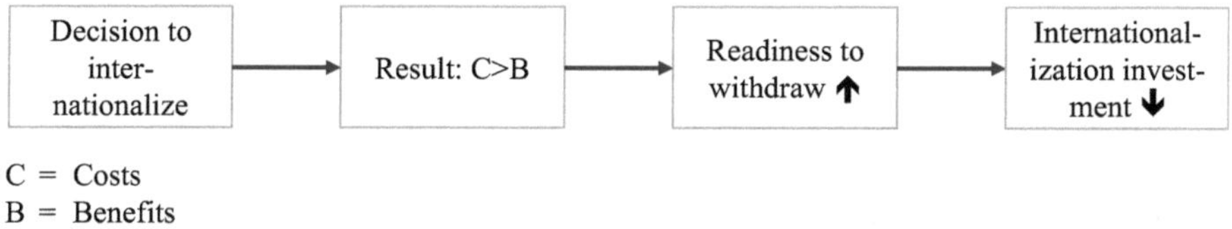

Fig. 3.14 Impact of a failed course of action on internationalization process decision-making under rational choice circumstances. Source: Own figure

understand how rational, i.e., non-committed, decision-makers should handle failing courses of action. In a scenario of internationalization process decision-making, an initial internationalization investment is taken on the grounds of project economics.[216] As soon as the original objective of the attempted internationalization is missed, i.e., the resulting costs (C) are bigger than the corresponding benefits (B), decision-makers should be characterized by an increased readiness to withdraw from the course of action and should therefore reduce their internationalization investment, which has been associated with the chosen decision path (cf. Fig. 3.14).

In contrast, decision-makers under escalation of commitment should act differently.[217] Principally, their readiness to withdraw should also be increased due to the received negative economic feedback. The readiness, however, is balanced by the escalation bias in the form of psychological and social forces for persistence (e.g., a misperception of sunk costs, face-saving, etc.).[218] As a consequence, the internationalization process will be continued with a further—potentially worse—negative economic feedback in the next stage. While this should increase decision-makers' readiness to withdraw once more, the escalation bias is now enforced by structural

[216]For the sake of the development and discussion of hypotheses, internationalization process decision-making is reduced to decisions on (further) internationalization investments. Continued internationalization investments signify the maintenance of the internationalization process.

[217]Cf. Schwenk (1984, p. 117).

[218]Cf. Sects. 3.3.4.2 and 3.3.4.3 for more information on psychological and social forces for persistence.

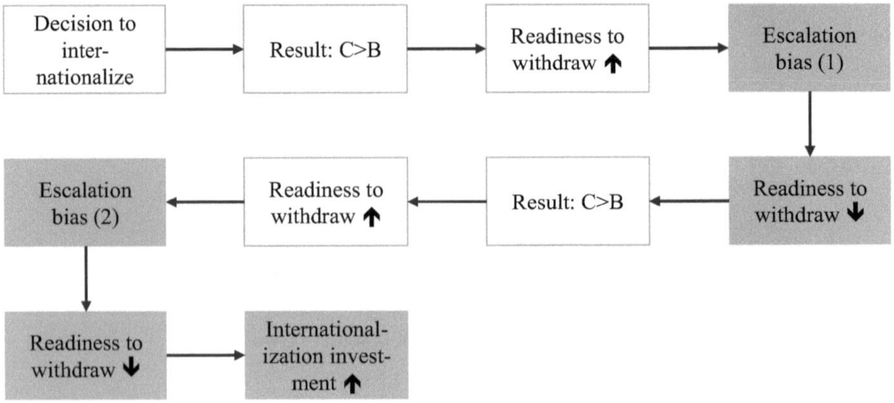

C = Costs
B = Benefits
(1) Psychological and social forces for persistence
(2) Structural forces for persistence

Fig. 3.15 Impact of a failed course of action on internationalization process decision-making under escalation of commitment. Source: Own figure

forces for persistence (e.g., adapted organizational structures and policy systems) as a consequence of an institutionalized internationalization process.[219] Ultimately, decision-makers under escalation of commitment should therefore continue their internationalization investment regardless of their success (cf. Fig. 3.15).

How do these considerations translate into hypotheses? Effectually, the here outlined causal chains imply that internationalization managers will act differently in dependence of the presence of an escalation bias (at a group level). Furthermore (at an individual level), there should be a relation between the individual degree of commitment of single decision-makers, i.e., their relative amount of resources committed, and their undertaken internationalization investment in the next stage of the internationalization process because escalation of commitment forms a self-perpetuating cycle. Thus, two hypotheses can be formulated:

Hypothesis 1a At the group level, managerial decision-makers in internationalization processes, who are under escalation of commitment, will rather act contrary to the logic of rational choices compared to a non-committed peer-group. This means that they will continue to raise internationalization investments regardless of the resultant economic success of the venture.

[219]Cf. Sect. 3.3.4.4 for more information on structural forces for persistence.

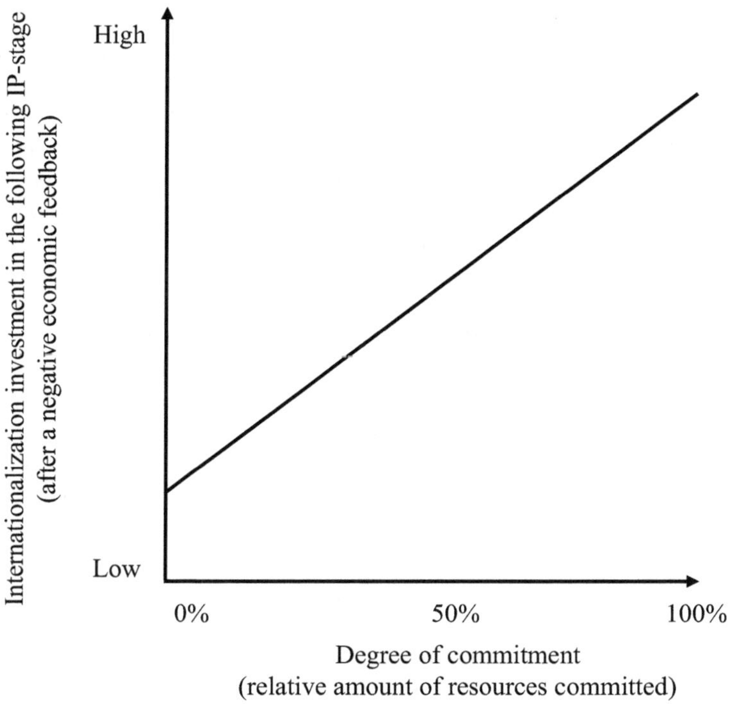

Fig. 3.16 Hypothesized relation between the degree of commitment and the internationalization investment in the following IP-stage. Source: Own figure

Hypothesis 1b At the individual level, managerial decision-makers will act increasingly contrary to the logic of rational choices with higher individual degrees of commitment. This means that the raised internationalization investment of a single internationalization manager will increase regardless of the resultant economic success of the venture but in dependence of the decision-maker's degree of commitment (Fig. 3.16).

3.3.7.2 Moderating Effect of Psychic Distance on the Impact of Escalation of Commitment on Internationalization Process Decision-Making (H2)

In international business research, the construct of psychic distance is one of the most cited and accepted concepts.[220] While the term has been brought up by Beckerman,[221] who studied intra-European trade flows, it is due to the scholars of

[220] Cf. Dow and Karunaratna (2006, pp. 578–579).

[221] Cf. Beckerman (1956, p. 38).

the Uppsala School of Thought that it has gained today's prominence.[222] Generally, psychic distance should not be confounded with geographical distance or any other exact measure. Instead, it refers to a certain dissimilarity or similarity of language, education, business practices, culture, and industrial development.[223] Johanson and Vahlne define psychic distance as "the sum of factors preventing the flow of information from and to the market".[224] The concept provides the basis for the assumption that psychically close countries and markets are better understood by companies that pursue an internationalization strategy. As a consequence, operating in psychically close markets should lead to increased chances of economic success. While the last argument is controversial, it is safe to say that high psychic distance to targeted markets will inhibit economic success during the early stages of internationalization processes.[225] One can argue that high psychic distance increases the uncertainty, which is associated with a market entry, and that it therefore increases the risk for international business ventures.[226]

Since high psychic distance increases the involved risk for companies, it could also have a moderating effect on the impact of escalation of commitment on internationalization process decision-making. Particularly in a scenario of high psychic distance to targeted markets, the involved risk might be perceived differently by committed and non-committed decision-makers.[227] In order to record a corresponding hypothesis, one should—similar to the previous section—first consider a rational, i.e., non-committed, decision-maker in an internationalization process. In a failing course of action, he/she has already been confronted with negative project economics since the initially targeted objective has been missed. As the associated costs have been bigger than the corresponding benefits, the decision-maker should be characterized by an increased readiness to withdraw from the decision path. Assuming that he/she wanted to continue the process nevertheless and given that the constellation is further complicated by the context of a high psychic distance towards the targeted market, the decision-maker will be confronted with a higher degree of uncertainty as well as risk. Thus, he/she should show an increased readiness to withdraw from the internationalization process a fortiori. Unlike in scenarios of low psychic distance, internationalization investments by rational decision-makers should therefore be smaller in high psychic distance contexts (cf. Fig. 3.17). In the alternative scenario of low psychic distance, rational decision-makers can be inclined to persist with the course of action (at minimal costs) due to the limited risk involved. As a consequence, this scenario could result in a similar behavioral pattern of rational actors and their counterparts under escalation of commitment (cf. the next paragraph).

---

[222]Cf. Brewer (2007, p. 44).

[223]Cf. Johnston et al. (2012, p. 38).

[224]Johanson and Vahlne (1977, p. 24).

[225]Cf. Magnusson and Boyle (2009, p. 77).

[226]Cf. O'Grady and Lane (1996, pp. 309–310).

[227]Cf. Kraus et al. (2015, pp. 1501 ff.).

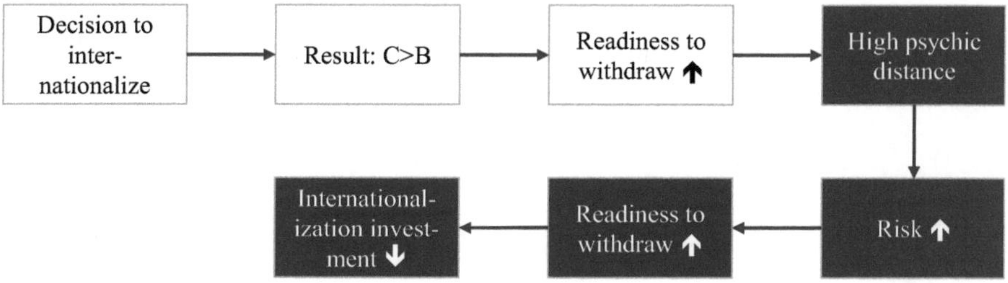

C = Costs
B = Benefits

Fig. 3.17 Effect of high psychic distance in failing internationalization processes under rational choice circumstances. Source: Own figure

Under escalation of commitment decision-makers are likely to misperceive the involved risk that goes along with a context of high psychic distance. This is best explained by Brockner, who applied the framing argument of Kahneman and Tversky and stated that decision-makers in a cycle of escalation of commitment have incurred losses (which present a negative frame) and that they are therefore likely to take higher risks in order to balance previous negative decision outcomes.[228] Within the reasoning of this logic, decision-makers will opt for a small chance of success regardless of the involved risk, which presents itself in the form of even higher losses. The increased readiness to withdraw from the internationalization process, which should be observable in the case of rationally proceeding decision-makers in contexts of high psychic distance, should therefore be balanced by the escalation bias in the form of a misperception of associated risks. Due to this lower risk assessment capacity, the readiness to withdraw should be in decline again and the internationalization investment will be maintained. In brief, one could argue that decision-makers under escalation of commitment tend to ignore the associated risk that is prevalent in a context of high psychic distance and that they maintain their internationalization investment regardless of the associated risk information (cf. Fig. 3.18). Naturally, this would also imply that they persist with the course of action in a scenario of low psychic distance.

The implications of psychic distance in the context of internationalization process decision-making lead to the assumption that there is a divergent behavioral pattern for decision-makers in dependence of the presence of an escalation bias. While non-committed managers should consider and react to the available information on psychic distance, their committed counterparts are likely to take their decision to maintain the internationalization process somewhat regardless of that information (cf. Fig. 3.19). This assumed divergent decision pattern should be especially prevalent in cases of high psychic distance and allows the formulation of the following hypothesis with regard to a potentially moderating effect of psychic distance on the impact of escalation of commitment on internationalization process decision-making.

[228]Cf. Brockner (1992, p. 51).

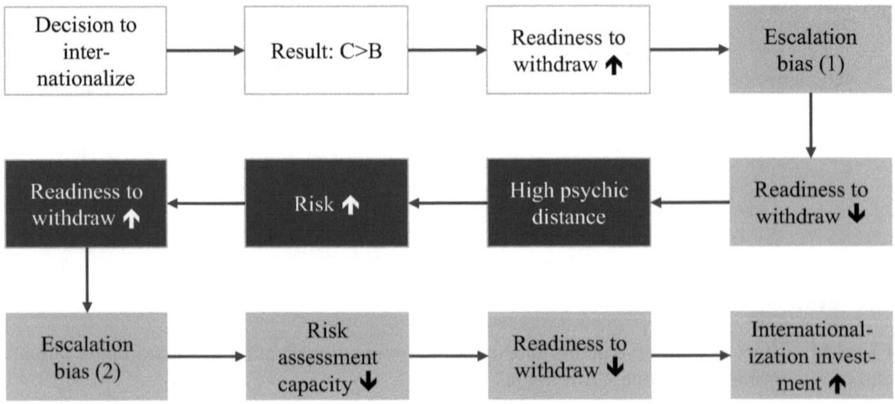

C = Costs
B = Benefits
(1) Previously discussed forces for persistence (psychological, social, and structural)
(2) Misperception of associated risks

Fig. 3.18 Effect of high psychic distance in failing internationalization processes under escalation of commitment. Source: Own figure

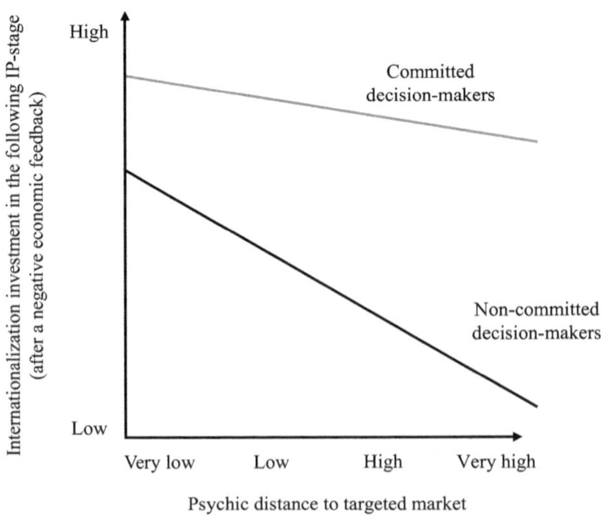

Fig. 3.19 Hypothesized moderating effect of psychic distance on the impact of escalation of commitment on internationalization processes. Source: Own figure

Hypothesis 2 Compared with a non-committed peer-group, managerial decision-makers in internationalization processes, who are under escalation of commitment, will increasingly diverge from the logic of rational choices with an increasing psychic distance to targeted markets.

3.3.7.3 Moderating Effect of the Establishment Chain Progress on the Impact of Escalation of Commitment on Internationalization Process Decision-Making (H3)

Similar to the implications of psychic distance, the establishment chain progress could also develop a moderating influence on the impact of escalation of commitment on internationalization process decision-making. The Uppsala School of Thought considers internationalization to be an incremental learning process, during which firms acquire knowledge about foreign markets gradually and during which they increase their commitment in respective countries step by step.[229] This is reflected in the establishment chain, according to which firms initially choose exports as the market entry of choice, and according to which they establish wholly owned subsidiaries only subsequently.[230] The different steps of the establishment chain can—like market entry modes in general—be structured in a hierarchical order along the amount of committed resources (i.e., from non-equity-based to equity-based).[231] The underlying assumption of the Uppsala School of Thought is that internationalization processes are per se risky as companies will be confronted with different market and institutional environments. In response to this risk, firms will try to commit as few resources as possible in the beginning of their internationalization process, thus reducing eventual capital losses in cases of internationalization failures. Therefore, the establishment chain progress is little initially. In later stages of the establishment chain, more capital becomes committed to respective foreign markets. While one might object that export-based internationalization also binds capital (because firms are still confronted with different market and institutional environments),[232] it is a relatively convincing argument to say that little establishment chain progress requires significantly less capital in comparison to later establishment chain stages. Consequentially, a failing internationalization path is potentially less costly during the early stages of the establishment chain.

Yet, how could the establishment chain progress develop a moderating influence on the impact of escalation of commitment on internationalization processes? As different forms of market entry involve different degrees of bounded capital, a withdrawal from

---

[229]Cf. Eriksson et al. (1997, p. 341) and Johanson and Vahlne (1977, p. 25); as well as Sect. 3.2.1.1 of the present study.

[230]Cf. Sect. 3.2.1.1 of the present study for a summary of the internationalization pattern according to the Uppsala School of Thought.

[231]Cf. Pan and Tse (2000, pp. 535–536).

[232]Cf. Morschett et al. (2010, p. 61) and Das et al. (2007, p. 867).

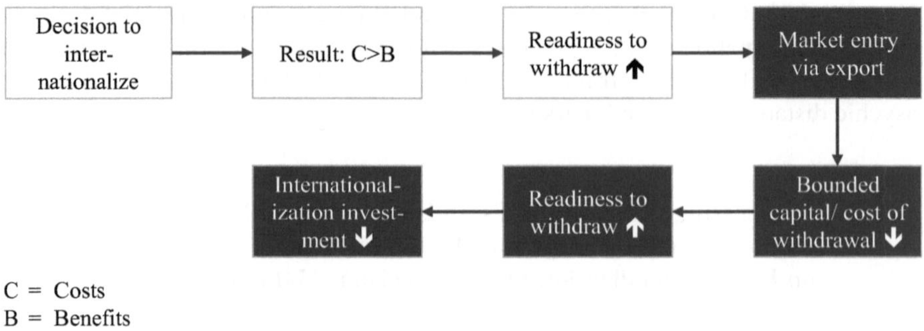

Fig. 3.20 Effect of little establishment chain progress in failing internationalization processes under rational choice circumstances. Source: Own figure

an internationalization process becomes associated with different degrees of withdrawal costs. Especially in scenarios of little establishment chain progress, this could be perceived differently by managerial decision-makers in dependence of their commitment. Following the argumentative proceeding of the previous two sections, a comparative approach between a rational, i.e., non-committed, decision-maker and a counterpart under escalation of commitment will be conducted. A rational internationalization manager, who has incurred losses due to previous internationalization process decisions, should already be marked by an increased readiness to withdraw from the decision path. Supposing that the decision-maker wanted to continue the course of action nevertheless and given that this happens in a context of little establishment chain progress (this means that exports have been the chosen form of market entry), he/she will now be confronted with little bounded capital and, therefore, lower costs of withdrawal (in comparison to equity-based market entries). As a consequence, the readiness to withdraw will increase and the decision-maker should seize the opportunity to exit the course of action at relatively low costs. Ultimately, the internationalization investment would be discounted once more (cf. Fig. 3.20). In the alternative scenario of an already advanced establishment chain progress, costs of withdrawal will be higher due to the equity-based market entry. Even though a rational decision-maker would account for the involved sunk costs, he/she will attempt to maintain the internationalization investment without further—or at best with minimal—resource allocations. A simple exit is not necessarily attractive due to the associated high costs of withdrawal. As for the previously addressed scenario of low psychic distance, this conclusion of the alternative scenario could bear a certain decision pattern similarity to the actions of committed managers (as explained in the next paragraph).

Principally, an internationalization manager under escalation of commitment should have difficulty to see the situation of varying withdrawal costs for what it is. Under escalation of commitment, decision-makers are marked by a reduced cost evaluation capacity as their decisions suffer from a misperception of associated costs. In a broader context of escalation of commitment, investment decisions are frequently taken without any regard to the associated costs as a consequence of the escalation bias (take the misperception of sunk costs or the focus on project

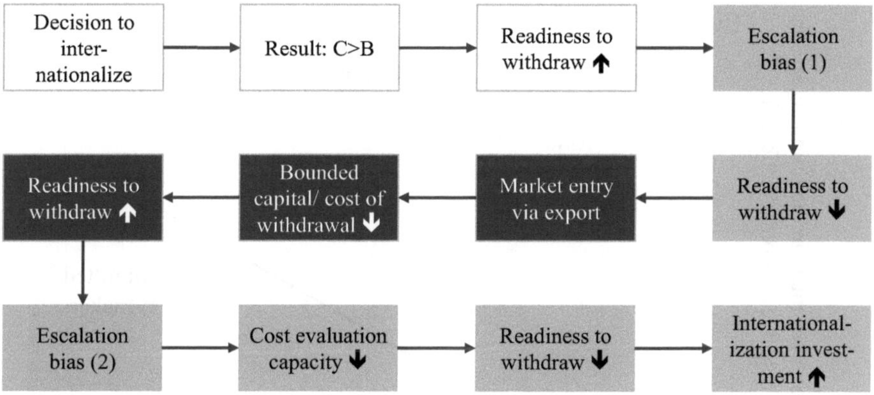

C = Costs
B = Benefits
(1) Previously discussed forces for persistence (psychological, social, and structural)
(2) Misperception of associated costs

Fig. 3.21 Effect of little establishment chain progress in failing internationalization processes under escalation of commitment. Source: Own figure

completion as examples).[233] If this is also true for judgment and decision-making in internationalization processes, reduced costs of withdrawal (as a result of non-equity-based market entry forms) will not be assessed as a convenient opportunity to pull out of a failing internationalization process. Instead, the readiness to withdraw from the course of action remains low due to the limited cost evaluation capacity. Ultimately, the internationalization investment would be reinforced (cf. Fig. 3.21). In the opposite scenario of an already advanced establishment chain, decision-makers under escalation of commitment should likewise persist with the course of action, as they are unaware of the involved sunk costs. As a result, they will—similar to rationally proceeding administrators—maintain the internationalization process without further modification.

The described implications of the establishment chain progress are somewhat comparable to the implications of psychic distance in the context of escalation of commitment in internationalization process decision-making. Once more, it can be assumed that there is a different behavioral pattern for decision-makers in dependence of the presence of an escalation bias since decision-makers under escalation of commitment will continue their internationalization investment regardless of the associated withdrawal costs and since rational internationalization managers will account for different degrees of withdrawal costs. This, however, will be especially identifiable in a scenario of little establishment chain progress, in which rational decision-makers exit the internationalization process while committed managers persist—regardless of the associated costs. In the alternative scenario of an already

[233]Cf. Arkes and Blumer (1985, pp. 124 ff.); see also Sect. 3.3.4.2.

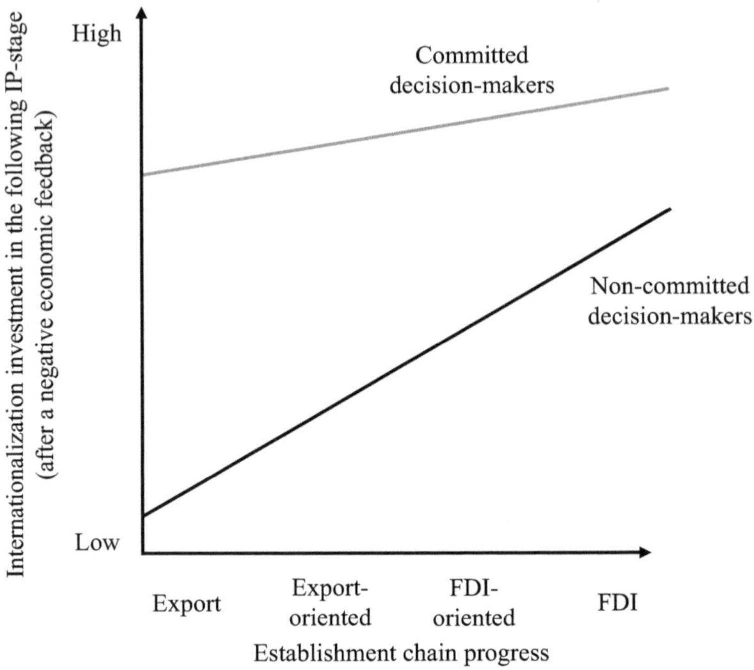

Fig. 3.22 Hypothesized moderating effect of the establishment chain progress on the impact of escalation of commitment on internationalization processes. Source: Own figure

advanced establishment chain progress, the decision-making pattern of committed and non-committed managers should converge since high withdrawal costs make an internationalization exit unattractive for both groups (cf. Fig. 3.22). Admittedly, Fig. 3.22 could seem somewhat tautological at first sight as one might object that it is quite clear that advanced establishment chain stages require higher internationalization investments in later periods. Thus, one might conclude that the establishment chain progress is not fully independent from following internationalization investments. This criticism, however, is off target. Figure 3.22—as well as the here developed Hypothesis 3—scrutinize the different decision-making pattern of committed and non-committed managers. The purpose is to highlight the dissimilar actions of decision-makers under escalation of commitment compared to a group of rational counterparts.

Hypothesis 3 Compared with a non-committed peer-group, managerial decision-makers in internationalization processes, who are under escalation of commitment, will increasingly converge towards the logic of rational choices with an increasing establishment chain progress.

3.3.8 *Section Conclusion*

Section 3.3 takes up the key insight of Sect. 3.2, in which it has been outlined that the U-Model is somewhat ambiguous with regard to its prescriptive and descriptive perspective as well as to its behavioral assumptions. Especially due to the lacking consideration of cognitive dispositions and behavioral biases in Johanson's and Vahlne's theory, it is justified to state that decision-makers are—at least implicitly—expected to act rationally, i.e., consistently and purposefully (with regard to their preferences). Against this background, the present section presents a critical approach to the rational choice content of the U-Model. In the context of bounded rationality, the decision-making assumptions of the U-Model are questioned. For this matter, the cognitive behavioral bias of escalation of commitment has been presented in depth. Decision-makers under escalation of commitment continue to allocate resources to failing courses of action, e.g., an unsuccessful internationalization process, as they include previous decision outcomes in ongoing decision problems. Escalation situations often present themselves as self-perpetuating cycles, which are determined by different factors in temporal dependence. Altogether, they contradict the premises of orthodox judgment and decision-making approaches. Escalation of commitment can thus be considered as a suitable representative of the limited cognitive capabilities of decision-makers under bounded rationality and serves well in order to look into the matter of bounded rationality in internationalization processes.

3.4 Chapter Conclusion

As a whole, the third chapter deals with the core subject of the present study as it raises the topic of escalation of commitment in internationalization process decision-making. Even though there have been different abstractions of the internationalization of firms in the past, the Uppsala IP Model of Johanson and Vahlne must be considered as the state-of-the-art in this discipline. Considering its high count of citations as well as the continued interest by academia, one can only conclude that the U-Model enjoys widespread recognition and approval. Often, this is connected with the claim that the U-Model is particularly realistic due to its processual perspective and due to its respect for limited information availability in internationalization processes. This, however, does not yet turn the approach into an example of the bounded rationality program. Despite the circumstance that the U-Model acknowledges that decision-makers' actions are limited by incomplete information, it considers them—at least implicitly—to be rationally proceeding administrators, who possess the cognitive capability to assess their options.

At the same time, however, one cannot help but realize that the U-Model is marked by certain inconsistencies with regard to its validity in behavioral decision-making realities. For example, failed internationalization steps, which have been

Hypothesis 1a	Hypothesis 1b
At the group level, managerial decision-makers in internationalization processes, who are under escalation of commitment, will rather act contrary to the logic of rational choices compared to a non-committed peer-group. This means that they will continue to raise internationalization investments regardless of the resultant economic success of the venture.	At the individual level, managerial decision-makers will act increasingly contrary to the logic of rational choices with higher individual degrees of commitment. This means that the raised internationalization investment of a single internationalization manager will increase regardless of the resultant economic success of the venture but in dependence of the decision-maker's degree of commitment.
Hypothesis 2	**Hypothesis 3**
Compared with a non-committed peer-group, managerial decision-makers in internationalization processes, who are under escalation of commitment, will increasingly diverge from the logic of rational choices with an increasing psychic distance to targeted markets.	Compared with a non-committed peer-group, managerial decision-makers in internationalization processes, who are under escalation of commitment, will increasingly converge towards the logic of rational choices with an increasing establishment chain progress.

Fig. 3.23 Summary of hypotheses. Source: Own figure

prominently covered in different media, such as the North-American activity of the British retailer Marks & Spencer or the international experiences of Wal-Mart in South Korea and Germany, are not foreseen in the U-Model. Against this background, the present chapter can be read as a critical assessment of the U-Model and as a check for objections in the form of bounded rationality in internationalization processes. For this purpose, escalation of commitment has been presented as an example of the cognitive limitations of decision-makers. The disposition of decision-makers to allocate further funds to failing courses of action could have a defining impact on internationalization process decision-making. Especially due to the different degrees of uncertainty that are connected with going international, and also due to the varying costs of withdrawal that are associated with different market entry forms, decision-makers in internationalization processes may be prone to an escalation bias. For an analysis of the issue of escalation of commitment in internationalization process decision-making, three hypotheses have been established (cf. Fig. 3.23).

References

Aharoni, Y. (1966). *The foreign investment decision process*. Boston: Harvard University.

Andersen, O. (1993). On the internationalization process of firms: A critical analysis. *Journal of International Business Studies, 24*(2), 209–231.

Andersson, S. (2000). The internationalization of the firm from an entrepreneurial perspective. *International Studies of Management and Organization, 30*(1), 63–92.

Arkes, H. R., & Blumer, C. (1985). The psychology of sunk cost. *Organizational Behavior and Human Decision Processes, 35*(1), 124–140.

Aronson, E. (1969). The theory of cognitive dissonance: A current perspective. *Advances in Experimental Social Psychology, 4*, 1–34.

Barkema, H. G., Bell, J. H. J., & Pennings, J. M. (1996). Foreign entry, cultural barriers, and learning. *Strategic Management Journal, 17*(2), 151–166.

Barton, S. L., Duchon, D., & Dunegan, K. J. (1989). An empirical test of Staw and Ross's prescriptions for the management of escalation of commitment behavior in organizations. *Decision Sciences, 20*(3), 532–544.

Bazerman, M. H., Giuliano, T., & Appelman, A. (1984). Escalation of commitment in individual and group decision making. *Organizational Behavior and Human Performance, 33*(2), 141–152.

Beauvois, J.-L., Joule, R.-V., & Brunetti, F. (1993). Cognitive rationalization and act rationalization in an escalation of commitment. *Basic and Applied Social Psychology, 14*(1), 1–17.

Beckerman, W. (1956). Distance and the pattern of intra-european trade. *The Review of Economics and Statistics, 38*(1), 31–40.

Benito, G. R. G. (2005). The review of economics and statistics. *The Review of Economics and Statistics, 5*(2), 235–251.

Benito, G. R. G., & Welch, L. S. (1997). De-internationalization. *Management International Review, 37*(S2), 7–25.

Björkman, I., & Forsgren, M. (2000). Nordic international business research. A review of its development. *International Studies of Management and Organization, 30*(1), 6–25.

Bobocel, D. R., & Meyer, J. P. (1994). Escalating commitment to a failing course of action: Separating the roles of choice and justification. *Journal of Applied Psychology, 79*(3), 360–363.

Bonaccorsi, A. (1992). On the relationship between firm size and export intensity. *Journal of International Business Studies, 23*(4), 605–635.

Bragger, J. D., Hantula, D. A., Bragger, D., Kirnan, J., & Kutcher, E. (2003). When success breeds failure: History, hysteresis, and delayed exit decisions. *Journal of Applied Psychology, 88*(1), 6–14.

Brewer, P. A. (2007). Operationalizing psychic distance: A revised approach. *Journal of International Marketing, 15*(1), 44–66.

Brockner, J. (1992). The escalation of commitment to a failing course of action: Toward theoretical progress. *Academy of Management Review, 17*(1), 39–61.

Brockner, J., Houser, R., Birnbaum, G., Lloyd, K., Deitcher, J., Nathanson, S., et al. (1986). Escalation of commitment to an ineffective course of action: The effect of feedback having negative implications for self-identity. *Administrative Science Quarterly, 31*(1), 109–126.

Brockner, J., & Rubin, J. Z. (1985). *Entrapment in escalating conflicts: A social psychological analysis*. New York: Springer.

Brockner, J., Rubin, J. Z., Fine, J., Hamilton, T. P., Thomas, B., & Turetsky, B. (1982). Factors affecting entrapment in escalating conflicts: The importance of timing. *Journal of Research in Personality, 16*(2), 247–266.

Brockner, J., Rubin, J. Z., & Lang, E. (1981). Face-saving and entrapment. *Journal of Experimental Social Psychology, 17*(1), 68–79.

Brockner, J., Shaw, M. C., & Rubin, J. Z. (1979). Factors affecting withdrawal from an escalating conflict: Quitting before it's too late. *Journal of Experimental Social Psychology, 15*(5), 492–503.
Buckley, P. J. (2004). The role of China in the global strategy of multinational enterprises. *Journal of Chinese Economic and Business Studies, 2*(1), 1–25.
Buckley, P. J., & Casson, M. (1991). *The future of the multinational enterprise* (2nd ed.). London: Macmillan.
Buckley, P. J., & Casson, M. C. (2009). The internalisation theory of the multinational enterprise: A review of the progress of a research agenda after 30 years. *Journal of International Business Studies, 40*(9), 1563–1580.
Buckley, P. J., Devinney, T. M., & Louviere, J. J. (2007). Do managers behave the way theory suggests? A choice-theoretic examination of foreign direct investment location decision-making. *Journal of International Business Studies, 38*(7), 1069–1094.
Caldwell, D. F., & O'Reilly, C. A. (1982). Responses to failure: The effects of choice and responsibility on impression management. *Academy of Management Journal, 25*(1), 121–136.
Carlson, S. (1966). *International business research*. Uppsala: Acta Universitatis Upsaliensis.
Cavusgil, S. T. (1984). Differences among exporting firms based on their degree of internationalization. *Journal of Business Research, 12*(2), 195–208.
Chenhall, R., & Morris, D. (1991). The effect of cognitive style and sponsorship bias on the treatment of opportunity costs in resource allocation decisions. *Accounting, Organizations and Society, 16*(1), 27–46.
Chong, V. K., & Syarifuddin, I. (2010). Escalation of commitment to unprofitable projects: An experimental investigation of the effect of conformity pressure and self-esteem. *Accounting, Accountability and Performance, 16*(1–2), 1–23.
Chulkov, D. (2007). Economics of escalation: When is escalation of commitment rational for managers and for firms? *International Journal of Business Research, 7*(5), 44–51.
Conlon, D. E., & Garland, H. (1993). The role of project completion information in resource allocation decisions. *Academy of Management Journal, 36*(2), 402–413.
Conlon, E. J., & Wolf, G. (1980). The moderating effects of strategy, visibility, and involvement on allocation behavior: An extension of Staw's escalation paradigm. *Organizational Behavior and Human Performance, 26*(2), 172–192.
Cyert, R. M., & March, J. G. (1963). *A behavioral theory of the firm*. Prentice-Hall: Englewood Cliffs.
Das, S., Roberts, M. J., & Tybout, J. R. (2007). Market entry costs, producer heterogeneity, and export dynamics. *Econometrica, 75*(3), 837–873.
Denison, C. A. (2009). Real options and escalation of commitment: A behavioral analysis of capital investment decisions. *The Accounting Review, 84*(1), 133–155.
Donthu, N., & Unal, B. (2014). Identifying escalation of commitment in B2B new product development projects using data envelopment analysis. *Journal of Business and Industrial Marketing, 29*(3), 209–214.
Dow, D., & Karunaratna, A. (2006). Developing a multidimensional instrument to measure psychic distance stimuli. *Journal of International Business Studies, 37*(5), 578–602.
Dunning, J. H. (1979). Explaining changing patterns of international production: In defence of the eclectic theory. *Oxford Bulletin of Economics and Statistics, 41*(4), 269–295.
Dunning, J. H. (1980). Toward an eclectic theory of international production: Some empirical tests. *Journal of International Business Studies, 11*(1), 9–31.
Dunning, J. H. (1988). The eclectic paradigm of international production: A restatement and some possible extensions. *Journal of International Business Studies, 19*(1), 1–31.
Dunning, J. H. (2000). The eclectic paradigm as an envelope for economic and business theories of MNE activity. *International Business Review, 9*(2), 163–190.
Duxbury, D. (2012). Sunk costs and sunk benefits: A re-examination of re-investment decisions. *The British Accounting Review, 44*(3), 144–156.

Eriksson, K., Johanson, J., Majkgård, A., & Sharma, D. D. (1997). Experiential knowledge and costs in the internationalization process. *Journal of International Business Studies, 28*(2), 337–360.

Festinger, L. (1957). *A theory of cognitive dissonance*. Stanford: Stanford University Press.

Fishburn, P. C. (1981). Subjective expected utility: A review of normative theories. *Theory and Decision, 13*(2), 139–199.

Fletcher, R. (2001). A holistic approach to internationalisation. *International Business Review, 10*(1), 25–49.

Forsgren, M. (2002). The concept of learning in the Uppsala internationalization process model: A critical review. *International Business Review, 11*(3), 257–277.

Forsgren, M., & Johanson, J. (2010). A dialogue about the Uppsala modell of internationalization. In U. Andersson & U. Holm (Eds.), *Managing the contemporary multinational* (pp. 283–304). Cheltenham: Edward Elgar.

Fox, F. V., & Staw, B. M. (1979). The trapped administrator: Effects of job insecurity and policy resistance upon commitment to a course of action. *Administrative Science Quarterly, 24*(3), 449–471.

Garland, H., & Newport, S. (1991). Effects of absolute and relative sunk costs on the decision to persist with a course of action. *Organizational Behavior and Human Decision Processes, 48*(1), 55–69.

Ghosh, D. (1997). De-escalation strategies: Some experimental evidence. In *Behavioral research in accounting* (Vol. 9, pp. 88–112).

Goffman, E. (1959). *The presentation of self in everyday life*. New York: Doubleday.

Goodman, P. S., Bazerman, M., & Conlon, E. (1980). Institutionalization of planned organizational change. In B. M. Staw & L. L. Cummings (Eds.), *Research in organizational behavior* (Vol. 2, pp. 215–246). Greenwich: JAI Press.

Hadjikhani, A. (1997). A note on the criticisms against the internationalization process model. *Management International Review, 37*(S2), 43–66.

Hambrick, D. C. (2007). Upper echelons theory: An update. *Academy of Management Review, 32*(2), 334–343.

Hambrick, D. C., & Mason, P. A. (1984). Upper echelons: The organization as a reflection of its top managers. *Academy of Management Review, 9*(2), 193–206.

Hammond, P. J. (1998). Subjective expected utility. In S. Barberà, P. J. Hammond, & C. Seidl (Eds.), *Handbook of utility theory* (pp. 213–271). Dordrecht: Kluwer.

Hannan, M. T., & Freeman, J. (1984). Structural Inertia and organizational change. *American Sociological Review, 49*(2), 149–164.

Harvey, P., & Victoravich, L. M. (2009). The influence of forward-looking antecedents, uncertainty, and anticipatory emotions on project escalation. *Decision Sciences, 40*(4), 759–782.

He, X., & Mittal, V. (2007). The effect of decision risk and project stage on escalation of commitment. *Organizational Behavior and Human Decision Processes, 103*(2), 225–237.

Hennart, J.-F. (1982). *A theory of multinational enterprise*. Ann Arbor: University of Michigan Press.

Hutzschenreuter, T., Pedersen, T., & Volberda, H. W. (2007). The role of path dependency and managerial intentionality: A perspective on international business research. *Journal of International Business Studies, 38*(7), 1055–1068.

Johanson, J., & Vahlne, J.-E. (1977). The internationalization process of the firm – A model of knowledge development and increasing foreign market commitments. *Journal of International Business Studies, 8*(1), 23–32.

Johanson, J., & Vahlne, J.-E. (1990). The mechanism of internationalisation. *International Marketing Review, 7*(4), 11–24.

Johanson, J., & Vahlne, J.-E. (2003). Business relationship learning and commitment in the internationalization process. *Journal of International Entrepreneurship, 1*(1), 83–101.

Johanson, J., & Vahlne, J.-E. (2006). Commitment and opportunity development in the internationalization process: A note on the Uppsala internationalization process model. *Management International Review, 46*(2), 165–178.

Johanson, J., & Vahlne, J.-E. (2009). The Uppsala internationalization process model revisited: From liability of foreignness to liability of outsidership. *Journal of International Business Studies, 40*(9), 1411–1431.

Johanson, J., & Wiedersheim-Paul, F. (1975). The internationalization of the firm – Four Swedish cases. *Journal of Management Studies, 12*(3), 305–323.

Johnston, W. J., Khalil, S., Jain, M., & Cheng, J. M. S. (2012). Determinants of joint action in international channels of distribution: The moderating role of psychic distance. *Journal of International Marketing, 20*(3), 34–49.

Jones, E. E., & Pittman, T. S. (1982). Toward a general theory of strategic self-presentation. In *Psychological perspectives on the self* (Vol. 1, pp. 231–262). Hillsdale: Lawrence Erlbaum.

Judge, T. A., Erez, A., & Bono, J. E. (1998). The power of being positive: The relation between positive self-concept and job performance. *Human Performance, 11*(2–3), 167–187.

Kalinic, I., Sarasvathy, S. D., & Forza, C. (2014). 'Expect the unexpected': Implications of effectual logic on the internationalization process. *International Business Review, 23*(3), 635–647.

Kelly, D., & Amburgey, T. L. (1991). Organizational inertia and momentum: A dynamic model of strategic change. *Academy of Management Journal, 34*(3), 591–612.

Kish-Gephart, J. J., & Campbell, J. T. (2015). You don't forget your roots: The influence of CEO social class background on strategic risk taking. *Academy of Management Journal, 58*(6), 1614–1636.

Kraus, S., Ambos, T. C., Eggers, F., & Cesinger, B. (2015). Distance and perceptions of risk in internationalization decisions. *Journal of Business Research, 68*(7), 1501–1505.

Ku, G. (2008). Learning to de-escalate: The effects of regret in escalation of commitment. *Organizational Behavior and Human Decision Processes, 105*(2), 221–232.

Kunz, J. (2013). Die psychologische und ökonomische Perspektive in der BWL: Eine Diskussion am Beispiel der Literatur zum Escalation of Commitment. *Die Betriebswirtschaft, 73*(3), 205–219.

Li, J. (1995). Foreign entry and survival: Effects of strategic choices on performance in international markets. *Strategic Management Journal, 16*(5), 333–351.

Luo, Y., & Peng, M. W. (1999). Learning to compete in a transition economy: Experience, environment, and performance. *Journal of International Business Studies, 30*(2), 269–295.

Luostarinen, R. (1979). *Internationalization of the firm: An empirical study of the internationalization of firms with small and open domestic markets with special emphasis on lateral rigidity as a behavioral characteristics in strategic decision-making*. Helsinki: Helsinki School of Economics.

Magnusson, P., & Boyle, B. A. (2009). A contingency perspective on psychic distance in international channel relationships. *Journal of Marketing Channels, 16*(1), 77–99.

Matthyssens, P., & Pauwels, P. (2000). Uncovering international market-exit processes: A comparative case study. *Psychology and Marketing, 17*(8), 697–719.

McCain, B. E. (1986). Continuing investment under conditions of failure: A laboratory study of the limits to escalation. *Journal of Applied Psychology, 71*(2), 280–284.

McCarthy, A. M., Schoorman, F. D., & Cooper, A. C. (1993). Reinvestment decisions by entrepreneurs: Rational decision-making or escalation of commitment? *Journal of Business Venturing, 8*(1), 9–24.

Melin, L. (1992). Internationalization as a strategy process. *Strategic Management Journal, 13*(S2), 99–118.

Moon, H. (2001a). Looking forward and looking back: Integrating completion and sunk-cost effects within an escalation-of-commitment progress decision. *Journal of Applied Psychology, 86*(1), 104–113.

Moon, H. (2001b). The two faces of conscientiousness: Duty and achievement striving in escalation of commitment dilemmas. *Journal of Applied Psychology, 86*(3), 533–540.
Moon, H., & Conlon, D. E. (2002). From acclaim to blame: Evidence of a person sensitivity decision bias. *Journal of Applied Psychology, 87*(1), 33–42.
Morschett, D., Schramm-Klein, H., & Swoboda, B. (2010). Decades of research on market entry modes: What do we really know about external antecedents of entry mode choice? *Journal of International Management, 16*(1), 60–77.
Moser, K., Wolff, H. G., & Kraft, A. (2013). The de-escalation of commitment: Predecisional accountability and cognitive processes. *Journal of Applied Social Psychology, 43*(2), 363–376.
Nathanson, S., Brockner, J., Brenner, D., Samuelson, C., Countryman, M., Lloyd, M., et al. (1982). Toward the reduction of entrapment. *Journal of Applied Social Psychology, 12*(3), 193–208.
Nordström, K. A. (1991). *The internationalization process of the firm – Searching for new patterns and explanations*. Stockholm: Stockholm School of Economics.
Northcraft, G. B., & Wolf, G. (1984). Dollars, sense, and sunk costs: A life cycle model of resource allocation decisions. *Academy of Management Review, 9*(2), 225–234.
O'Grady, S., & Lane, H. W. (1996). The psychic distance paradox. *Journal of International Business Studies, 27*(2), 309–333.
Oesterle, M.-J. (1993). *Joint Ventures in Russland*. Wiesbaden: Gabler.
Oesterle, M.-J. (1999). Fiktionen der Internationalisierungsforschung. In J. Engelhard & W. A. Oechsler (Eds.), *Internationales Management* (pp. 219–245). Wiesbaden: Gabler.
Oviatt, B. M., & McDougall, P. P. (1994). Toward a theory of international new ventures. *Journal of International Business Studies, 25*(1), 45–64.
Oviatt, B. M., & McDougall, P. P. (2005). Defining international entrepreneurship and modeling the speed of internationalization. *Entrepreneurship Theory and Practice, 29*(5), 537–554.
Pan, Y., & Tse, D. K. (2000). The hierarchical model of market entry modes. *Journal of International Business Studies, 31*(4), 535–554.
Papadopoulos, N., & Denis, J. E. (1988). Inventory, taxonomy and assessment of methods for international market selection. *International Marketing Review, 5*(3), 38–51.
Penrose, E. (2009). *The theory of the growth of the firm* (4th ed.). Oxford: Oxford University Press.
Perks, K. J., & Hughes, M. (2008). Entrepreneurial decision-making in internationalization: Propositions from mid-size firms. *International Business Review, 17*(3), 310–330.
Petersen, B., Pedersen, T., & Sharma, D. D. (2003). The role of knowledge in firms' internationalization process: Wherefrom and whereto. In A. Blomstermo & D. D. Sharma (Eds.), *Learning in the internationalization process of firms*. Cheltenham: Edward Elgar.
Rao, V. S., & Monk, A. (1999). The effects of individual differences and anonymity on commitment to decisions: Preliminary evidence. *The Journal of Social Psychology, 139*(4), 496–515.
Reid, S. (1983). Firm internationalization, transaction costs and strategic choice. *International Marketing Review, 1*(2), 44–56.
Reid, S. D., & Rosson, P. J. (1987). Managing export entry and expansion: An overview. In S. D. Reid & P. J. Rosson (Eds.), *Managing export entry and expansion* (pp. 3–20). New York: Praeger.
Rialp, A., Rialp, J., & Knight, G. A. (2005). The phenomenon of early internationalizing firms: What do we know after a decade (1993–2003) of scientific inquiry? *International Business Review, 14*(2), 147–166.
Ross, J., & Staw, B. M. (1986). Expo 86: An escalation prototype. *Administrative Science Quarterly, 31*(2), 274–297.
Ross, J., & Staw, B. M. (1993). Organizational escalation and exit: Lessons from the Shoreham nuclear power plant. *Academy of Management Journal, 36*(4), 701–732.
Rubin, J. Z., & Brockner, J. (1975). Factors affecting entrapment in waiting situations: The Rosencrantz and Guildenstern effect. *Journal of Personality and Social Psychology, 31*(6), 1054–1063.
Rugman, A. M. (2009). *The Oxford Handbook of international business* (2nd ed.). New York: Oxford University Press.

Rugman, A. M., & Verbeke, A. (2007). Liabilities of regional foreignness and the use of firm-level versus country-level data: A response to Dunning et al. (2007). *Journal of International Business Studies, 38*(1), 200–205.
Savage, L. J. (1972). *The foundations of statistics* (2nd ed.). New York: Dover.
Schmid, S. (2002). Die Internationalisierung von Unternehmungen aus der Perspektive der Uppsala-Schule. *WiSt-Wirtschaftswissenschaftliches Studium, 31*(7), 387–392.
Schmidt, J. B., & Calantone, R. J. (2002). Escalation of commitment during new product development. *Journal of the Academy of Marketing Science, 30*(2), 103–118.
Schulz, A. K.-D., & Cheng, M. M. (2002). Persistence in capital budgeting reinvestment decisions – Personal responsibility antecedent and information asymmetry moderator: A note. *Accounting and Finance, 42*(1), 73–86.
Schulz-Hardt, S., Thurow-Kröning, B., & Frey, D. (2009). Preference-based escalation: A new interpretation for the responsibility effect in escalating commitment and entrapment. *Organizational Behavior and Human Decision Processes, 108*(2), 175–186.
Schwenk, C. R. (1984). Cognitive simplification processes in strategic decision-making. *Strategic Management Journal, 5*(2), 111–128.
Sharp, D. J., & Salter, S. B. (1997). Project escalation and sunk costs: A test of the international generalizability of agency and prospect theories. *Journal of International Business Studies, 28*(1), 101–121.
Singer, M. S., & Singer, A. E. (1986). Individual differences and the escalation of commitment paradigm. *Journal of Social Psychology, 126*(2), 197–204.
Sivanathan, N., Molden, D. C., Galinsky, A. D., & Ku, G. (2008). The promise and peril of self-affirmation in de-escalation of commitment. *Organizational Behavior and Human Decision Processes, 107*(1), 1–14.
Sleesman, D. J., Conlon, D. E., McNamara, G., & Miles, J. E. (2012). Cleaning up the Big Muddy: A meta-analytic review of the determinants of escalation of commitment. *Academy of Management Journal, 55*(3), 541–562.
Soman, D. (2001). The mental accounting of sunk time costs: Why time is not like money. *Journal of Behavioral Decision Making, 14*(3), 169–185.
Staw, B. M. (1976). Knee-deep in the big muddy: A study of escalating commitment to a chosen course of action. *Organizational Behavior and Human Performance, 16*(1), 27–44.
Staw, B. M. (1981). The escalation of commitment to a course of action. *Academy of Management Review, 6*(4), 577–587.
Staw, B. M. (1997). The escalation of commitment: An update and appraisal. In Z. Shapira (Ed.), *Organizational decision making* (pp. 191–215). Cambridge: Cambridge University Press.
Staw, B. M., & Ross, J. (1987). Behavior in escalation situations: Antecedents, prototypes, and solutions. In *Research in organizational behavior* (Vol. 9, pp. 39–78). Greenwich: JAI Press.
Staw, B. M., & Ross, J. (1989). Understanding behavior in escalation situations. *Science, 246*(4927), 216–220.
Street, M. D., & Anthony, W. P. (1997). A conceptual framework establishing the relationship between groupthink and escalating commitment behavior. *Small Group Research, 28*(2), 267–293.
Sullivan, D., & Bauerschmidt, A. (1990). Incremental internationalization: A test of Johanson and Vahlne's thesis. *Management International Review, 30*(1), 19–30.
Tang, M.-J. (1988). An economic perspective on escalating commitment. *Strategic Management Journal, 9*(S1), 79–92.
Teece, D. J. (1986). Transactions cost economics and the multinational enterprise: An assessment. *Journal of Economic Behavior and Organization, 7*(1), 21–45.
Teger, A. I. (1980). *Too much invested to quit*. New York: Pergamon.
Thaler, R. (1980). Toward a positive theory of consumer choice. *Journal of Economic Behavior and Organization, 1*(1), 39–60.
Ting, H. (2011). The effects of goal distance and value in escalation of commitment. *Current Psychology, 30*(1), 93–104.

Turnbull, P. W. (1987). A challenge to the stages theory of the internationalization process. In S. D. Reid & P. J. Rosson (Eds.), *Managing export entry and expansion* (pp. 21–40). New York: Praeger.

Turner, R. G. (1977). Self-consciousness and anticipatory belief change. *Personality and Social Psychology Bulletin, 3*(3), 438–441.

Vahlne, J.-E., & Johanson, J. (2013). The Uppsala model on evolution of the multinational business enterprise – From internalization to coordination of networks. *International Marketing Review, 30*(3), 189–210.

Walsh, J. P., & Henderson, C. M. (1989). An attributional analysis of decisions about making commitments. *The Journal of Social Psychology, 129*(4), 533–549.

Welch, L. S., & Wiedersheim-Paul, F. (1980). Initial exports – A marketing failure? *Journal of Management Studies, 17*(3), 333–344.

Whyte, G. (1986). Escalating commitment to a course of action: A reinterpretation. *Academy of Management Review, 11*(2), 311–321.

Whyte, G. (1993). Escalating commitment in individual and group decision making: A prospect theory approach. *Organizational Behavior and Human Decision Processes, 54*(3), 430–455.

Wolff, H. G., & Moser, K. (2008). Choice, accountability, and effortful processing in escalation situations. *Zeitschrift für Psychologie [Journal of Psychology], 216*(4), 235–243.

Wong, K. F. E., Kwong, J. Y. Y., & Ng, C. K. (2008). When thinking rationally increases biases: The role of rational thinking style in escalation of commitment. *Applied Psychology, 57*(2), 246–271.

Wong, K. F. E., Yik, M., & Kwong, J. Y. (2006). Understanding the emotional aspects of escalation of commitment: The role of negative affect. *Journal of Applied Psychology, 91*(2), 282–297.

Zaheer, S. (1995). Overcoming the liability of foreignness. *Academy of Management Journal, 38*(2), 341–363.

Zhang, L., & Baumeister, R. F. (2006). Your money or your self-esteem: Threatened Egotism promotes costly entrapment in losing endeavors. *Personality and Social Psychology Bulletin, 32*(7), 881–893.

Chapter 4
Empirical Analysis of Escalation of Commitment in Internationalization Process Decision-Making

Up to this point, the present study has dealt with the identification as well as with the development of the research problem. In order to analyze bounded rationality in internationalization processes, the present fourth chapter will attempt to identify the display of escalation of commitment in internationalization decision-making empirically. The here-applied structural setup of the study (first the problem identification and development, then the empirical analysis) can be considered as a standard procedure in research processes.[1] With regard to the empirical analysis, the following Sect. 4.1 will outline the applied methodological approach for the present study. This is necessary because a sound empirical analysis requires a closer look at the selection of the underlying research methodology. Section 4.2 is dedicated to the quantitative-empirical analysis of the research problem, and Sect. 4.3 presents a qualitative-empirical illustration of this study's subject.

4.1 Selection of the Underlying Research Methodology

There are different forms of accessing research problems empirically. Fundamentally, empirical research methods can be differentiated in quantitative and qualitative approaches. These two access-forms are often regarded as diametrically opposed. Yet in fact, a combination of both research approaches can yield fruitful results with regard to the in-depth coverage of research problems. For the present study, such a mixed-methods setup has been selected. On the one hand, a randomized experiment under laboratory circumstances has been conducted in order to uncover the decision-making processes in a simulated internationalization context. On the other hand, two case examples will illustrate the topic of escalation of commitment in internationalization process reality and add profundity to the

[1] Cf. Angerer et al. (2006, p. 115).

B. Röber, *Escalation of Commitment in Internationalization Processes*, MIR Series in International Business, https://doi.org/10.1007/978-3-319-69102-2_4

quantitative-empirical analysis. It is the overall aim of the present Sect. 4.1 to give an introduction to the selected research methods of this dissertation. First, the different empirical access-forms to research problems will be presented under particular attention to mixed-methods (Sect. 4.1.1). Subsequently, laboratory experiments (Sect. 4.1.2) and case analyses (Sect. 4.1.3) will be introduced as quantitative-empirical and qualitative-empirical research methods respectively.

4.1.1 Benefit and Application of Mixed-Methods in Social Sciences

Quantitative and qualitative research approaches must be considered as fundamentally different. Some authors go as far as to refer to the two categories as opposing research paradigms.[2] Considering that a paradigm is an intellectual conception that enjoys universal acclaim in academia,[3] it remains debatable whether or not 'paradigm' is a suitable term in this context. It is, however, clear how the two categories are differentiated. Social science scholars, who follow the quantitative approach, treat their observations in a similar manner as natural science researchers treat theirs. As in natural sciences, for example, it is their underlying assumption that generally applicable laws can be identified, which allow conclusions with regard to the individual level. Furthermore, insights must provide time- and context-free generalizations. In order to arrive at such generalizations, any potential interference of the researcher must be avoided, and research conclusions must be objective.[4] As a result, quantitative research is often built on numerical and statistical data analyses, which require a quantification of an observed, predefined segment of reality and which provide seemingly robust conclusions with regard to hypothesized causes and effects. In research practice, quantitative empirics are commonly consulted in order to test established theories.

However, the application of natural sciences standards in social sciences disciplines raises the obvious question, whether generally applicable laws can actually be identified for the latter. Social behavior is always defined by the objectives, motives, and free will of individuals. As these defining factors have the potential to change over time, social behavior is clearly neither time- nor context-free.[5] Thus, generally applicable laws might simply not exist in social sciences and corresponding methodological approaches are possibly an illusion of scholars. Certainly, advocates of quantitative-empirical research approaches have presented methodological advancements against the background of these doubts.[6]

[2]Cf. Angerer et al. (2006, p. 117).
[3]Cf. Kuhn (2012, pp. 11 ff.).
[4]Cf. Johnson and Onwuegbuzie (2004, p. 14).
[5]Cf. Angerer et al. (2006, p. 117).
[6]Cf. Mayring (2001, p. 2).

Nevertheless, scholars of the qualitative approach refrain from quantitative measurements because of the questionable applicability of numerical and statistical methods in social sciences. They acknowledge that time- and context-free generalizations are neither possible nor desirable for their disciplines. In addition, causes and effects for observed phenomena can never be fully differentiated in social sciences.[7] Conclusions in this regard will always—at least partially—remain a product of the mind of the researcher. On the basis of these objections, scholars of the qualitative approach promote the collection of data material, which is based on verbalized and interpreted observations of reality (e.g., in the form of interviews).[8] The benefit of such qualitative data collections lies in the open-end character of corresponding research methods (i.e., no predefined segments of reality are under analysis). This allows more flexible discussions of research problems at the price of less (statistical) generalizability of research results. In research practice, qualitative empirics are commonly consulted in order to develop theories.

Considering the presented dichotomous perspective on quantitative and qualitative approaches, one must conclude that corresponding research methods have both benefits and shortcomings. However, there is a third perspective. Both approaches can also be seen as ideal complements if they are jointly applied in order to cover a single research question.[9] With this idea in mind, more and more scholars are promoting mixed-methods, i.e., the combination of quantitative-empirical and qualitative-empirical analyses, as an empirical research methodology, which is increasingly recognized as a third research approach.[10] Currently, however, there is no univocal understanding of the underlying requirements and criteria for mixed-methods. Quite the contrary, the discussion on a suitable definition is open, and authors who claim to apply mixed-methods use the term for different research designs.[11] Creswell and Plano Clark have possibly identified the common denominator for the field of mixed-methods research: "Its central premise is that the use of quantitative and qualitative approaches, in combination, provides a better understanding of research problems than either approach alone."[12] The benefit of a combination lies in several reasons: First, it has the potential of an increased profundity of studies because more analytical perspectives can be considered. Second, methodological disadvantages of one method can be compensated for by the other.[13] Third, mixed-methods allow theory development and testing at the same time because they build on a predefined segment of reality as well as on open-end research methods.

---

[7]Cf. Johnson and Onwuegbuzie (2004, p. 14).

[8]Cf. Angerer et al. (2006, pp. 117–118).

[9]Cf. Creswell (2014, p. 4) and Angerer et al. (2006, pp. 119).

[10]Cf. Johnson et al. (2007, pp. 112–113).

[11]Cf. Creswell (2010, pp. 45 ff.) and Tashakkori and Creswell (2007, pp. 3–4).

[12]Creswell and Plano Clark (2011, p. 5).

[13]Cf. Johnson and Onwuegbuzie (2004, p. 21).

With the support of such arguments, the application of mixed-methods research is growing in the field of social and behavioral sciences.[14] Also in the sub-discipline of business and economics, an increased usage of mixed-methods is identifiable despite a traditionally marginal importance of qualitative research in this area.[15] Yet regardless of their current popularity, one must also see that mixed-methods still represent a methodological niche. In 2011, Cameron and Molina-Azorin, who examined different content analyses (in several other publications) across the fields of management research, reported that 76% of studies built on quantitative research methods, 14% applied mixed-methods, and 10% used qualitative research approaches. Inter alia, they also referred to the results of a study of Hurmerinta-Peltomäki and Nummela, who investigated the prevalence of mixed-methods in four influential journals in the sphere of international business.[16] In 2006, the authors assessed that mixed-methods research was still underrepresented compared to singularly quantitative-empirical or qualitative-empirical studies. In total, only 17% of the reviewed publications applied mixed-methods research approaches in international business. Despite its year of publication, the study of Hurmerinta-Peltomäki and Nummela does not seem to have lost much of its contemporary relevance as current publications still tend to build predominantly on singularly quantitative-empirical methods as well as on singularly qualitative-empirical approaches.

This, however, seems to be a rather unfortunate status quo. Hurmerinta-Peltomäki and Nummela highlighted quite rightfully that international business is a research field that requires innovative methodological designs. They argued that today's international firms are confronted with constant and quick changes of business environments (e.g., changing national and legal boundaries, new business models, etc.). Therefore, the context of international business research is also subject to changes. It increasingly includes matters from peripheral research disciplines. Thus, methodological approaches in international business have to face the challenge of reflecting the changes in international business reality. Established single-method research approaches, however, are probably not always fit to meet these requirements. Instead, "holistic, multidisciplinary, and multi-method research" is necessary in order to deliver a comprehensive picture of international business.[17]

The present study attempts to deliver such a comprehensive picture for the analysis of the role of bounded rationality in the form of escalation of commitment in internationalization processes. With the potential benefits of mixed-methods in mind, it builds on a randomized experiment as a quantitative-empirical approach, and it is furthermore accompanied by an analysis of two cases as a qualitative-empirical approach. Mayring refers to this specific order of analysis as a

[14] Cf. Cameron and Molina-Azorin (2011, p. 267).

[15] Cf. Starr (2012, p. 238).

[16] Cf. Hurmerinta-Peltomäki and Nummela (2006, pp. 439 ff.); the authors included International Business Review, Journal of International Business Studies, Journal of World Business, and Management International Review in their analysis.

[17] Hurmerinta-Peltomäki and Nummela (2006, p. 452).

Fig. 4.1 Consolidated design of quantitative and qualitative studies. Source: Own figure, based on Mayring (2001, p. 8)

'consolidated design' (cf. Fig. 4.1). The quantitative-empirical study addresses the hypotheses and discloses the statistical findings. Subsequently, the results are consolidated with additional qualitative-empirical insights. The benefit of this order of analysis lies in an increased interpretation capability because identified causalities can be additionally substantiated with open-end observations.[18]

4.1.2 Randomized Experiments as a Quantitative-Empirical Research Method

Experimental studies present different research methods, which allow the purposeful manipulation of independent variables.[19] Typically, the term 'experiment' refers to a randomized research design ('randomized experiment'), which is also applied for the present study.[20] The name implies that test subjects are randomly assigned to treatment and control groups and that the researcher has no influence on the specific group allocation. This prototype, however, must be distinguished from quasi experiments and field experiments. Quasi experiments bear a lot of similarity to their randomized counterparts.[21] The fundamental difference lies in the assignment of subjects, which is not coincidental. In the course of the renowned Hawthorne Experiments, for example, the participating women were already non-randomly assigned to their work groups when the actual empirical analysis began.[22] Randomized as well as quasi experiments are conducted under laboratory circumstances. This distinguishes them from field experiments, which are conducted in the natural surroundings of research subjects, who are not aware of the experiment.[23] In business and economics, for example, this could mean that actual business processes

[18]Cf. Mayring (2001, p. 12).

[19]Cf. the seminal works of R. A. Fisher on experimental studies, above all Fisher (1966).

[20]Cf. Sect. 4.2.

[21]Cf. Campbell and Stanley (1963, p. 34).

[22]The Hawthorne experiments of Roethlisberger and Dickson (1949, pp. 1 ff.), refer to a series of experimental studies, which have been conducted in the Hawthorne production plant of the Western Electric Company. Against the background of Taylorism and scientific management, the research objective was the improvement of productivity.

[23]Cf. Kühl (2009, pp. 534 ff.).

are observed and compared. Clearly, such a 'real-life' observation of business processes implies a full immersion into operative and administrative tasks over a longer period of time (in order to generate reliable results). Practically, this presupposes that a researcher has the opportunity to 'look over the shoulders' of managers. As such a research design requires a substantial degree of cooperation on the managers' end, it is justified to be skeptical about the likelihood of such a research design being put effectively into action in business and economics (since it remains doubtful whether or not managers are actually willing to cooperate to the described extent).

This is a downside that studies applying randomized experiments do not have to cope with. Furthermore, it is their distinct possibility to control the research process, which gives them a decisive advantage over other quantitative-empirical research methods. The experimenter does not only develop a simulated scenario as an experimental setting, but he/she has furthermore the opportunity to intervene in the observation process in order to create a perfect fit between his/her research problem and the research environment. In the context of business and economics, for example, this would mean that the resource endowment, available information, decision options, as well as potential benefits for test subjects are under control. As these factors are consistently exposed to interfering influences under non-laboratory circumstances, other quantitative-empirical research methods must always account for the latter. With randomized experiments, however, interfering influences are largely absent, and therefore observed effects can always be traced to an initially conducted manipulation of independent variables. Thus, endogeneity—a common problem for non-laboratory, non-experimental quantitative-empirical research methods—does not pose a problem.[24] In consequence, it is legitimate that pertinent classics in research methodology literature praise randomized experiments for their aptitude to identify causal effects.[25]

Despite this distinct benefit of randomized experiments, certain downsides must also be taken into consideration. First and foremost, this refers to the questionable representativeness of simulated scenario settings of laboratory experiments. As with any simulation, it has to be critically checked whether the experimental setting does actually match realistic circumstances.[26] Muzafer Sherif, one of the pioneers of social psychology, criticized that some studies—in his area of competence at least—suffer from a "community-centrism" of the investigating researchers, for example.[27] He emphasized the danger of "artificiality" and lacking life-like situations in laboratory experiments.[28] This critique also relates to the question of who comes into consideration as test subjects. In social sciences, students are frequently

---

[24]Cf. Reeb et al. (2012, pp. 211 ff.) and Langer (2007, col. 420–421).

[25]Cf. Rubin (1974, pp. 688 ff.), Fisher (1966, p. 7), and Campbell and Stanley (1963, pp. 2–4).

[26]Cf. Kühl (2009, p. 551).

[27]Sherif (1936, p. 25).

[28]Sherif (1936, p. 68).

participating in experiments as decision-making representatives for various decision contexts.[29] Particularly in management studies, actual managers are commonly not available for participation. As a result, the motivational drivers of actual decision-makers remain a 'black box' for researchers.[30] The lacking availability of actual decision-makers leads to the consultation of student samples who take over the role of professionals. The obvious problem with this practice lies in the question of whether students have the sufficient skills to take over the part of professionals.[31] Staw, who consulted a student sample for his initial experiment on escalation of commitment himself,[32] recently summarized the different views on this issue in a well-balanced manner.[33] On the one hand, one could indeed argue that the consultation of a student sample leads to less external validity than the consultation of professionals, who cope with actual managerial problems on a daily basis. On the other hand, one must also see that JDM research is mostly targeting processes of the human mind, which are "more hard-wired than socialized".[34] Potential cognitive dispositions in this regard cannot be effectively counteracted with professional skills. Therefore, "nearly any subject will do".[35] Escalation of commitment, for example, remains an issue for professional decision-makers even if selfsame are aware of their disposition. Experienced managers are not immune to this behavioral bias. Thus, the consultation of a student sample would be suitable because the respective participants are as prone to the bias as professionals. Between the different views on this issue, the truth should be located somewhere in the middle. Ultimately, the research setting must be cautiously selected against the background of the research field and objective.[36]

An additional downside of randomized experiments concerns the risk of a manipulative influence—conscious or not—of the experimenter. As with most primary data collections, the researcher has the possibility to influence the sample, i.e., to impinge on test subjects in a hypotheses-supporting manner. Furthermore, test subjects can act differently under simulated laboratory circumstances compared to their actions in reality. This issue emerges particularly if the test subjects do not take the experimental research setting seriously because of a lack of consequences of their actions. As a result, experiments always run a risk of documenting non-representative, distorted behavior. In order to compensate for these downsides, the experimenter has to disclose the data collection process as transparently as possible. Furthermore, an incentive-based reward scheme needs to be established in order to integrate effective consequences for test subjects. For experimental

[29]Cf. Peterson (2001, pp. 450 ff.).

[30]Cf. Lawrence (1997, pp. 1 ff.).

[31]Cf. Falk and Heckman (2009, p. 537).

[32]Cf. Sect. 3.3.2 of the present study.

[33]Cf. Staw (2010, p. 411).

[34]Staw (2010, p. 411).

[35]Staw (2010, p. 411).

[36]Cf. Thomas (2011, p. 288) and Staw (2010, p. 411).

research in business and economics, for example, remuneration should be connected to any monetary decision that test subjects take during a simulation.[37] While it is ultimately not possible to dissolve a 'play-like' character of experiments entirely, an incentive-based reward scheme diminishes this particular negative consequence of the research method.[38]

Considering the advantages as well as disadvantages of randomized experiments as a quantitative-empirical research method, one could summarize that they are marked by a high internal and a low external validity. The internal validity of an empirical research method describes the quality of its causation.[39] It allows a statement whether the hypothesized and identified relation between independent and dependent variables is actually valid.[40] Thus, for research methods with high internal validity, one could say with relative certainty that any observed effect on the dependent variable is also caused by a variation of the independent variable. As mentioned above, under laboratory circumstances no interfering factors need to be taken into account. Therefore, a causal interpretation of identified effects is feasible with laboratory experiments.[41] In contrast, external validity describes the generalizability as well as representativeness of an empirical research method. It allows a statement whether the setting of a research method matches realistic circumstances. Ideally, empirical research methods are based on a large randomized sample, which draws a representative picture of reality. Methods with low external validity, such as laboratory experiments, imply a simplified research setting, which does not fully reflect the actual complexities of reality.[42] Interestingly, Dobbins and colleagues, who examined some of the early criticism on the questionable external validity of laboratory experiments, concluded that this is less of a problem than it seems to be. According to their opinion, experiments provide the clear benefit of rigorously testing theories and of increasing researchers' understanding of decision-making behavior. Such understanding can gain external validity as it is applied subsequently in field research.[43]

As an applied research methodology in international business, randomized experiments have only played a minor role in the past. This statement is supported by Zellmer-Bruhn and colleagues, who argued in the pages of the Journal of International Business Studies that "experiments are largely absent from international business literature."[44] Furthermore, Yang and colleagues, who investigated "what is common practice in international business research methodology",[45]

---

[37] Cf. Camerer and Hogarth (1999, p. 8).
[38] Cf. Langer (2007, col. 425).
[39] Cf. Schram (2005, p. 226).
[40] Cf. Bortz and Döring (2006, p. 53).
[41] Cf. Bortz and Döring (2006, p. 57).
[42] Cf. Kühl (2009, p. 552).
[43] Cf. Dobbins et al. (1988, p. 285).
[44] Zellmer-Bruhn et al. (2016, p. 399).
[45] Yang et al. (2006, p. 601).

Table 4.1 Data collection methods for empirical studies, 1992–2003

Type of study	Pct. IBJ	JIBS	IMR	IBR	JIM	JWB	MIR	Number of articles
Survey	60.3	51.8	67.7	60.2	65.5	58.9	65.7	782
Mail survey	37.6	34.2	38.2	35.1	47.9	27.7	44.4	487
Administered questionnaire	11.9	11.6	21.4	9.7	6.7	8.9	10.7	154
Personal interview	9.9	5.4	6.4	14.3	10.9	20.5	9.5	128
Telephone interview	1.0	0.5	1.8	1.2	0.0	1.8	1.2	13
Secondary data (e.g. database, case study)	32.7	42.6	17.7	34.0	24.8	38.4	32.5	424
Other (e.g. content analysis, focus group, intercept, panel)	4.9	4.0	11.8	4.6	3.6	0.9	1.8	63
Experiment	2.1	1.6	2.7	1.2	6.1	1.8	0.0	27
Total	100.0	100.0	100.0	100.0	100.0	100.0	100.0	100.0
Number of articles	1296	371	220	259	165	112	169	1296

Source: Yang et al. (2006, p. 607)
Percentages based on empirical articles only
IBJ International Business Journals including JIBS, IMR, IBR, JIM, JWB, and MIR, *JIBS* Journal of International Business Studies, *IMR* International Marketing Review, *IBR* International Business Review, *JIM* Journal of International Marketing, *JWB* Journal of World Business, *MIR* Management International Review

revealed that the prevalence of experimental studies was remarkably low in the major journals (cf. Table 4.1). For the time frame of 1992–2003, only 0–6.1% of the published empirical articles were based on experimental research approaches (in dependence of the journal under examination).[46] The low share of experimental studies is surprising, if one considers that international business research is often confronted with endogeneity problems as a result of a disproportionate reliance on observational data and non-experimental quantitative-empirical research methods.[47]

While the results of Yang and colleagues seem to be somewhat outdated from today's stance, they highlight the novelty of randomized experiments as a research method in IB. So far, IB scholars advocate corresponding research approaches only occasionally. Buckley and colleagues, for example, argued that experiments can present a helpful method in order to understand complex decision-making processes in international business.[48] In light of this statement, and considering that escalation of commitment emerges in complex decision-making processes, randomized

[46]Cf. Yang et al. (2006, p. 605).

[47]Cf. Reeb et al. (2012, pp. 211 ff.).

[48]Cf. Buckley et al. (2007, p. 1066), who made their statement in the context of decision-making processes for FDI.

experiments seem to be a suitable quantitative-empirical research method for the present study. This thinking is additionally substantiated by Hutzschenreuter and colleagues, who acknowledged that studies that applied structured experimentation are fit to investigate the "human factor" in international business.[49] Principally, the human factor takes any deviation from rational choice behavior—and therefore also escalation of commitment—into account. However, one might object that a randomized experiment only investigates the escalation bias at the individual level and, as a result, that it is not an ideal method to shed light on to the matter of escalation of commitment in large multinational firms. Then again, this criticism can be rebutted with three arguments. First, even within the Uppsala School of Thought the importance of the individual for the internationalization process of firms is highlighted because it is people who acquire market knowledge and take commitment decisions.[50] Second, based on methodological individualism one could argue that organizations consist of individuals and that individual behavior constitutes the smallest unit of organizational decision-making. Ultimately, the three-stage model of the escalation process of Staw and Ross could be consulted because it relates individual decision-making (in Stage 1) with institutionalized decisions at the organizational level (in Stage 3).[51] Considering these arguments, one could very well conclude that randomized experiments are not only an appropriate method for the identification of escalation of commitment at the individual level but that they can turn out equally helpful in a bigger organizational context, such as the internationalization process of a firm.

4.1.3 Case Studies as a Qualitative-Empirical Research Method

As mentioned before, the present study is not limited to the application of a quantitative-empirical research method. Within the consolidated mixed-methods setup, a qualitative-empirical approach is additionally implemented in order to add more profundity to the empirical investigation of the research problem. For this purpose, two cases will be presented as illustrations of the matter of escalation of commitment in internationalization process decision-making in business reality.[52] In a general context, case study research is conducted for a better understanding of the underlying behavior and motivations of individuals and organizations across social sciences disciplines.[53] The better understanding is a result of the consideration of context observations, which are not necessarily included in studies based

[49]Hutzschenreuter et al. (2007, p. 1064).

[50]Cf. Petersen et al. (2003, p. 40) and Forsgren (2002, p. 269).

[51]Cf. Sect. 3.3.5 for more information on the three-stage model of the escalation process.

[52]Cf. Sect. 4.3.

[53]Cf. Leonard-Barton (1990, p. 249).

exclusively on quantitative-empirical methods.[54] Especially when it comes to subconscious cognitive processes, case-study research can prove to be a valuable source for insights. This is also related to the open-end character of qualitative-empirical research methods, which has the potential to contribute to insights that were not considered in the research process until then.[55]

Case studies offer a broad range of research designs and present a rather complex, heterogeneous field. In this regard, John Gerring considers the term as a "definitional morass".[56] For business and economics at least, the contributions of Robert K. Yin, who established a twofold definition, are quite predominant. First, a case study offers a specific scope. It "investigates a contemporary phenomenon in depth and within real-world context, especially when the boundaries between phenomenon and context may not be clearly evident".[57] Second, a case study is marked by certain features. This refers above all to the count of variables, which is not limited a priori. It is not limited because a case study considers the previously mentioned context factors, which may go beyond predefined variables and which unfold during the investigation process. In consideration of this openness, a thorough case study analysis builds on multiple sources of evidence.[58] Furthermore, it "benefits from the prior development of theoretical propositions".[59]

Notwithstanding this basis, case studies differ with regard to their objective as well as to their design.[60] They can, for example, aim at a description, an exploration, or an explanation of research problems. The purpose of a descriptive case study lies in an accurate portrayal of an investigated phenomenon in a realistic context. Exploratory case studies aim at a development as well as at an identification of current and additional research problems respectively. Lastly, the purpose of explanatory cases lies in a clarification of the 'hows' and 'whys' of a research problem.[61] In addition, the design of the case study presents a distinctive criterion. Although case study research is commonly considered to be an informal empirical method (compared to quantitative-empirical approaches), one can fundamentally differ between a single-case and a multiple-case design. Commonly, the former presents a detailed 'within analysis' of a critical case. The latter, in contrast, reviews two or more cases and allows for a cross case synthesis. This design gives the researcher the opportunity to search for general patterns across cases once they have been analyzed individually.[62]

[54]Cf. Blanco Ramírez (2016, p. 19).

[55]Cf. Woodside (2010, p. 2).

[56]Gerring (2007, p. 17).

[57]Yin (2014, p. 16).

[58]Cf. the comments on triangulation in Sect. 4.3.1 of the present study.

[59]Yin (2014, p. 17).

[60]Cf. Yin (2012, p. 7).

[61]Cf. Yin (2014, p. 238) and Woodside (2010, pp. 11 ff.).

[62]Cf. Miles et al. (2014, pp. 33–34), Yin (2014, pp. 50 ff.), and Eisenhardt (1989, p. 540).

While case study research offers some methodological benefits, certain downsides must also be taken into account.[63] First and foremost, this refers to the questionable rigorousness of case study research. As corresponding research designs require only a low degree of formality, research results should be handled with critical caution and healthy skepticism as they may present a low degree of validity. Furthermore, case study research has to deal with a limited statistical generalizability—especially if only a single case has been consulted.[64] For certain research questions these aspects can present a significant drawback. Therefore, it is fair to say that case study research offers pros and cons (much like any other research method). The drawbacks are particularly apparent if case studies are the only applied empirical research method. At the same time, however, cases have the potential to deliver particularly profound results, if they are consulted as a complementary research method besides a quantitative approach.[65] Often, empirical research finds itself in a struggle between rigor, i.e., the methodological soundness, and relevance, i.e., the applicability in reality.[66] Mixed-methods, however, have the potential to combine the benefits of rigor as well as of relevance, if a case study perspective is implemented.

Against the background of this beneficial complementarity, the present study implements a descriptive, multiple-case study. The underlying objective behind the integration of such a qualitative-empirical method is a description of the phenomenon of escalation of commitment in a realistic context. More precisely, the aim is to illustrate the effect of this behavioral bias in international business practice and, thereby, to increase the analytical profundity of the study. With such an illustration, further empirical evidence can be added besides the quantitative-empirical analysis. In fact, case study research is often applied in order to investigate judgment and decision-making processes in business reality.[67] After all, even Johanson and Vahlne consulted the cases of four Swedish firms as a qualitative-empirical basis for their U-Model.

4.2 Randomized Experiment for the Analysis of Escalation of Commitment in Internationalization Process Decision-Making

The present section attends to the quantitative-empirical analysis of the question of whether or not there is substantial evidence for the display of bounded rationality in the form of escalation of commitment in internationalization process decision-

[63]Cf. Yin (2012, p. 5).

[64]Cf. Yin (2014, pp. 19–20).

[65]Cf. Flyvbjerg (2011, p. 314).

[66]Cf. Gulati (2007, pp. 775 ff.).

[67]Cf. Eisenhardt and Zbaracki (1992, pp.17 ff.).

making. For this purpose—and as previously highlighted—a randomized experiment has been conducted in order to test the study's underlying hypotheses.[68] The structure of the present section is somewhat typical for experimental studies.[69] First, the setup of the experiment, i.e., the preparations as well as the details of the procedure, is introduced (Sect. 4.2.1). Subsequently, the benefit and the insights of a preliminary pretest are disclosed (Sect. 4.2.2). Finally, the statistical results of the randomized experiment will be outlined (Sect. 4.2.3) and discussed (Sect. 4.2.4).

4.2.1 Setup of the Randomized Experiment

As the cornerstone of the experiment, a simulated internationalization process scenario has been developed and manipulated in order to investigate the occurrence of an escalation bias of test subjects. Against the background of the previously indicated necessity of full transparency and disclosure in the context of primary data consultations,[70] it is essential to provide the reader with sufficient information on the conduct of the experiment before the results are outlined. This refers to four areas: the utilized variables as well as the respective operationalizations (Sect. 4.2.1.1); the test subjects, randomization, and data collection of the experiment (Sect. 4.2.1.2); the procedure itself (Sect. 4.2.1.3); and the applied statistical methods (Sect. 4.2.1.4).

4.2.1.1 Variables and Operationalization

One of the challenges of experimental studies lies in the translation of verbalized hypotheses into statistically measurable counterparts. Such an operationalization requires a quantifiable measure, which enables the experimenter to document the effects that surface during the process of data collection, i.e., during the phase of structured experimentation.[71] Against this background, it is appropriate to recall briefly the hypotheses for the present study. Hypotheses 1a and 1b cover the general impact of escalation of commitment on internationalization process decision-making.[72] The former postulates (at the group level) that managerial decision-makers in internationalization processes, who are under escalation of commitment, will continue to raise internationalization investments regardless of the resultant economic success of the venture. The latter specifies that a single internationalization manager will continue to raise his/her internationalization investment regardless of the

[68]Cf. Sect. 3.3.7 for the development of hypotheses.
[69]Cf. Manning et al. (1987, pp. 251 ff.), as an example.
[70]Cf. Sect. 4.1.2 for the indication.
[71]Cf. Kühl (2009, p. 538).
[72]Cf. Sect. 3.3.7.1 on the development of hypotheses.

resultant economic success of the venture but in dependence of the decision-maker's degree of commitment. In addition, Hypotheses 2 and 3 cover a moderating effect of psychic distance as well as of the establishment chain progress on the impact of escalation of commitment on internationalization process decision-making. More specifically, Hypothesis 2 postulates that the choices of a group of committed test subjects will increasingly diverge from the decisions of a group of non-committed test persons with increasing psychic distance to the target market. According to Hypothesis 3, a group of committed test subjects will increasingly converge towards the decisions of a group of non-committed test persons with an increasing establishment chain progress.

Dependent Variable

The 'internationalization investment' of test subjects serves as the dependent variable. Continued internationalization investments translate into a continued internationalization process. For a better comparability between subjects, it is measured as the ratio of invested resources (in the current decision-making period) to available resources instead of absolute numbers. A withdrawal from the internationalization process equates to an internationalization investment of zero.

Independent Variables

Considering the postulates of the hypotheses, two independent variables must be accounted for. Both relate to the commitment of test subjects. Fundamentally, one must consider whether or not a subject is already committed to a course of action. Therefore, a dummy variable 'commitment', with the categories of 'committed' and 'non-committed', is used. Subjects are considered to be committed if they carried out a resource allocation in the beginning of the internationalization process, i.e., respective subjects are responsible for their actions. In addition, the specific 'degree of commitment' of a single test person must also be included under particular attention of Hypothesis 1b. The degree is measured as the ratio of the accumulated internationalization investment of a decision-maker (of the previous decision-making periods) to his/her initially available resources. One might object that the dependent variable 'internationalization investment' is not fully independent from the 'degree of commitment' of a decision-maker since both variables are built on a decision-maker's investment. Yet, this objection is only seemingly: The 'internationalization investment' is only concerned by the current decision-making period, whereas the 'degree of commitment' is concerned by the previous decision-making periods up to the present. Therefore, the two variables are indeed independent despite the circumstance of their resemblance.

Moderating Variables

For the investigation of a moderating effect of 'psychic distance', cultural distance is introduced as a less abstract proxy measure. Cultural distance is expressed in values between zero (full cultural congruence) to 100 (full cultural incongruence). Higher values of cultural distance imply an increased risk of failure for internationalizing companies because of an associated higher level of uncertainty.[73] With regard to a moderating effect of the 'establishment chain progress', the number of employees assigned to a foreign market serves as a proxy measure. Fewer workforces abroad, for example, go along with export-based establishment chain stages and imply low withdrawal costs for internationalizing firms.

These operationalizations present significant yet permissible simplifications of more complex realities. For example, the understanding of commitment in the U-Model goes beyond the relatively simple ratio of accumulated internationalization investments to initially available resources. The same applies to the operationalization of psychic distance and establishment chain progress. According to the U-Model, psychic distance is not only related to cultural factors. It is additionally put together from differences in language, education, business practices, and industrial development. With regard to the establishment chain progress, it is needless to say that different market entry forms bear further complexities than the involved number of employees in a foreign market. In consideration of these simplifications, one must keep in mind that the degree of commitment, psychic distance, and the establishment chain progress are strictly treated with simplified or proxy measures.

4.2.1.2 Test Subjects, Data Collection, and Randomization

Subjects of the experiment were altogether 100 female and male postgraduate students at the University of Stuttgart, Germany. The participants were required to pursue (or to have completed) coursework in the fields of business and economics. As discussed in Sect. 4.1.2, the consultation of students as representatives of executives is relatively common in social sciences laboratory experiments. Concerns whether students have the sufficient skills to take over the part of managers can be rebutted with a reference to Staw, according to whom they could come very well into question for studies that investigate problems that are "more hard-wired than socialized".[74] With regard to escalation of commitment, this argumentation makes sense: There are no signs that a specific skillset lowers the odds of being affected by an escalation bias in JDM processes. Professional decision-makers, experienced managers for example, are not immune to this cognitive disposition despite their experience.[75] Therefore, relatively inexperienced students may also be consulted as subjects. Furthermore, one should recall that even Staw's initial (experimental) study on escalation of commitment was based on a consultation of students.[76]

[73]Cf. Sect. 3.3.7.2.

[74]Staw (2010, p. 411).

[75]See also Sect. 4.1.2 in this regard.

[76]Cf. Staw (1976, p. 38).

The data collection period lasted from July to November 2014 and was conducted in four separate appointments. It was supported by the insights of a preliminary pretest, which has been conducted with a smaller sample in order to check for the overall operability of the experiment.[77] Test subjects were assigned randomly and evenly to a treatment or control group. The experimenter had no influence on the randomization, i.e., the group assignment was entirely coincidental. Major differences between the samples with regard to the participants' age and educational background were ruled out because there was already a high degree of similarity across all participants in the first place (after all, test subjects were exclusively university students). Furthermore, subjects were only permitted to participate in a single appointment as a preventative measure against distorted experimentation effects.

4.2.1.3 Procedure

With only one exception, the treatment and the control group were confronted with similar decision contexts in the simulated internationalization process scenario. The essential difference lay in the fact that the treatment group was exposed to a certain level of commitment as well as to the involved forces for persistence.[78] This approach is commonly known as a 'between-subjects-design'. Unlike a 'within-subjects-design', it presents two groups with slightly different context information in an attempt to identify causal effects.[79] This identification is possible as any deviating effect between the groups must be triggered by the different context of the experimental scenario.[80] In the case of the present experiment, any deviating effect must be traced to the difference of commitment exposure between subjects.

The procedure of the experiment can roughly be divided in a basic scenario, which presented a simulation of the underlying internationalization process in a general context, as well as in an interlude of the scenario, in which some context information regarding the involved psychic distance and establishment chain progress was modified. Obviously, it was necessary to conceal any information on the research problem and motivation from the test subjects. For the experiment, subjects received a paper-based copy of the simulated internationalization process scenario.

Basic Scenario

In accordance with the three-stage model of the escalation process of Staw and Ross, the basic scenario of the simulated internationalization process consisted of three consecutive decision-making rounds. Every round signified the end of a 3 year

---

[77]The insights of the pretest are presented in Sect. 4.2.2.2.

[78]Cf. Sect. 3.3.4 for a specification of the forces for persistence.

[79]A 'within-subject-design', which has not been applied for the present study, presents all subjects with all context variations.

[80]Cf. Homburg (2012, p. 274).

period in which the circumstances of the scenario had changed. Prior to the first decision-making round, subjects were familiarized with the background of the scenario. The participants were told that they were employed by the fictional Swabian firm 'SAG', which showed typical characteristics for firms that are addressed by the U-Model: It was a medium-sized to large (i.e., 8000 employees, 1.5 billion euros of turnover) supplier of industrial goods. In addition, test subjects were informed that the firm was founded in 1980 and that it went through a phase of rapid growth initially. In the recent past, however, the company was confronted with a stagnating development. In response to this stagnation, the firm decided to pursue an international expansion strategy and to enter a new international market.

1. Round 1

The aim of the first round was to develop an initial level of commitment among the participants of the treatment group. Therefore, the (non-committed) control group was excluded in this stage of the experiment. Subjects of the treatment group, however, found themselves in the role of an internationalization manager, who had to take a decision concerning a new market choice as part of SAG's internationalization process. They had an internationalization budget of 50 million euros at their disposition and were requested to maximize the returns on their investment. Fifty million euros in the simulated scenario were equivalent to 5 € in reality. This amount was previously paid out and served as remuneration to the participants. Subjects were told that relative profits and losses in the simulation were directly applicable to their remuneration (as explained in Sect. 4.1.2, an incentive-based remuneration system reduces the 'play-like' character of experiments). Hereupon, subjects were presented with two target markets, A and B. There were no significant differences between these markets. Both countries were shaped by similar degrees of economic development, a stable market economy, comparable population sizes, and an equal cultural distance to SAG's domestic market Germany. For the purpose of the experiment, it was irrelevant which country the subjects selected. More important at this stage was the initial development of commitment to a specific course of action. For this purpose, it was essential that the participants made explicitly 'their' internationalization decision because this brought up a sense of responsibility and, thus, increased their commitment. Furthermore, subjects were informed that SAG expected to 'break-even' within 3 years in either market, i.e., until the next decision round. Optimistic estimations, however, also saw the possibility of a 25% return on investment (ROI) after 3 years. Thus, project economics were promising for market A as well as for market B (as foreseen by the first stage of the three-stage model of the escalation process).

At the end of the first round, subjects of the treatment group were asked to take an internationalization decision and to invest an amount between 10 and 40 million euros, i.e., between 1 and 4 € effectively, in either country. Ten million euros was the required minimal investment in order to secure a minimal degree of commitment among test subjects. In addition, no more than 40 million euros were distributable because 10 million euros served as a reserve for later decision-making rounds.

2. Round 2

In the second round, subjects of the treatment group were confronted with a negative feedback and a critical review of the first decision-making period. Regardless of the chosen target market, all participants in the experiment were informed that 'their' internationalization choice fell short of expectations. Neither a 25% ROI nor the 'break-even point' were reached. All resource allocations from the previous round were retained by the experimenter.[81] Furthermore, subjects were told that a solid forecast for the future development of SAG in the new market was hardly possible. Thus, the previously promising project economics turned into a questionable or even negative factor. At the same time, however, test subjects were confronted with a dilemma because psychological and social forces for persistence were introduced into the simulation. As a psychological impulse, they were reminded of their confident market analysis in the first round as well as of their responsibility to reach the objective of the international expansion. As a social impulse, subjects received the information that the project team for the internationalization was of the opinion that the current process was not wrong. Any change to the decision path would have been interpreted as fickle action by their side. Furthermore, it was stated that the management board was willing to support the test subject if he/she wanted to persist with the chosen course of action in the next decision stage despite the fact that the initial target was missed after 3 years.

The second round was also the first round of participation for the control group. Respective subjects received the information that they substituted an internationalization manager, who took an internationalization decision 3 years ago. This design of the simulation was inspired by the initial study of Staw on escalation of commitment. In his original version, a subject of a control group was told that he/she substituted a colleague in a R&D project.[82] In the present experiment, subjects of the control group knew that their predecessor had reason to believe that a 25% ROI or at least a break-even was feasible. Likewise, however, subjects knew that the initial targets were missed. Thus, they were well informed about the once promising and now questionable or negative project economics. There was no introduction of psychological and social impulses for persistence to the control group because the newly appointed subjects had no previous decision to justify (against themselves or others).

Finally, the treatment and the control group were separately asked to take a decision for or against continued investments in the internationalization process. The budget of the subjects of the treatment group was defined by the initial 50 million euros, minus the respective investments in the previous Round 1. Subjects of the

[81] As a positive feedback, i.e., a financial profit, was neither wanted nor foreseen in the course of the experiment, no participant had an honest chance to generate a profit. Instead, all test subjects received ultimately 5 € of remuneration for their time and effort regardless of the undertaken internationalization decision. Of course, this information was only disclosed at the end of the experiment.

[82] Cf. Staw (1976, pp. 27 ff.) and Sect. 3.3.2 of the present study.

control group received a 'cloned' budget. This means that there was a doppelganger of every participant of the treatment group, who received the same amount of resources. In contrast to Round 1, all subjects—regardless of the group allocation—had the opportunity to withdraw from the internationalization process at the cost of 2.5 million euros (0.25 € effectively). In doing so, they had the opportunity to safeguard the remainder of their initial budget and to keep it as remuneration. In case of continued investments, however, the minimal reinvestment-amount had to be 5 million euros, while another 5 million euros had to serve as a reserve for an additional third decision round (0.50 € effectively).

3. Round 3

After another three fictional years, test subjects of the treatment group (that is to say, the ones who decided to continue the internationalization process) were informed that SAG was still in dire straits in the new international market and that the future outlook remained insecure. Furthermore, it was indicated that there was now an increased pressure to justify the market entry decision in front of the SAG management board. Given the time that had passed since the initial internationalization decision (6 years after all), project economics needed to be evaluated as negative and not just as questionable any longer. Notwithstanding, the psychological and social factors for persistence of the previous decision round were left largely unmodified: On the one hand, subjects were—once again—reminded that their initial market analysis was seemingly flawless in order to increase their decision confidence as well as their self-justification ability. On the other hand, they were told that a strategic turn-around at this point could lead to the criticism that they reacted too late. Another wrong decision would have entailed a compromising effect on subjects' careers. In addition to the largely unmodified psychological and social forces for persistence, a new structural dimension was introduced in the experimental simulation (as foreseen by the third stage of the three-stage model of the escalation process). For this, subjects were informed that the project team, which was already relatively convinced of the internationalization decision in the previous round, was now certain that the new market presence constituted a 'core element' of SAG's strategy. To some extent, this highlighted that the internationalization process was institutionalized at this point.

The remaining participants of the control group received the identical project information as the treatment group. Therefore, the unsatisfactory situation of SAG in the new market was clear to every participant in the experiment regardless of the group allocation. As in the previous round, the control group was not confronted with psychological and social forces for persistence because the corresponding participants were ultimately not responsible for the enacted internationalization decision. They were, however, informed that the fictional project team was in favor of an additional allocation of resources to the new market. This means that the control group was confronted with the structural dimension of escalation of commitment. Such a procedure was justified because an institutionalized internationalization process should have affected newly appointed managers as much as the ones who were initially responsible for the internationalization decision.

	Scenario context	Decision alternatives (investments in €)	
		Treatment group (n = 50)	Control group (n = 50)
Round 1	• Internationalization decision; development of commitment • Presentation of promising internationalization project economics	Invest x_1 $\{1.0 \leq x_1 \leq 4.0\}$	
Round 2	• Questionable or negative internationalization project economics • Partial introduction of psychological and social forces for persistence	Invest y_1 or withdraw $\{0.5 \leq y_1 \leq 5.0 - x_1 - 0.5\}$	Invest y_2 or withdraw $\{0.5 \leq y_2 \leq 5.0 - x_1 - 0.5\}$
Round 3	• Negative internationalization project economics • Unmodified psychological and social forces for persistence • Introduction of structural forces for persistence	Invest z_1 or withdraw $\{0,5 \leq z_1 \leq 5,0 - x_1 - y_1\}$	Invest z_2 or withdraw $\{0,5 \leq z_2 \leq 5,0 - x_1 - y_2\}$

Fig. 4.2 Basic scenario of the randomized experiment. Source: Own figure

At the end of the third round, the remaining participants of the treatment and of the control group were once again separately asked whether or not they wanted to continue the internationalization process. At this point, test subjects were free to invest their remaining budgets without a maximal limit (since no fourth decision round was conducted). As in the previous round, however, the minimal reinvestment had to be 5 million euros (0.50 € effectively). A withdrawal from the internationalization process was also possible at the (unchanged) cost of 2.5 million euros (0.25 € effectively). Figure 4.2 presents an informative overview of the three rounds of the basic scenario of the randomized experiment.

Interlude of the Basic Scenario

As mentioned in the beginning of this section, the procedure of the experiment did not only involve the basic scenario of a simulated internationalization process but it also included an interlude, in which some context information regarding the involved psychic distance and establishment chain progress were modified. The purpose of this interlude was to observe how an increase or a decrease in psychic distance and establishment chain progress interacts with the impact of escalation of commitment on internationalization process decision-making.[83] For this purpose,

[83]Cf. Sects. 3.3.7.2 and 3.3.7.3 for the causal argumentation of a potentially moderated effect due to psychic distance and establishment chain progress.

the treatment and the control group were interrupted with two additional rounds between the second and the third round of the basic scenario. In Round 2.1 the psychic distance information was modified, and in Round 2.2 the establishment chain context was altered. In order to simultaneously test for an increase as well as for a decrease, the treatment and the control group were split up and divided into two subclasses (i.e., four subgroups in total). Thus, 25 subjects constituted one subgroup. From a methodological stance, this is a relevant piece of information because standard literature on the execution of experimental studies requires an assignment of at least 20 subjects for every group in order to deliver a robust analysis.[84]

1. Round 2.1

After the test subjects took their decision for or against continued internationalization investments in the second decision round, they were required to indicate how they would have decided if the scenario was altered in the then described manner. Half of the participants of the treatment, as well as half of the control group, were told that the cultural distance to the target market was lower than previously believed. As explained in Sect. 4.2.1.1, cultural distance serves as a proxy variable for psychic distance and is expressed in values between zero (full cultural congruence) and 100 (full cultural incongruence). In the basic scenario, the cultural distance was defined to be 50. In the interlude for the first half of participants, it was initially reduced to 25 and then lowered even further to a value of five. In addition, the participants received the information that low cultural distance implies less uncertainty and therefore less risk with regard to the outcome of the internationalization process. After the modification of the psychic distance information, the participants were asked how they would have reacted in the light of this altered decision context, and they were given the opportunity to reconsider their previous choice in Round 2 on an optional basis.[85] Obviously, the aim of this alteration was the presentation of a stimulus for increased internationalization investments (in comparison to the second decision-making round).

In contrast, the two other halves of the treatment and control group were told that the cultural distance to the target market was higher than initially believed. In their interlude, it was first increased to a value of 75 and then raised even further to 95. Accordingly, they were informed that high psychic distance implies more uncertainty and more risk with regard to the outcome of the internationalization process. Hereupon, concerned test subjects were also given the chance to reconsider their decision of the second round. This time, the intention behind the procedure was to provide a stimulus for reduced internationalization investments and more internationalization exits.

[84]Cf. Hair et al. (2010, p. 453).

[85]The decisions during the interlude, however, had no effect on the proceedings of the basic scenario (i.e., the third round still connected to the original second round).

2. Round 2.2

The second round of the interlude was structurally similar to the previous Round 2.1. This time, however, half of the treatment and half of the control group were confronted with the information that SAG required fewer employees in the target market than initially assumed. The assigned workforce to a foreign market serves as a proxy variable for the establishment chain progress. This is based on the reasoning that the number of employees abroad is related to the degree of international involvement. For example, a market entry via exports requires commonly fewer employees than a market entry via FDI. With fewer employees, less capital is bounded in the foreign market and withdrawal costs are lower.[86] In the basic scenario, SAG required 100 employees in the foreign market. This corresponded to withdrawal costs of 2.5 million euros (or 0.25 € effectively). In the interlude for the first half of the participants, the number of employees was first lowered to 60 and then to 20. This corresponded to withdrawal costs of 1.5 and 0.5 million euros (0.15 € and 0.05 € effectively). Exactly as in Round 2.1, the participants had once more the opportunity to reconsider their previous choice in the second round of the basic scenario on an optional basis. The reduction of the assigned employees presented a good opportunity to withdraw from the new market at relatively low costs. Thus, it served as a stimulus for reduced internationalization investments and more internationalization exits.

At the same time, the second halves of the treatment and control group were confronted with a raised number of employees in the foreign market (first 140, then 180). As a consequence, the withdrawal costs were raised to 3.5 million and 4.5 million euros (0.35 € and 0.45 € effectively). This alteration presented a stimulus to persist with the chosen course of action because the withdrawal costs were now almost as high as the minimal re-investment of 5 million euros (or 0.50 € effectively) for a continued internationalization process. Figure 4.3 presents an informative overview of the interlude of the basic scenario of the randomized experiment.

4.2.1.4 Statistical Methods

Standard textbook literature on the application of statistical methods for social sciences studies considers the analysis of variance (ANOVA) to be the most useful instrument for the evaluation of experiments.[87] An ANOVA is applied in order to investigate the effect of one or more independent variables, also known as factors, on one or more dependent variables.[88] With regard to the dependent variable, it allows for the identification and analysis of significant differences among the means of different groups.[89] Thus, an ANOVA presents an ideal instrument for the

[86]Cf. Sect. 3.3.7.3 for the line of argumentation in this regard.

[87]Cf. Huber et al. (2014, pp. 43 ff.) and Backhaus et al. (2011, pp. 157 ff.).

[88]Cf. Backhaus et al. (2011, p. 158).

[89]Cf. Huber et al. (2014, p. 43).

	Scenario context	Decision alternatives (investments in €)			
		Treatment group (n = 50)		Control group (n = 50)	
Round 2	• Questionable or negative internationalization project economics • Partial introduction of psychological and social forces for persistence	Invest y_1 or withdraw $\{0.5 \leq y_1 \leq 5.0 - x_1 - 0.5\}$		Invest y_2 or withdraw $\{0.5 \leq y_2 \leq 5.0 - x_1 - 0.5\}$	
Round 2.1	• Modified information: • Lower *or* higher cultural distance to the international target market	Reconsideration possibility			
		Invest $y_{1.1}$ or withdraw $\{0.5 \leq y_{1.1} \leq 5.0 - x_1 - 0.5\}$	Invest $y_{1.2}$ or withdraw $\{0.5 \leq y_{1.2} \leq 5.0 - x_1 - 0.5\}$	Invest $y_{2.1}$ or withdraw $\{0.5 \leq y_{2.1} \leq 5.0 - x_1 - 0.5\}$	Invest $y_{2.2}$ or withdraw $\{0.5 \leq y_{2.2} \leq 5.0 - x_1 - 0.5\}$
	• Modified information: • Much lower *or* much higher cultural distance to the international target market	Reconsideration possibility			
		Invest $y_{1.1}$ or withdraw $\{0.5 \leq y_{1.1} \leq 5.0 - x_1 - 0.5\}$	Invest $y_{1.2}$ or withdraw $\{0.5 \leq y_{1.2} \leq 5.0 - x_1 - 0.5\}$	Invest $y_{2.1}$ or withdraw $\{0.5 \leq y_{2.1} \leq 5.0 - x_1 - 0.5\}$	Invest $y_{2.2}$ or withdraw $\{0.5 \leq y_{2.2} \leq 5.0 - x_1 - 0.5\}$
Round 2.2	• Modified information: • Fewer *or* more employees assigned to the international venture	Reconsideration possibility			
		Invest $y_{1.1}$ or withdraw $\{0.5 \leq y_{1.1} \leq 5.0 - x_1 - 0.5\}$	Invest $y_{1.2}$ or withdraw $\{0.5 \leq y_{1.2} \leq 5.0 - x_1 - 0.5\}$	Invest $y_{2.1}$ or withdraw $\{0.5 \leq y_{2.1} \leq 5.0 - x_1 - 0.5\}$	Invest $y_{2.2}$ or withdraw $\{0.5 \leq y_{2.2} \leq 5.0 - x_1 - 0.5\}$
	• Modified information: • Many fewer *or* many more employees assigned to the international venture	Reconsideration possibility			
		Invest $y_{1.1}$ or withdraw $\{0.5 \leq y_{1.1} \leq 5.0 - x_1 - 0.5\}$	Invest $y_{1.2}$ or withdraw $\{0.5 \leq y_{1.2} \leq 5.0 - x_1 - 0.5\}$	Invest $y_{2.1}$ or withdraw $\{0.5 \leq y_{2.1} \leq 5.0 - x_1 - 0.5\}$	Invest $y_{2.2}$ or withdraw $\{0.5 \leq y_{2.2} \leq 5.0 - x_1 - 0.5\}$
Round 3	• Negative internationalization project economics • Unmodified psychological and social forces for persistence • Introduction of structural forces for persistence	Invest z_1 or withdraw $\{0,5 \leq z_1 \leq 5,0 - x_1 - y_1\}$		Invest z_2 or withdraw $\{0,5 \leq z_2 \leq 5,0 - x_1 - y_2\}$	

Fig. 4.3 Interlude of the basic scenario of the randomized experiment. Source: Own figure

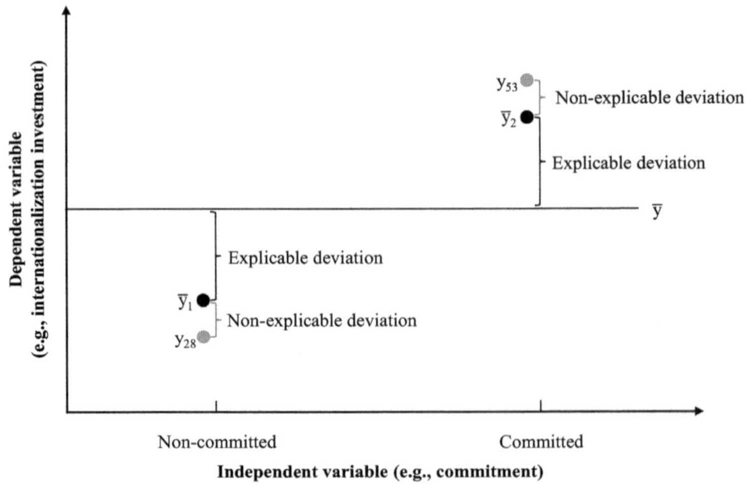

Fig. 4.4 Explicable and non-explicable deviation with an ANOVA. Source: Backhaus et al. (2011, p. 162)

comparison of different groups, such as committed and non-committed test subjects. It is, however, limited to its group orientation. An ANOVA explains the deviation of group means from a total mean but allows no further conclusions with regard to single values.[90] In other words, it can explain the variance between groups but not within groups. This is best illustrated with Fig. 4.4. The independent variable of the ANOVA could explain the deviation of the two group mean values $\bar{y}_1$ and $\bar{y}_2$ from a total mean value $\bar{y}$. Further conclusions with regard to the intra-group deviation, however, are not feasible. This means that the deviation of single values, such as y_{28} and y_{53}, from the respective group mean are not explicable with an ANOVA.

An ANOVA is a suitable statistical instrument for the evaluation of three of the four postulated hypotheses, which have been developed for the present study. Hypothesis 1a argues that managerial decision-makers under escalation of commitment will continue to raise internationalization investments regardless of the resultant economic success of the venture (unlike their non-committed counterparts). Thus, the independent nominal factor 'commitment' influences the dependent metric variable 'internationalization investment'.[91] This hypothesis is approached with a one-way ANOVA (i.e., a single factor and a single dependent variable).[92] Hypotheses 2 and 3 postulate that managerial decision-makers under escalation of commitment will deviate from the logic of rational choices (compared with their non-committed

[90]Cf. Backhaus et al. (2011, pp. 161–162).

[91]With an ANOVA, the dependent variable needs to be measured on a metric scale and independent factors need to be measured at least on a nominal scale; cf. Backhaus et al. (2011, p. 158).

[92]Hypothesis 1a could have been equally tested with a t-test because it is equivalent to the F-test of an ANOVA as long as only two group means are compared.

counterparts) in dependence of certain levels of psychic distance and establishment chain progress respectively.[93] Thus, the independent factor 'commitment' influences the dependent variable 'internationalization investment' in combination with the moderating ordinal variables 'psychic distance' and 'establishment chain progress'. These two hypotheses will be approached with a two-way ANOVA. This alternative ANOVA design allows for an evaluation of the effect of two independent factors on a single dependent variable. It assesses the main effect of both factors individually and enables the consideration of an interaction effect. Obviously, the latter is of particular interest for the context of the postulated moderating effect of psychic distance and establishment chain progress.

In contrast to the hypotheses above, Hypothesis 1b is affected by the analytical limitation of an ANOVA. It postulates that the internationalization investment of a single internationalization manager will increase in dependence of the decision-maker's individual 'degree of commitment'. Hence, this hypothesis does not address a comparison between groups. Instead, it covers the group of committed internationalization managers in more detail. As a result, an ANOVA is not suitable as a statistical evaluation method due to its group orientation. In order to cover this hypothesis, a simple linear regression is conducted with the 'degree of commitment' as an independent variable. The combination of the statistical methods for the analysis of Hypotheses 1a and 1b allows for an in-depths evaluation of the basic scenario of the randomized experiment. In this manner, it is not only possible to review the effect of escalation of commitment with a group perspective but, furthermore, it is feasible to draw a more specific picture of the group of committed subjects. Figure 4.5 presents an informative overview of the study-underlying hypotheses, concerned variables, as well as the applied statistical methods.

4.2.2 *Pretest Insights*

As stated in Sect. 4.2.1.2, a preliminary pretest has been conducted prior to the final data collection phase.[94] This step provided a range of benefits (Sect. 4.2.2.1) and yielded encouraging results (Sect. 4.2.2.2).

4.2.2.1 Benefit of a Pretest

As the perception of provided information in social science experiments may vary, the implementation of a pretest is advisable for test-theoretical considerations.[95] In the light of potential misinterpretations by test subjects, it helps to assess the overall

[93]See also Fig. 3.23 for a concise summary of hypotheses.

[94]The final data collection period lasted from July to November 2014 (cf. Sect. 4.2.1.2).

[95]Cf. Eschweiler et al. (2007, p. 6).

Dependent variable: 'Internationalization investment'			
Hypothesis	Moderating variable	Independent variable	Statistical method
H1a: At the group level, managerial decision-makers in internationalization processes, who are under escalation of commitment, will rather act contrary to the logic of rational choices compared to a non-committed peer-group. This means that they will continue to raise internationalization investments regardless of the resultant economic success of the venture.		• 'Commitment'	• One-way ANOVA
H1b: At the individual level, managerial decision-makers will act increasingly contrary to the logic of rational choices with higher individual degrees of commitment. This means that the raised internationalization investment of a single internationalization manager will increase regardless of the resultant economic success of the venture but in dependence of the decision-maker's degree of commitment.		• 'Degree of commitment'	• Simple linear regression
H2: Compared with a non-committed peer-group, managerial decision-makers in internationalization processes, who are under escalation of commitment, will increasingly diverge from the logic of rational choices with an increasing psychic distance to targeted markets.	• 'Psychic distance'	• 'Commitment'	• Two-way ANOVA
H3: Compared with a non-committed peer-group, managerial decision-makers in internationalization processes, who are under escalation of commitment, will increasingly converge towards the logic of rational choices with an increasing establishment chain progress.	• 'Establishment chain progress'	• 'Commitment'	• Two-way ANOVA

Fig. 4.5 Overview of hypotheses, variables, and applied statistical methods. Source: Own figure

operability of the experiment. First, this refers to the comprehensibility of the experiment. A pretest with a significantly smaller sample size helps to ensure that the test subjects of the final large-scale experiment understand and process the given information as intended. This is somewhat connected to a second benefit: The pretest also helps to assess whether or not the conducted manipulation was fruitful and resulted in a measurable effect.[96] Especially under laboratory circumstances, it is not necessarily said that the independent variables unfold their manipulation

[96]Often, experimental studies refer to a manipulation check for this purpose (and then they do not necessarily include a pretest). In the present study, the manipulation is tested with the help of the pretest.

effect as planned because they may be unnoticed by test subjects.[97] The pretest provides an insight of participants' awareness of the independent factors and thereby verifies the effectiveness of the manipulation. Finally, a pretest gives a first impression regarding the duration of the experiment as well as other interfering factors that have not been considered by the experimenter and which are thus unintended.[98]

4.2.2.2 Pretest Findings

Against the background of these benefits, a pretest has also been conducted for the present study. Besides a check of the overall comprehensibility of the experiment, the main objective of the pretest was to inquire whether or not the commitment of the pretest's treatment group was successfully developed (after all, a requirement in order to test any of the study-underlying hypotheses). To fulfill the objective, the pretest needed to show a clear difference between the decision outcomes of the treatment and of the control group. Furthermore, the respective subjects also needed to assess the relevance of the previous internationalization investments differently for their subjective decision-making process (less relevant for committed test subjects, more relevant for non-committed test subjects). Thus, a potential difference between the decision outcomes would be traceable to the perceived relevance of previous internationalization investments. For this purpose, a short survey has been implemented at the end of the pretest, in which the participants were asked to indicate how substantial some of the implied information was for their decision outcome. Test subjects were asked to self-assess the relevance of the fact that they were already invested in the second and third decision round on a scale between one (irrelevant) and 10 (very relevant). Other than that, the setup of the pretest was identical to the final stage of the experiment. Obviously, however, the total sample size consisted of only 20 students for the pretest. Test subjects, who participated in the pretest, were excluded from the final large-scale experiment.

The pretest worked as expected. Throughout the pretest, the treatment and control group results were clearly distinct. The participants of the treatment group invested 65%, 52.25%, and 53.5% of their funds in the first, second, and third round respectively. Nobody withdrew from the chosen internationalization path until Round 3, in which three out of ten test subjects withdrew from the internationalization process. In contrast, the participants of the control group invested merely 33.49% and 36.81% of their available resources in the second and third round.[99]

---

[97]Consider, for example, a scenario context, in which the effect of good weather on sales numbers is investigated. If test subjects do not perceive the different weather conditions as intended by the experimenter, any causation in this regard must be invalid.

[98]Cf. Brake (2009, p. 401).

[99]Keep in mind that the control group was excluded from the first decision round (cf. Sect. 4.2.1.3) in order to ensure that the treatment group was relatively more committed.

Furthermore, four out of ten of test subjects withdrew already in the second round and one additional student withdrew in the third round. The differing decision outcomes are indicative for an effective manipulation of the independent factor 'commitment'. This interpretation is additionally substantiated with the participants' assessment of the relevance of the previous investments for their decision outcome: The treatment group only assessed a moderate relevance with a mean value of 4.7 while the control group attached greater relevance to this fact with a mean value of 7.7. This allows the assumption that the control group of the pretest was more aware of the factual events during the simulation.

Overall, the pretest does not only show that the internationalization simulation was clear and comprehensible for the test subjects but it also highlights that the initial internationalization decision of the treatment group (in the first round) resulted in an effective manipulation of the independent factor 'commitment'.

4.2.3 Presentation of the Statistical Results

In the present section, the statistical results of the randomized experiment will be outlined. The applied structure is similar to the section on the development of the hypotheses[100]: First, the general impact of escalation of commitment on the simulated internationalization process is covered (Sect. 4.2.3.1). This part is put together from the one-way ANOVA results at the group level (for the analysis of Hypothesis 1a) as well as from the simple linear regression results at the individual level (for the analysis of Hypothesis 1b). Second and third, the two-way ANOVA results covering potential moderating effects of 'psychic distance' (Sect. 4.2.3.2) as well as of 'establishment chain progress' (Sect. 4.2.3.3) are presented respectively (for the analysis of Hypotheses 2 and 3).

4.2.3.1 Measured General Impact of Escalation of Commitment on the Simulated Internationalization Process

Group Level

At the group level, the conducted one-way ANOVA supports the assumption that the disposition of an increased commitment among decision-makers leads to higher investments and persistence in the internationalization processes of firms—even in times of failure. In the second round ($F = 9.243$, $p < 0.01$; cf. Table 4.2) as well as in the third round ($F = 5.769$, $p < 0.05$; cf. Table 4.3) of the simulated internationalization process scenario, statistically significant decision-making differences between the group of committed and non-committed test subjects were measurable.

[100]Cf. Sect. 3.3.7.

Table 4.2 Test of between-subjects effects (H1a), Round 2

Dependent variable: Internationalization investment (Round 2)						
Source	Type III sum of squares	df	Mean square	F	Sig.	Partial eta squared
Corrected model	0.806[a]	1	0.806	9.243	0.003	0.086
Intercept	15.775	1	15.775	180.972	0.000	0.649
Commitment	0.806	1	0.806	9.243	**0.003****	0.086
Error	8.543	98	0.087			
Total	25.124	100				
Corrected total	9.348	99				

Source: Own table
[a]$R^2 = 0.086$ (adjusted $R^2 = 0.077$)
*$p < 0.05$; **$p < 0.01$; ***$p < 0.001$

Table 4.3 Test of between-subjects effects (H1a), Round 3

Dependent variable: Internationalization investment (Round 3)						
Source	Type III sum of squares	df	Mean square	F	Sig.	Partial eta squared
Corrected model	0.637[a]	1	0.637	5.769	0.019	0.071
Intercept	20.567	1	20.567	186.243	0.000	0.710
Commitment	0.637	1	0.637	5.769	**0.019***	0.071
Error	8.393	76	0.110			
Total	32.078	78				
Corrected total	9.030	77				

Source: Own table
[a]$R^2 = 0.071$ (adjusted $R^2 = 0.058$)
*$p < 0.05$; **$p < 0.01$; ***$p < 0.001$

Table 4.4 Descriptive statistics (H1a)

	Dependent variable: Internationalization investment (Round 2)			Dependent variable: Internationalization investment (Round 3)		
Commitment	Mean	Standard deviation	N	Mean	Standard deviation	N
Committed	0.4869	0.27445	50	0.6170	0.32308	47
Non-committed	0.3074	0.31467	50	0.4323	0.34598	31
Total	0.3972	0.30729	100	0.5436	0.34244	78

Source: Own table

A decomposition of the different decision-making rounds reveals that the group of committed test subjects invested significantly more capital for the maintenance of the internationalization process despite its unfavorable outcome throughout the simulation ($Mean_{(Round\ 2)} = 0.4869$, $M_{(Round\ 3)} = 0.6170$; cf. Table 4.4). In contrast, the

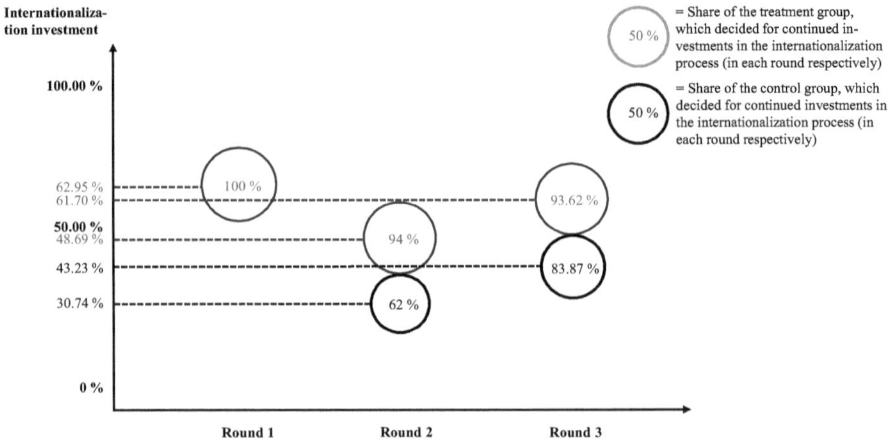

Fig. 4.6 Illustration of the basic scenario results. Source: Own figure

non-committed peer group was much more reluctant with regard to an additional funding of the internationalization process ($M_{(\text{Round 2})} = 0.3074$, $M_{(\text{Round 3})} = 0.4323$; cf. Table 4.4).

These numbers are best illustrated with the above Fig. 4.6. It shows quite clearly the contrast between the group of committed and non-committed test subjects. In the first decision-making round, all of the participants of the treatment group had to opt for one of the two presented target markets. Thus, 100% decided for an investment initially. In average, test subjects of the treatment group allocated 62.95% of their funds to one of the available target markets. In the second round, 94% decided for continued investments in the internationalization process at an average reinvestment rate of 48.69% of their remaining capital. In the third round, 93.62% of the remaining treatment group (i.e., 88% of its initial basis) allocated an additional 61.7% of their residual funds to the internationalization process. After three decision rounds, only 6 out of 50 participants of the treatment group seized the opportunity to withdraw from the internationalization process at some point during the simulation.

In contrast, only 62% of the participants of the control group decided for continued investments in the second decision-making round (at an average reinvestment rate of 30.74% of their remaining funds).[101] In the third round, 83.87% of the remaining control group (i.e., 52% of its initial basis) allocated an additional 43.23% of their available capital to the internationalization process. Ultimately, 24 out of 50 participants of the control group seized the opportunity to withdraw from the internationalization process at some point during the simulated internationalization process.

[101]The control group was excluded from the first decision round, which served only for the development of the commitment of the treatment group.

Individual Level

The analysis at the group level, however, does not yet allow for an empirical insight into the effect of commitment at the individual level of a single internationalization manager. Yet, this insight is necessary in order to fully understand the impact of escalation of commitment on internationalization process decision-making. In order to compensate for this shortcoming, the present study includes a simple linear regression covering the relation between an internationalization manager's individual degree of commitment and his/her internationalization investments in failing courses of action. Thus, it includes the individual perspective in addition to the analysis at the group level. The simple linear regression has been conducted for the second and third decision-making round respectively and covers the group of committed internationalization managers in more detail. This means that the investigated population for the second round is identical with the treatment group ($N = 50$) since the concerned participants were the only ones who were subjected to a certain degree of commitment (cf. Table 4.5). In the third decision-making round, however, there is a population influx. Besides the share of the treatment group that opted for continued investments in the previous round (94%, equating to 47 subjects), there is also the share of the control group that opted for further internationalization investments (62%, equating to 31 subjects). By the time of the third decision-making round, these test subjects were also committed to their course of action (although to a smaller extent). Therefore, they were added to the investigated population (equating a total of $N = 78$; cf. Table 4.9).

For the second decision-making round, the correlation examining the relation between the decision-maker's degree of commitment and his/her internationalization investment was significant at the 0.001 level and in the expected positive direction ($r = 0.714$; cf. Table 4.6 and Fig. 4.7).

The regression revealed that the independent variable ('degree of commitment') accounted for 51% ($R^2 = 0.510$; cf. Table 4.7) of the variability in the dependent variable ('internationalization investment').[102] The regression was statistically significant ($p < 0.001$; cf. Table 4.8).

Also for the third decision-making round, the correlation examining the relation between the decision-maker's degree of commitment and his/her internationalization investment was significant at the 0.001 level and in the expected positive direction ($r = 0.571$; cf. Table 4.10 and Fig. 4.8).

With regard to the regression results, it can be stated that the independent variable ('degree of commitment') accounted for 32.6% ($R^2 = 0.326$; cf. Table 4.11) of the variability in the dependent variable ('internationalization investment') in the third decision-making round. As for the second round, the regression was statistically significant ($p < 0.001$; cf. Table 4.12).

[102]The marginally higher R^2 in Fig. 4.7 (compared to Table 4.7) can be attributed to rounding differences in MS Excel (used for the figure) and in IBM SPSS (used for the table).

Table 4.5 Descriptive statistics (H1b), Round 2

	Mean	Std. deviation	N
Internationalization investment (Round 2)	0.4869	0.27445	50
Degree of commitment	0.5036	0.15455	50

Source: Own table

Table 4.6 Correlations (H1b), Round 2

		Internationalization investment (Round 2)	Degree of commitment
Pearson correlation	Internationalization investment (Round 2)	1.000	0.714
	Degree of commitment	0.714	1.000
Sig. (1-tailed)	Internationalization investment (Round 2)		0.000
	Degree of commitment	0.000	
N	Internationalization investment (Round 2)	50	50
	Degree of commitment	50	50

Source: Own table

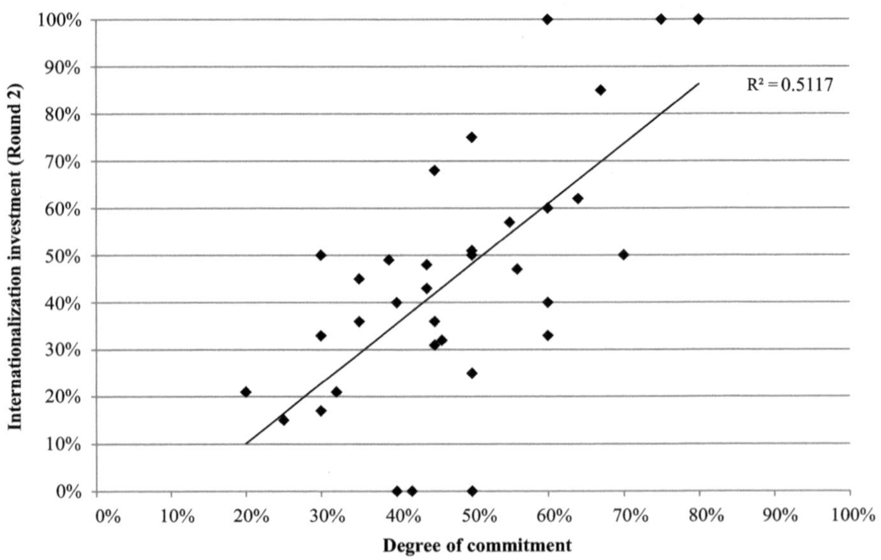

Fig. 4.7 Scatterplot (H1b), Round 2. Source: Own figure

Table 4.7 Model summary (H1b), Round 2

Model	R	R^2	Adjusted R^2	Std. error of the estimate
1	0.714[a]	0.510	0.500	0.19412

Source: Own table
[a]Predictors: (Constant), degree of commitment

Table 4.8 Coefficients[a] (H1b), Round 2

	Unstandardized coefficients		Standardized coefficients		
Model	B	Std. error	Beta	t	Sig.
1 (Constant)	−0.152	0.094		−1.606	0.115
Degree of commitment	1.268	0.179	0.714	7.067	**0.000*** **

Source: Own table
[a]Dependent variable: Internationalization investment (Round 2)
*$p < 0.05$; **$p < 0.01$; ***$p < 0.001$

Table 4.9 Descriptive statistics (H1b), Round 3

	Mean	Std. deviation	N
Internationalization investment (Round 3)	0.5436	0.34244	78
Degree of commitment	0.6077	0.21525	78

Source: Own table

Table 4.10 Correlations (H1b), Round 3

		Internationalization investment (Round 3)	Degree of commitment
Pearson correlation	Internationalization investment (Round 3)	1.000	0.571
	Degree of commitment	0.571	1.000
Sig. (1-tailed)	Internationalization investment (Round 3)		0.000
	Degree of commitment	0.000	
N	Internationalization investment (Round 3)	78	78
	Degree of commitment	78	78

Source: Own table

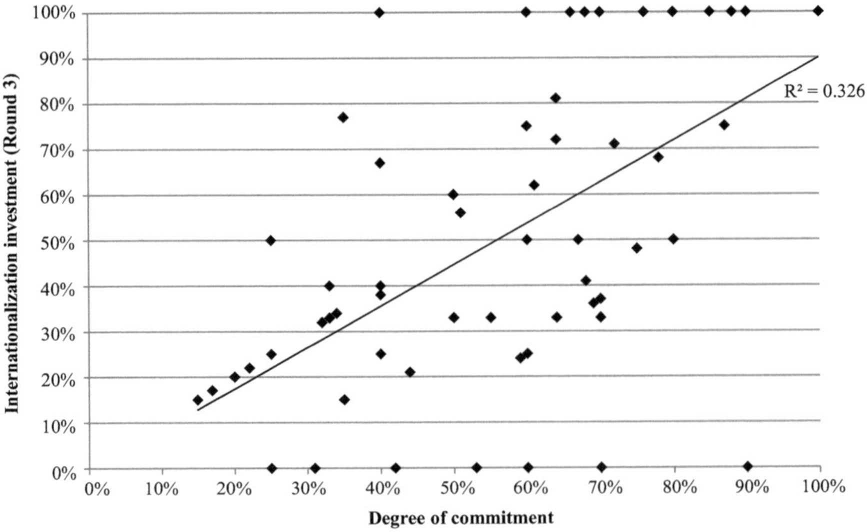

Fig. 4.8 Scatterplot (H1b), Round 3. Source: Own figure

Table 4.11 Model summary (H1b), Round 3

Model	R	R^2	Adjusted R^2	Std. error of the estimate
1	0.571[a]	0.326	0.318	0.28289

Source: Own table
[a]Predictors: (Constant), degree of commitment

Table 4.12 Coefficients[a] (H1b), Round 3

	Unstandardized coefficients		Standardized coefficients		
Model	B	Std. error	Beta	t	Sig.
1 (Constant)	−0.009	0.096		−0.091	0.928
Degree of commitment	0.909	0.150	0.571	6.069	**0.000*****

Source: Own table
[a]Dependent variable: Internationalization investment (Round 3)
*$p < 0.05$; **$p < 0.01$; ***$p < 0.001$

4.2.3.2 Measured Effect of Psychic Distance on the Impact of Escalation of Commitment

In consideration of the risk-altering implications of psychic distance, the present study also investigates a possible divergent decision-making pattern for committed and non-committed decision-makers in an internationalization context of increasing psychic distance. It is the hypothesis that committed test subjects tend to ignore the associated risk, which is prevalent in situations of high psychic distance, and that they maintain their internationalization investments regardless of this specific

Table 4.13 Test of between-subjects effects (H2)

Dependent variable: Internationalization investment						
Source	Type III sum of squares	df	Mean square	F	Sig.	Partial eta squared
Corrected model	3.533[a]	3	1.178	12.810	0.000	0.164
Intercept	31.527	1	31.527	342.905	0.000	0.636
Commitment	1.446	1	1.446	15.733	0.000	0.074
Psychic distance	1.705	1	1.705	18.545	0.000	0.086
Commitment * psychic distance	0.382	1	0.382	4.152	**0.043***	0.021
Error	18.020	196	0.092			
Total	53.080	200				
Corrected total	21.553	199				

Source: Own table
[a]$R^2 = 0.164$ (adjusted $R^2 = 0.151$)
*$p < 0.05$; **$p < 0.01$; ***$p < 0.001$

decision context.[103] Thus, there could be a statistically measurable interaction term between the independent variable 'commitment' and the moderating variable 'psychic distance'. In order to test for such a moderating effect, a two-way ANOVA has been conducted. The data stems from the interlude of the basic scenario.

The data analysis supports the assumption that psychic distance has a moderating effect on the impact of escalation of commitment on internationalization process decision-making. As it can be concluded from Table 4.13, a statistically significant interaction term between 'commitment' and 'psychic distance' was measurable ($F = 4.152$, $p < 0.05$). This means that the prevalence of commitment as well as the psychic distance context had a simultaneous influence on the decision-making outcome of the participants in the simulated internationalization process.

A closer look at the different levels of psychic distance, to which the participants were exposed, reveals that the average internationalization investment of the committed test subjects ($M_{(\text{very low PD})} = 0.5533$, $M_{(\text{low PD})} = 0.5081$, $M_{(\text{high PD})} = 0.4421$, $Mean_{(\text{very high PD})} = 0.4248$) as well as of the control group ($M_{(\text{very low PD})} = 0.5007$, $M_{(\text{low PD})} = 0.3953$, $M_{(\text{high PD})} = 0.2399$ $M_{(\text{very high PD})} = 0.1120$) decreased with an increasing psychic distance to the targeted market. In high and very high psychic distance contexts, however, the control group allocated significantly less capital in comparison to the treatment group (cf. Table 4.14).

The following Fig. 4.9 illustrates these numbers accordingly. For both groups, lower levels of psychic distance come along with higher internationalization investments. Thus, there is a common trend. Nonetheless, there is a moderating effect because the participants reacted differently in high and very high psychic distance situations in dependence of their commitment. This is expressed in the

[103]Cf. Hypothesis 2, Sect. 3.3.7.2.

Table 4.14 Descriptive statistics (H2)

Dependent variable: Internationalizatioftn investment				
Commitment	Psychic distance	Mean	Std. deviation	N
Committed	Very low	0.5533	0.26935	25
	Low	0.5081	0.26258	25
	High	0.4421	0.33809	25
	Very high	0.4248	0.36944	25
	Total	0.4821	0.31271	100
Non-committed	Very low	0.5007	0.32655	25
	Low	0.3953	0.28509	25
	High	0.2399	0.32024	25
	Very high	0.1120	0.22926	25
	Total	0.3120	0.32452	100
Total	Very low	0.5270	0.29744	50
	Low	0.4517	0.27718	50
	High	0.3410	0.34152	50
	Very high	0.2684	0.34286	50
	Total	0.3970	0.32910	200

Source: Own table

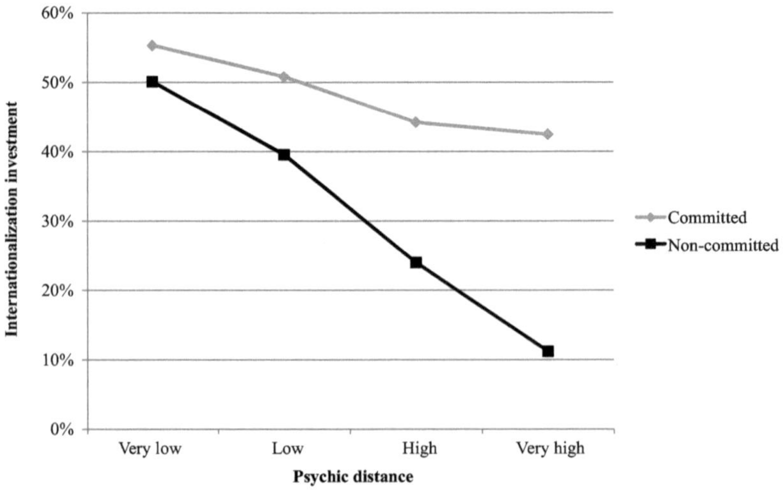

Fig. 4.9 Ordinal interaction of commitment and psychic distance. Source: Own figure

increasing spacing between the two graphs in Fig. 4.9, which depicts an ordinal interaction between the commitment of the test subjects and the psychic distance decision-making context.[104]

[104]Ordinal interactions can be distinguished from hybrid and disordinal interactions; cf. Leigh and Kinnear (1980, p. 842).

4.2.3.3 Measured Effect of the Establishment Chain Progress on the Impact of Escalation of Commitment

Besides psychic distance, different levels of establishment chain progress may also unfold a moderating effect on the impact of escalation of commitment on internationalization process decision-making. As little establishment chain progress requires significantly less capital in comparison to later establishment chain stages, a failing internationalization path is potentially less costly during its early stages. Yet, decision-makers under escalation of commitment are marked by a reduced cost evaluation capacity.[105] Therefore, the present study investigates the hypothesis that test subjects under escalation of commitment misperceive the reduced withdrawal costs that are associated with the early stages of the establishment chain progress in internationalization processes, and that they will maintain their decision path without further modification—unlike their non-committed counterparts.[106]

The data analysis, however, contradicts the hypothesis. As it can be concluded from Table 4.15, there is no significant interaction term between 'commitment' and 'establishment chain progress' ($F = 0.002$, $p = 0.961$). Thus, there is no reason to assume that the establishment chain progress has a moderating effect on the impact of escalation of commitment on internationalization process decision-making based on the statistical results. This means that the prevalence of commitment as well as the establishment chain progress may have an impact on the decision outcome separately, but that there is no simultaneous influence.

Table 4.16 shows that the average internationalization investment of the committed test subjects ($Mean_{(20)} = 0.3451$, $M_{(60)} = 0.4098$, $M_{(140)} = 0.5045$,

Table 4.15 Test of between-subjects effects (H3)

Dependent variable: Internationalization investment						
Source	Type III sum of squares	df	Mean square	F	Sig.	Partial eta squared
Corrected model	1.626[a]	3	0.542	5.986	0.001	0.084
Intercept	28.566	1	28.566	315.419	0.000	0.617
Commitment	0.820	1	0.820	9.055	0.003	0.044
Establishment chain progress	0.806	1	0.806	8.900	0.003	0.043
Commitment * establishment chain progress	0.000	1	0.000	0.002	**0.961**	0.000
Error	17.751	196	0.091			
Total	47.943	200				
Corrected total	19.377	199				

Source: Own table
[a]$R^2 = 0.084$ (adjusted $R^2 = 0.070$)

[105]Cf. Sect. 3.3.7.3 for the respective argumentation.

[106]Cf. Hypothesis 3, Sect. 3.3.7.3.

Table 4.16 Descriptive statistics (H3)

Dependent variable: Internationalization investment				
Commitment	Establishment chain progress	Mean	Std. deviation	N
Committed	20 (Export-oriented)	0.3451	0.25603	25
	60	0.4098	0.24713	25
	140	0.5045	0.30512	25
	180 (FDI-oriented)	0.5085	0.29691	25
	Total	0.4420	0.28174	100
Non-committed	20 (Export-oriented)	0.2250	0.27829	25
	60	0.2779	0.27909	25
	140	0.3603	0.36729	25
	180 (FDI-oriented)	0.3923	0.37056	25
	Total	0.3139	0.32874	100
Total	20 (Export-oriented)	0.2850	0.27151	50
	60	0.3438	0.26926	50
	140	0.4324	0.34202	50
	180 (FDI-oriented)	0.4504	0.33745	50
	Total	0.3779	0.31204	200

Source: Own table

$M_{(180)} = 0.5058$) as well as of the control group ($M_{(20)} = 0.2250$, $M_{(60)} = 0.2779$, $M_{(140)} = 0.3603$, $M_{(180)} = 0.3923$) increased with growing numbers of employees in the target market, i.e., in later establishment chain stages.[107] This does not speak for a moderating effect because there seems to be equidistance between the internationalization investments of the treatment as well as of the control group for each of the different establishment chain stages, ranging from 20 (export-oriented) to 180 (FDI-oriented).

The lack of an interaction term is clear to see in the following Fig. 4.10. For both groups, later establishment chain stages lead to higher internationalization investments. Unlike for the case of psychic distance, there is no moderating effect because the participants reacted very similarly to the establishment chain variations in the simulated internationalization process scenario. This is expressed in the almost constant spacing between the two graphs, which shows that there is no significant interaction between the commitment of the test subjects and the varied establishment chain stages.

[107]The index values represent the workforce that was assigned to the foreign market in the simulated IP scenario (ranging from 20 to 180); they serve as a proxy measure and indicate the establishment chain progress (from early to later stages). Cf. the procedure of the experiment (Sect. 4.2.1.3).

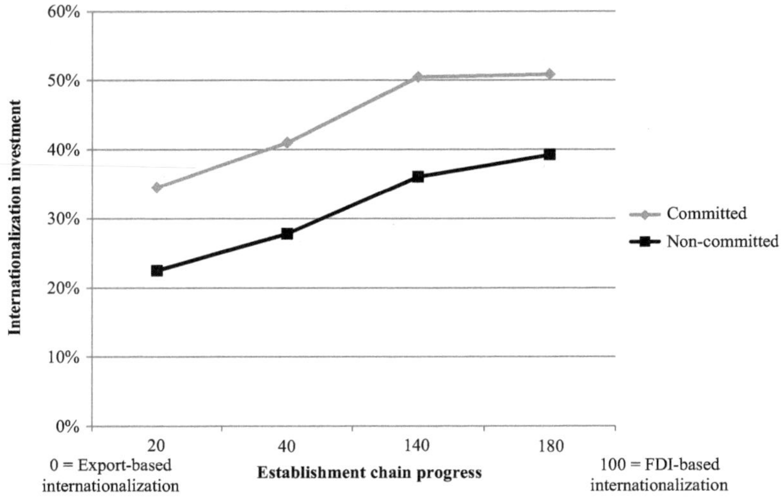

Fig. 4.10 No interaction of commitment and establishment chain progress. Source: Own figure

4.2.4 Discussion of the Results

For the analysis of the issue of escalation of commitment as a representative of bounded rationality in internationalization process decision-making, the previously established hypotheses will be discussed with the help of the quantitative-empirical results in the following. The applied structure follows the logic of the previous sections. First, the display of a general impact of escalation of commitment on IP decision-making will be discussed (Sect. 4.2.4.1). Subsequently, the moderating effect of psychic distance (Sect. 4.2.4.2) and the lack of a moderating effect of the establishment chain progress (Sect. 4.2.4.3) will be argued.

4.2.4.1 Display of Escalation of Commitment in Internationalization Process Decision-Making

The statistical results support Hypothesis 1a and 1b (cf. Fig. 4.11). Therefore, it can reasonably be assumed that escalation of commitment has an impact on the internationalization process decision-making of managerial administrators. The randomized experiment highlighted that committed test subjects were affected by the psychological, social, and structural forces for persistence to which they were exposed during the randomized experiment because they continued to raise internationalization investments regardless of their economic success.

This is manifested in the significant decision-making differences between the treatment and control group. With 94% and 93.62%, the share of committed test persons, who continued the internationalization process despite its failing outcome, was continuously high throughout the decision-making stages of the experiment. At

	Alternative hypothesis	Sig.	Assessment null hypothesis	Assessment alt. hypothesis
H1a	At the group level, managerial decision-makers in internationalization processes, who are under escalation of commitment, will rather act contrary to the logic of rational choices compared to a non-committed peer-group. This means that they will continue to raise internationalization investments regardless of the resultant economic success of the venture.	0.003 (Round 2) 0.019 (Round 3)	Rejected	**Supported**
H1b	At the individual level, managerial decision-makers will act increasingly contrary to the logic of rational choices with higher individual degrees of commitment. This means that the raised internationalization investment of a single internationalization manager will increase regardless of the resultant economic success of the venture but in dependence of the decision-maker's degree of commitment.	0.000 (Round 2) 0.000 (Round 3)	Rejected	**Supported**

Fig. 4.11 Assessment of Hypotheses H1a and H1b. Source: Own figure

the individual level, one can furthermore record a clear relation between the individual degree of commitment of a decision-maker and his/her internationalization investment: The internationalization investment of single test subjects increased regardless of the resultant economic success but in dependence of their individual degree of commitment. This, however, is in direct contradiction to the postulate of the U-Model, according to which all test persons should have limited their international engagement to a tolerable risk.

In contrast, non-committed and rather rational decision-makers are apparently characterized by an increased readiness to withdraw from an internationalization process once the attempted internationalization targets are missed. The control group, which was not exposed to an escalation bias, paid more consideration to the signals of internationalization process failure, tended to follow the implicit rational choice principles of the U-Model, and withdrew more frequently from the internationalization process in order to secure the remaining funds. This has led to an average internationalization investment rate, which was significantly lower for non-committed participants throughout the simulated internationalization process scenario. All of this supports the assumption that decision-makers in internationalization processes are indeed prone to an escalation bias, which causes an increased persistence in failing courses of action. Therefore, (also unsuccessful) internationalization processes may in fact be maintained due to the escalation of commitment of the decision-makers in charge (cf. Fig. 4.12).

The display of escalation of commitment during the simulated internationalization process is indicative for a significant shortcoming of the currently prevailing perspective within the field of internationalization process literature, the seminal U-Model. Apparently—and contrary to the theoretical postulate—the internationalization process

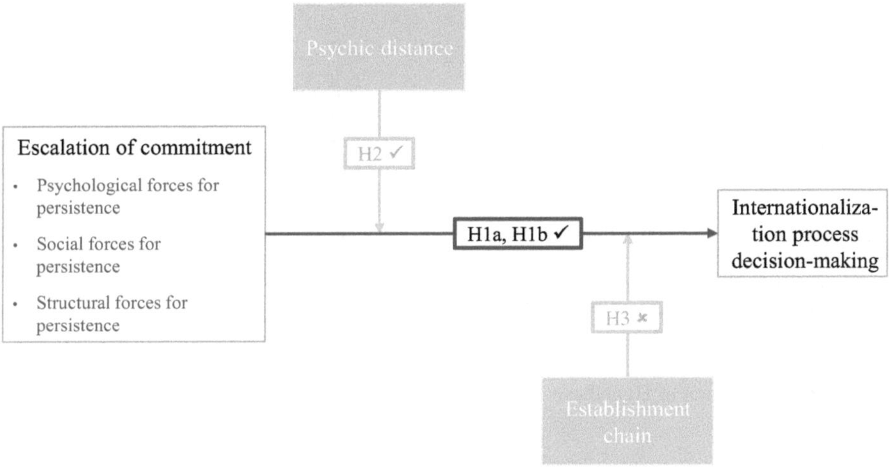

Fig. 4.12 Hypotheses 1a and 1b in the research model. Source: Own figure

of firms does not only depend on an interplay between state (market knowledge and market commitment) and change aspects (commitment decisions and current activities). The fact that managerial decision-makers in internationalization processes are prone to escalation of commitment shows that managers do not always possess the ability to evaluate their options rationally and that they do not always ponder between the perceived and tolerable market risks. Therefore, new commitment decisions are not necessarily taken on the basis of existing market knowledge and market commitments. This highlights that the commitment dimension is in fact more complex than postulated by the U-Model, which tends to ignore the limited cognitive capability of decision-makers and which overstresses their rational decision-making powers. Despite the U-Model's internal logic and plausibility, it does not seem to recognize the bounded rationality of decision-makers sufficiently.

4.2.4.2 Moderating Effect of Psychic Distance

Besides demonstrating the impact of escalation of commitment on internationalization process decision-making, the statistical results also support the second hypothesis of the present study: The risk increasing implications of high psychic distance moderate the impact of escalation of commitment on internationalization process decision-making (cf. Fig. 4.13). With increasing levels of psychic distance to the target market, it has been possible to show a divergent internationalization investment pattern for decision-makers in dependence of the presence of an escalation bias. In the context of growing psychic distance, committed test subjects acted increasingly against rational choice principles in the simulation.

In a scenario of very low psychic distance to the target market, the treatment and control group drew relatively similar conclusions with regard to the maintenance of

	Alternative hypothesis	Sig.	Assessment null hypothesis	Assessment alt. hypothesis
H2	Compared with a non-committed peer-group, managerial decision-makers in internationalization processes, who are under escalation of commitment, will increasingly diverge from the logic of rational choices with an increasing psychic distance to targeted markets.	0.043	Rejected	**Supported**

Fig. 4.13 Assessment of Hypothesis 2. Source: Own figure

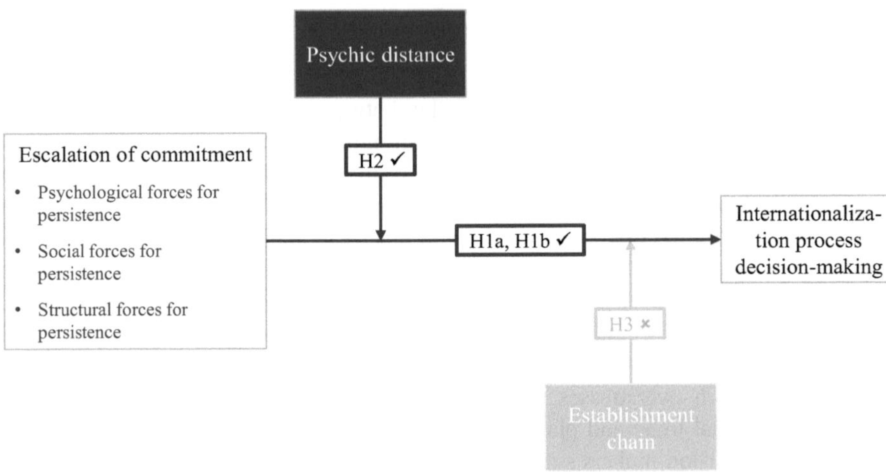

Fig. 4.14 Hypothesis 2 in the research model. Source: Own figure

the internationalization process. In such a situation, the committed test subjects decided to invest 55.33% of their remaining capital in the internationalization process, while the non-committed peer-group allocated a similarly high share with 50.07%. The gap, however, widened with every additional level of psychic distance that has been added to the simulation. In situations of very high psychic distance, the treatment group invested 42.48% of their funds, whereas the control group allocated a mere 11.2% to the target market. As psychic distance presented the only altered variable at this stage of the experiment, it must have had a moderating influence on the impact of the escalation bias on the internationalization process, and it must have entailed the divergent decision-making pattern (cf. Fig. 4.14).

The moderating effect can be traced back to the lower risk assessment capacity, with which decision-makers under escalation of commitment have to cope. Due to this disposition, the treatment group seems to have misjudged the increased risk, which resulted from the higher level of uncertainty in situations of high psychic distance. The concerned test subjects opted for a small chance of success at the risk of even higher losses: With the hope of balancing the unfavorable internationalization development, the treatment group maintained its decision path with a rather extensive capital allowance regardless of the risk increasing context alterations in the simulation. This, of course, contradicts the idea of purposefully proceeding internationalization managers. Rational decision-makers, such as the control group, are already rather reluctant with regard to continued investments in failing courses of action. An additional confrontation with higher levels of psychic distance leads to an even higher readiness to withdraw from an internationalization process among such decision-makers.

Thus, the quantitative-empirical analysis for the second hypothesis highlights that the issue of escalation of commitment as a representative of bounded rationality has a specific effect in the context of internationalization process decision-making. It shows that the impact of the escalation bias is aggravating with increasing psychic distance levels to target markets because affected internationalization managers are departing more and more from an objectively rational basis. In addition to the general impact of escalation of commitment on internationalization process decision-making, this aspect emphasizes even more that the bounded rationality of decision-makers presents a factor that IP-theories—including the U-Model—should account for. Apparently, the currently prevailing idea of rationally, i.e., consistently and purposefully, acting decision-makers is somewhat far-fetched. Cognitive dispositions are a decision-making factor that IB-theorists should consider more than they do today.

4.2.4.3 Lack of a Moderating Effect of the Establishment Chain Progress

Unlike for the case of increasing psychic distance, there is no statistical evidence in support of the third hypothesis of the present study: The establishment chain progress had no moderating impact on the effect of escalation of commitment during the simulated internationalization process (cf. Fig. 4.15). The applied variations to the number of employees that have been assigned to the simulated target market (as a proxy for the establishment chain progress) did not bring a convergent decision-making pattern of test subjects to light. In contrast to the previously outlined considerations,[108] decision-makers under escalation of commitment did not make their internationalization investment regardless of the associated establishment chain stages. Instead, they seemed to account for the reduced withdrawal

[108]Cf. Sect. 3.3.7.3.

	Alternative hypothesis	Sig.	Assessment null hypothesis	Assessment alt. hypothesis
H3	Compared with a non-committed peer-group, managerial decision-makers in internationalization processes, who are under escalation of commitment, will increasingly converge towards the logic of rational choices with an increasing establishment chain progress.	0.961	Supported	**Rejected**

Fig. 4.15 Assessment of Hypothesis 3. Source: Own figure

costs in scenarios of little establishment chain progress and they took the opportunity to exit the internationalization process as much as their counterparts of the control group.

This is manifested in the relatively similar decision-making pattern of the treatment and control group. Regardless of the prevalence of a commitment bias, test subjects reacted almost identically to the establishment chain context variations during the simulation. When there were already 180 employees assigned to the target market, i.e., the withdrawal costs were high due to a FDI-oriented market entry mode, the committed test subjects decided to invest 50.85% of their remaining capital while the non-committed peer-group allocated 39.23% of its funds. When there were only 20 employees assigned to the international venture, i.e., the withdrawal costs were low due to an export-oriented market entry mode, the treatment group allocated 34.51% of its funds whereas the control group invested 22.5% of its remaining capital. As in the case of psychic distance context variations, these numbers reveal a gap between the internationalization investments of the treatment and control group. Contrary to the hypothesis, however, the gap did not narrow with an increasing establishment chain progress. At any establishment chain stage, the internationalization investment of the treatment group was around 12 percentage points above the numbers of the control group. This demonstrates that there was no measurable interaction between the prevalence of a commitment bias and the establishment chain progress (cf. Fig. 4.16).

Thus, the statistical results do not support the assumption that the reduced cost evaluation capacity of committed decision-makers translates into neglect for lower withdrawal costs during the early stages of an internationalization process. Yet, what could explain the rejection of the third hypothesis? First, at a statistical level this could be traced to a violation of the premises for the conduct of a two-way

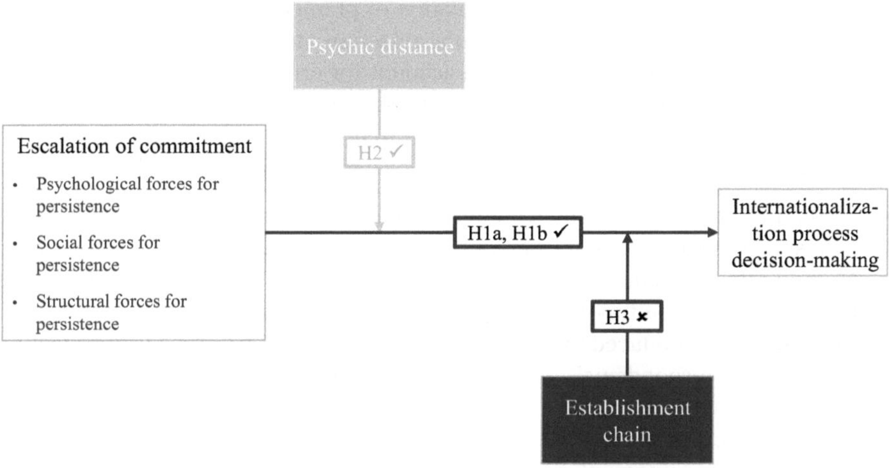

Fig. 4.16 Hypothesis 3 in the research model. Source: Own figure

ANOVA. When these are violated, the obtained statistical results may be misleading.[109] Essentially, the following premises apply for the conduct of an ANOVA[110]:

- No outliers
- Randomized group assignment
- Groups bigger than 20 subjects
- Variance homogeneity
- Normal distribution

While the first three premises have been fulfilled, it was not possible to assess variance homogeneity and normal distribution for this part of the conducted analysis. A Levene test for the assessment of the equality of variances demonstrated that an assumption of equal variances across the treatment and control group was not valid ($p < 0.01$). A Kolmogorov-Smirnov test for the assessment of normal distribution yielded the insight that the internationalization investments of the treatment group violated the respective premise repeatedly, i.e., in cases of FDI- as well as in cases of export-oriented internationalizations ($p < 0.05$; $p < 0.01$). These violations, however, can be cured if the test subjects are evenly divided among the different groups of the experiment.[111] Since the treatment as well as the control group were put together from 50 students each, and since every subgroup of the interlude of the basic scenario consisted of 25 test subjects evenly, the setup of

[109]Cf. Keselman et al. (1998, p. 351).
[110]Cf. Huber et al. (2014, p. 63).
[111]Cf. Huber et al. (2014, p. 63).

the experiment compensated for the violation of premises.[112] Therefore, this issue could have hardly been responsible for the rejection of the third hypothesis.

Second, methodological deficits can account for erroneous statistical results in quantitative-empirical studies. Above all, the so-called fallacy of common method biases has the potential to influence the research outcome in a distorting way.[113] These errors arise from having one or more of the following sources[114]:

- Method effects produced by a common source or rater (i.e., the dependent and independent variables stem from a single data source and result in a 'self-report')
- Method effects produced by 'item characteristics' (i.e., the item form affects the research results due to—for example—the respondents' personal preferences)
- Method effects produced by 'item context' (i.e., the context of the data collection affects the respondents' results due to—for example—the respondents' interpretations)
- Method effects produced by 'measurement context' (i.e., the obtained measures are shaped by contextual influences in the form of time, location, and media implications)

Common method biases, however, are usually consulted when hypothesis-confirming research results are critically tested, especially when a detected relation between dependent and independent variables is doubted. Nevertheless, it is worthwhile to take a closer look at the 'item characteristics' of the establishment chain progress in the context of the experimental setup of the present study. In the simulation, the different establishment chain stages were operationalized with different numbers of employees assigned to the foreign market. This went along with different levels of withdrawal costs for the test subjects. As a consequence, lower numbers of employees implied lower withdrawal costs. Thus, the 'item characteristic' of a situation of little establishment chain progress included a direct monetary incentive for the participants to exit the internationalization process. This aspect could have contributed more than initially assumed to the actions of the decision-makers—regardless of their group allocation and commitment. Eventually, the 'item characteristic' worked 'too well' as it provided too much of an incentive to withdraw from the IP. This issue could at least partially explain the rejection of the third hypothesis of the present study.

One might argue that a scenario of high psychic distance and much decision-making uncertainty—as for the analysis of the second hypothesis—should bear some similarity in this regard. Such a scenario implies more risk for the test subjects' capital and therefore it provides an indirect financial incentive to exit the internationalization process. Yet, the 'item characteristics' of a scenario of high

---

[112]In fact, this measure has been taken for all ANOVA-based hypotheses prior to the quantitative-empirical analysis. Thus, a violation of the premises can be equally ruled out for the statistical results regarding Hypothesis 1a and Hypothesis 2.

[113]Cf. Podsakoff et al. (2003, pp. 879 ff.).

[114]Cf. Podsakoff et al. (2003, pp. 881 ff.).

psychic distance are substantially different from the 'item characteristics' of the establishment chain progress: While the latter are marked by a low degree of abstraction (due to the form of a direct monetary incentive), the former are marked by a high degree of abstraction (due to the form of the rather intangible and indirect consequences of the construct of psychic distance). Since the higher degree of abstraction of a scenario of high psychic distance renders the scenario's 'item characteristics' (i.e., the financial incentive to exit the internationalization process) less noticeable, there is no substantive reason to assume a common method bias in this regard.

4.3 Two Cases as an Illustration of Escalation of Commitment in Internationalization Process Reality

Despite the rejection of the third hypothesis of the quantitative-empirical study, the previous section has offered relatively solid indicators confirming the impact of escalation of commitment on internationalization process decision-making as well as validating the moderating influence of psychic distance. Admittedly, however, the randomized experiment presents a somewhat abstract and highly theoretical investigation method for this matter—irrespective of its rigorousness.[115] For this reason and by integrating the presentation and analysis of two cases from international business practice, the present study wants to demonstrate that escalation of commitment is by no means only an academic and theoretical issue in internationalization processes. As it has already been outlined in the beginning of this chapter, with such a consolidated mixed-methods research design further empirical evidence is added to the quantitative-empirical study and a comprehensive picture concerning the role of bounded rationality in the form of escalation of commitment in internationalization processes can be drawn.

4.3.1 Case Design, Case Selection, Data Collection, and Analysis

Qualitative-empirical case study research bears the opportunity to consider context observations, which may provide a better understanding of the researched field and which are not necessarily looked upon by solely quantitative methods.[116] As for most research methods, the general aim of case studies is to identify recurring key

[115]Cf. Sect. 4.1.2 for an account of the advantageous rigorousness of randomized experiments.

[116]Cf. Blanco Ramírez (2016, p. 19), Voss et al. (2002), and Eisenhardt (1989, p. 546), and Sect. 4.1.3 of the present study.

elements or so-called 'themes'.[117] Despite this common basis, qualitative empiricists provide a great multitude of different case study designs, which serve different purposes. The abundance of case study types is underlined by Baxter and Jack, who distinguish—sometimes with a low degree of selectiveness—between explanatory, exploratory, descriptive, intrinsic, instrumental, and collective case studies as different categories.[118] Most significantly, however, one can draw a line between single-case and multiple-case designs, which are commonly considered to be more robust.[119] While the former attempt to generate new insights with the in-depth analysis (or 'within analysis') of a single subject, the latter follow a certain replication logic with the consideration and comparison of several cases. From these two alternatives, only a multiple-case design provides the possibility to search for patterns across cases and to arrive at generalizations.[120] Yet, even within the field of multiple-case designs, one can furthermore separate approaches that try to identify similarities from others that assess differences across cases.[121] Against the background of this diversity of case study research possibilities, certain measures must be taken in order to secure the quality of the qualitative-empirical procedure. First, the choice of a case study design must be well evaluated in consideration of the research objective. Second, reliability and validity must be ensured with a transparent documentation of the qualitative-empirical research process.

It is the objective of the qualitative-empirical part of the present study to illustrate the matter of escalation of commitment in international business practice. Thus, the research objective is much more marked by a descriptive than by any other intent. Yin acknowledges that many case studies "have description as their main objective" and highlights the purposefulness of a multiple-case design in this regard due to its replication logic.[122] In accordance with this line of reasoning, a multiple-case design has been chosen for the following. Overall, this design should add profundity to the present study and support the insights that were gained with the quantitative-empirical analysis. Yet, which cases to select specifically? Quite regularly, internationalization attempts are marked by a lack of success.[123] Theoretically, there should hence be a sizeable pool of potential cases for further analysis. Yet, unsuccessful internationalization attempts are not necessarily well suited for the study of escalation of commitment in internationalization processes per se because the causes for failure can be manifold. There are two examples from the recent past, however, that come to mind for the context of escalation of commitment, which have received substantial media attention (in Germany at least). First, there is the merger of Daimler-Benz and Chrysler.[124] The

[117]Cf. Ayres et al. (2003, p. 880).
[118]Cf. Baxter and Jack (2008, pp. 547 ff.).
[119]Cf. Baxter and Jack (2008, pp. 550) and Eisenhardt and Graebner (2007, p. 27).
[120]Cf. Piekkari et al. (2009, pp. 571–572).
[121]Cf. Piekkari et al. (2009, pp. 571–572).
[122]Yin (2012, p. 39).
[123]Cf. Bianchi and Ostale (2006, pp. 140).
[124]Cf. Oesterle et al. (2011, pp. 196–197).

two companies decided to pool their businesses in 1998 and aimed at becoming the world's most successful and most renowned automotive manufacturer by 2001. Despite the fact that this target has been missed, the merger period lasted until 2007. Second, the German manufacturer of plush toys Margarete Steiff GmbH shifted its production to China in 2004 in order to lower the manufacturing costs of its goods. This, however, came at the price of significant shortcomings with regard to product quality as well as delivery times. While the company's hopes were therefore not fulfilled, the decision to produce abroad was only reversed after the passing of 4 more years. Due to the considerable persistence of the companies under consideration, both cases allow for the assumption that the respective internationalization process decisions were somewhat affected by escalation of commitment. Therefore, it seems reasonable to consult these two cases for further analysis. It is, however, not possible to reflect the entire internationalization processes of the two firms in a single case study due to their respective temporal lengths. By concentrating on the above mentioned merger period of DaimlerChrysler as well as on the years between 2004 and 2008 in the case of Steiff, the following pages provide only a comprehensive overview of two escalation-relevant periods in time. In the first case, it is possible to observe the IP decision-making during an already advanced psychic distance and establishment chain stage. Thus, it is about the further intensification of an already advanced internationalization process.[125] In the second case, it is possible to observe an earlier phase of internationalization (in terms of the establishment chain progress at least).

In consideration of the reliability and validity of the present study one might object that the consultation of only two cases thwarts the increased robustness that is common for multiple-case studies. Eisenhardt, for example, raises doubt regarding the empirical power of studies that are based on fewer than four cases.[126] This would present a valid point, if the qualitative-empirical analysis was the only analytical method applied in the present study. Yet here, the cases serve mainly as an illustration of the escalation phenomenon in internationalization process reality and for an underpinning of the quantitative-empirical results. For this reason, the analysis of only two cases seems to be an appropriate measure. One can defend the chosen design furthermore with the fact that Eisenhardt made her point in the specific context of theory building, which does not apply here. Last but not least, the author herself faced considerable criticism in this debate from other qualitative empiricists for her argument.[127] Another frequent problem of case study research lies in its low degree of internal validity.[128] In order to balance this deficit slightly, the following analysis of the cases is built upon analytical pattern-matching. This method attempts to discover whether an empirically identified pattern in one case

[125]Cf. Fisch and Oesterle (2003, p. 2).

[126]Cf. Eisenhardt (1989, p. 545).

[127]Some authors, for example, criticize that Eisenhardt's case studies will always remain somewhat superficial as they lack context considerations—in contrast to thorough single case studies. Cf. Piekkari et al. (2009, pp. 571–572), for a deeper elaboration on this matter.

[128]Low internal validity casts doubt upon causal conclusions; cf. Sect. 4.1.2.

can be identified in others as well.[129] In other words, the following analysis tries to find similarities with regard to escalation of commitment across the cases of DaimlerChrysler and Steiff in China. It is the assumption that the different phases of the three-stage-model of the escalation process of Staw and Ross can be identified as a recurring pattern for both of the chosen cases.[130] Finally, the quality of the analysis is enhanced by triangulation, i.e., by the usage of multiple sources of information, which should contribute to the construct validity of the study.[131]

Yet, what are the sources of information that have been consulted for the following analysis? Conventionally, interviews are the most dominant data source in case study research, especially in the field of international business.[132] Other insights, however, such as group discussions, observations, and public documents, can provide an equally fruitful basis for case study research.[133] The present analysis of the cases of DaimlerChrysler and Steiff in China is primarily built around a structured revision of news articles concerning these companies. For this purpose, the five most circulated and relevant financial as well as business newspapers from Germany have been screened for the search terms 'DaimlerChrysler' and 'Steiff' (cf. Table 4.17). In March and April of 2016, the newspapers were accessed with the 'wiso database' of the provider GBI-Genios, which claims to provide the largest (electronic) gathering of German literature in the fields of economics and social sciences.[134] The screening concentrated on financial and business newspapers from Germany because this is where the two firms under consideration have (or have had, respectively) their headquarters. Admittedly, this procedure could bear the risk of an ethnocentric, German perspective. The media coverage on the merger of Daimler-Benz and Chrysler, for example, differed sometimes quite significantly in Germany and in the USA. In order to compensate for this risk, the present study reflects critically on the search results and takes an objective position. In effect, this means that news articles, which scrutinized the German position and which reported the US-American position, were included in the case analysis with particular attention.

Certainly, the search term screening concentrated on specific periods of time. For the case of DaimlerChrysler, the timeframe under consideration was from 1997 until 2008 (i.e., 1 year prior to the merger until 1 year after the disintegration).[135] For the case of Steiff in China, the data collection worked equivalently. Here the period under investigation was from 2003 until 2009 (because the company maintained its production line in China between 2004 and 2008). The screening

---

[129] Cf. Miles et al. (2014, p. 250).

[130] Cf. Sect. 3.3.5 for an overview of the three-stage model.

[131] For further information regarding the evaluation criteria for the quality of case study research designs, cf. Yin (2014, pp. 45 ff.), Maxwell (2013, pp. 121 ff.), and Pauwels and Matthyssens (2004, pp. 128–132).

[132] Cf. Piekkari et al. (2009, p. 581).

[133] Cf. Patton (2015, p. 14) and Grbich (2013, p. 123).

[134] Cf. Wiso (2016).

[135] The online achieve of FOCUS-MONEY, however, only stretches back until the year 2000.

Table 4.17 Ranking of the most circulated financial and business newspapers in Germany for the first quarter of 2016

Rank	Name	Paid circulation
1	Der Steuerzahler[a]	242,868
2	Guter Rat[b]	161,122
3	VDI Nachrichten[c]	153,600
4	**Capital**	**134,391**
5	**Wirtschaftswoche**	**125,450**
6	**FOCUS-MONEY**	**123,798**
7	**Handelsblatt**	**123,739**
8	**manager magazin**	**104,810**
9	brand eins	95,670
10	Euro	86,211

Source: Statista (2016)
[a]Published by the interest group '*Bund der Steuerzahler*' (Association of Taxpayers) and has therefore been excluded from the analysis
[b]Consumer magazine; has therefore been excluded from the analysis
[c]Published by the interest group '*Verein Deutscher Ingenieure*' (Association of German Engineers) and has therefore been excluded from the analysis

yielded 7677 articles on DaimlerChrysler and 65 on Steiff in China. Ultimately, 123 articles were 'directly relevant' for the former case, whereas 15 articles were pertinent for the latter (cf. Fig. 4.17).[136] Articles were considered to be 'directly relevant' for the case study, if the title or the first three sentences gave reason to believe that the text dealt specifically with the merger of DaimlerChrysler or, respectively, with the offshoring decision of Steiff. This was a necessary measure as not all articles on DaimlerChrysler as well as on Steiff covered topics relevant to the respective internationalization decisions. For example, articles that merely reported quarterly numbers or new product releases were left aside. The large discrepancy of published articles between the two cases is explained by the significantly higher media coverage on the publically listed DaimlerChrysler in comparison to the limited Margarete Steiff, which is a good example of the German *Mittelstand* (i.e., medium-sized companies).

As stated above, triangulation is applied in order to enhance the quality of the present analysis. Triangulation describes the simultaneous consultation of different data sources and the convergence of insights in order to ensure the consistency of one's findings.[137] Besides the structured analysis of relevant news articles, the annual reports of DaimlerChrysler AG serve as an additional data source for the first case. For the case of Margarete Steiff GmbH, an interview has been conducted with a senior management

[136]Cf. the appendix of the present study for a comprehensive list of the consulted newspaper articles.

[137]Cf. Yin (2014, p. 241) and Jick (1979, p. 602). Besides the combination of data sources for the qualitative-empirical analysis, one could furthermore consider the blending of a quantitative and a qualitative research method as a form of triangulation.

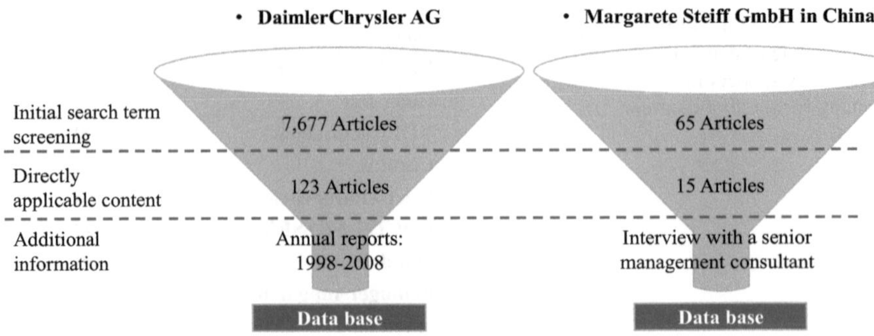

Fig. 4.17 Data base for the cases under analysis. Source: Own figure

consultant, who worked on behalf of the advisory board of the firm during the respective time frame under consideration.[138] The interview was structured in 12 questions, lasted about 1.5 h, and was electronically recorded on site. At the time under investigation, the interviewee provided support for the development of a new corporate strategy and had extensive insights into the decision-making processes of the management at the manufacturer of plush toys. He preferred to remain anonymous.

4.3.2 Description of the Cases

In order to conduct the cross case discussion, the present section will, as a first step, present both cases individually. For this purpose, the selected articles were read, substantiated with the additionally consulted sources, and summarized with regard to the research problem of the present study. The result will be documented in the following two sections. Section 4.3.2.1 presents the merger of Daimler-Benz and Chrysler. Section 4.3.2.2 provides the case of the production offshoring by Steiff to China. Based on the data material under consideration, the respective backgrounds will be reported in-depth in chronological order. Only subsequently, in Sect. 4.3.3, the cases will be compared and searched for a unifying and underlying pattern of escalation of commitment. A comprehensive list of the consulted newspaper articles, the source for the two cases under analysis, can be found in the appendix of the present study.

[138] As Steiff is a firm with limited liability, it does not need to publish extensive annual reports. The legally required financial statement of the firm is very limited with regard to its content and is thus not specifically listed here.

4.3.2.1 Merger of Daimler-Benz and Chrysler (1998–2007)

The merger of the German Daimler-Benz AG and the US-American Chrysler corporation presented the largest transatlantic pooling of businesses at the time and fell into a period that is sometimes strikingly referred to as 'merger-mania' today. Both firms aimed at further international development with the merger and, therefore, the step can be considered as a part of their respective internationalization processes. Under the supervision of the chairman of the Daimler-Benz executive board Jürgen Schrempp and the Chrysler CEO Robert Eaton, the shares of DaimlerChrysler AG became publicly listed by November 17th, 1998. The merger constituted the world's third largest automotive manufacturer and was largely met with universal acclaim, while there were only few skeptical voices. Chrysler had to cope often with significant competitive challenges throughout much of its history, but the company had its 'golden years' from 1983 to 1988 as well as from 1993 to 1998. These years were largely connected with the responsibility of Lee Iacocca, who served as Chrysler CEO from 1978 to 1992. He led the company out of the dire straits of the 1970s (in 1979 the firm was even saved by a government bailout) and hired Bob Lutz as the head for the global product development branch, who subsequently introduced successful models such as the firm's minivans and SUVs. By 1998, Chrysler was in an excellent position in North America in terms of sales numbers, yet in a weak spot globally. In retrospect, one can still say that Chrysler reached its competitive peak by the time of the merger with Daimler-Benz. Its German partner, primarily known for its core brand Mercedes-Benz, has undergone some strategic shifts in the time prior to the merger, but it has also proven to be a steady source for economic growth.[139] When Jürgen Schrempp's predecessor Edzard Reuter took over office in 1987, he was following the vision of turning Daimler-Benz into a diversified 'integrated technology group'. The corporation had significant liquidity and purchased a diverse portfolio of companies, such as electrical equipment producer AEG and aircraft manufacturers Dornier and Fokker. The 'integrated technology group' aimed at a diversification of risks and at the development of additional core competencies. By 1995, however, it became clear that the vision of the 'integrated technology group' did not hold its promises and Jürgen Schrempp took over control at Daimler-Benz. He, in return, not only reversed much of the 'integrated technology group', but he also had his very own vision for the firm. Schrempp wanted to turn Daimler-Benz into a global corporation, the so-called '*Welt AG*'. The target was to concentrate the corporation on its automotive core competency and to acquire international competitors in order to become ideally positioned for global competition. This has also been the subtext and the intention behind the merger with Chrysler. Financially, Daimler-Benz was well off. The final stand-alone annual report of the carmaker in 1997 reported a year-on-year growth of operating profit by 79% and a net income of 3.2 billion DM (which corresponded to a year-on-year growth rate of 15%).[140] Thus, both

[139]Cf. Kobrak and Oesterle (1999, pp. 70–76), for a concise yet thorough history of Daimler-Benz.

[140]Cf. Daimler-Benz (1998, Annual Report, p. 2).

firms—Daimler-Benz as well as Chrysler—were in relatively comfortable competitive positions by 1998.

What Have Been the Objectives Behind the Merger Decision?
Against the background of the good market positions that both companies possessed by the time of the merger, analysts and shareholders largely approved the plan to bring both car manufacturers together. One supporting argument was that both companies were well matched due to Chrysler's strong position in North America and Daimler-Benz's foothold in Europe. Vice versa, the American firm saw growth potentials in Europe and the Germans had room to develop in North America. Furthermore, analysts saw a significant potential to realize synergies. The joint usage of production capacities for the M-Class and for the Jeep Grand Cherokee, for example, provided the chance of savings in the three-digit range.[141] Further cost benefits were forecasted due to the usage of standard spare parts as well as due to a higher purchasing power of the merged group. Overall, industry pundits considered five billion DM to be a conservative estimate as the total sum of cost advantages.[142] In consideration of these optimistic voices, it is not much of a surprise to see that analysts issued recommendations to buy the newly listed DaimlerChrysler share and to see that shareholders largely agreed. In 1998, Dieter Kauffmann, who spoke for the association for the protection of private shareholders ('*Schutzgemeinschaft der Kleinaktionäre*'), declared himself in favor of the merger by saying that "they (n.b., the merging firms) turn the entire world into the marketplace of their cars".[143] According to DaimlerChrysler's annual report for 1998, 97.5% of Chrysler shareholders and 99.9% of Daimler-Benz shareholders agreed to the merger.[144] In the annual report, the company gave furthermore a precise objective concerning the project. The management wanted to turn the joint corporation into the world's most successful and renowned producer for cars, transportation products, and services by 2001. In 1999, the Handelsblatt newspaper reported that DaimlerChrysler sought to double its turnover within 10 years.[145] Skeptics, who expressed concern that the reputation of the Mercedes-Benz brand would have been damaged with the merger, were largely unheard. Earlier, however, Jürgen Schrempp admitted that he saw a challenge in merging two corporate cultures, yet he remained optimistic.[146]

What Happened Subsequently to the Merger Decision?
The first annual result of DaimlerChrysler was quite promising. The operating profit grew by 38% (relative to the numbers of both firms separately in 1997) and reached 8.6 billion euros.[147] The initial euphoria, however, soon passed and gave way to

---

[141]Cf. Handelsblatt (1999, Issue 100, p. 19) (cf. Appendix).

[142]Cf. Handelsblatt (1999, Issue 115, p. i03) (cf. Appendix).

[143]Handelsblatt (1998, Issue 101, p. 15) (cf. Appendix).

[144]Cf. DaimlerChrysler (1999, p. 11), Annual Report.

[145]Cf. Handelsblatt (1999, Issue 95, p. 1) (cf. Appendix).

[146]Cf. Handelsblatt (1998, Issue 101, p. 15) (cf. Appendix).

[147]Cf. DaimlerChrysler (1999, p. 2), Annual Report.

some more realistic voices, which highlighted the fact that the merger came with challenges at an institutional level. For example, two largely different legal systems needed to be integrated and the executive board had to be thinned out. By 1999, some observers recognized that the integration at DaimlerChrysler did not proceed as planned—contrary to repeated confirmations of Schrempp.[148] While some synergies were indeed quickly realized—especially for the procurement of the group—day-to-day difficulties needed to be confronted. Factually, Daimler and Chrysler continued to be separate entities in the eyes of its employees. Not least, this had to do with the large geographical distances that needed to be overcome between Auburn Hills in Michigan and Stuttgart in Germany (i.e., the firms' headquarters). Much of the decision power resided in Stuttgart, which contributed to an exodus of important Chrysler figureheads such as the already mentioned Bob Lutz and design-chief Thomas Gale. One could speculate that many of the top managers left willingly as they received a 'golden handshake'. Yet besides the top management, large fractions of Chrysler's development and design divisions also left for Ford and General Motors between 1998 and 2000. In addition, a fierce discount battle hit the North American market around the turn of the millennium. Subsequently, the previously very successful Chrysler branch slipped into 'red numbers' by the second half of 2000. Furthermore, the market share of DaimlerChrysler in North America dropped from 16.2% in 1998 to 13% in 2002.[149] By 2001, DaimlerChrysler fell some way short of its initial target to become the world's most successful and renowned producer for cars. Instead, the Chrysler division stumbled in the area between small profits and losses throughout the next few years (cf. Fig. 4.18). DaimlerChrysler reacted to this development with a series of turnaround programs.

Against the background of this development, the positive acclaim of shareholders and analysts for the merger of Daimler-Benz and Chrysler vanished entirely during the years between 2000 and 2005. It became more and more clear that "the merger of equals" (according to Schrempp and Eaton in 1998)[150] was more of an acquisition. By 2000, analysts began to call openly for a split-up of DaimlerChrysler and argued that a 'divorce' would be the most painless solution to the difficulties of the automotive manufacturer. DaimlerChrysler, however, was far from ready to give up on the vision of the global corporation at that time. In 2003, Schrempp argued against most indicators that DaimlerChrysler was splendidly positioned in the global automotive market. According to him, the corporation offered clearly defined brands for all market segments from small city cars to large trucks.[151] Schrempp stated furthermore that the vision of the global corporation had the support of the supervisory board and the employees of the firm. From today's perspective, he might not even have been wrong with this statement to a certain extent. When asked whether he still believed in the '*Welt AG*', Hilmar Kopper, chairman of the supervisory board

[148]Cf. manager magazin (1999, Issue 10, p. 12) (cf. Appendix).

[149]Cf. Wirtschaftswoche (2002, Issue 3, p. 44) (cf. Appendix).

[150]manager magazin (1998, Issue 9, p. 68) (cf. Appendix).

[151]Cf. manager magazin (2003, Issue 11, p. 58) (cf. Appendix).

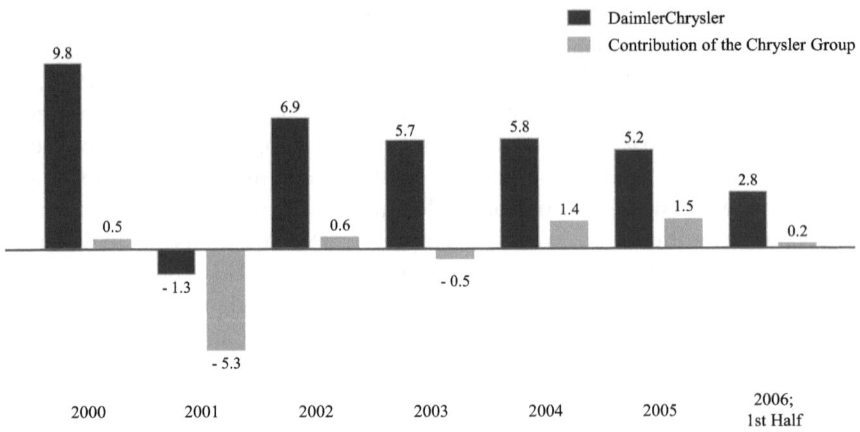

Fig. 4.18 Operating profit of DaimlerChrysler in billion euros. Source: Handelsblatt (2006, Issue 182, p. 13)

of DaimlerChrysler at the time, answered that he was very much convinced and that the firm was well positioned globally.[152] Dieter Zetsche, who was appointed CEO of Chrysler in 2000 and who chairs Daimler's executive board today, was convinced that the promises of the merger would have been fulfilled by 2004.[153] This benevolent view was also—at least implicitly—reflected in the annual reports of the firm. While these documents gave significant attention to the integration efforts shortly after the merger decision, the annual reports rarely covered this topic specifically in the 2000s. Investors, however, disagreed with the development of the firm. The share price fell considerably from about 85 € in the first quarter of 1999 to about 27 € in the second quarter of 2003 (cf. Fig. 4.19). At the time, the Handelsblatt newspaper compared the merger of Daimler-Benz and Chrysler with the flight of Icarus from ancient Greek mythology.[154]

The tide only turned in 2005 at DaimlerChrysler when Schrempp stepped down. He was substituted by the former head of Chrysler, Dieter Zetsche, who was praised for his crisis management in the USA. But when the American branch was yet again in dire straits in 2006 and 2007, it was he who decided to sell Chrysler to Cerberus Capital Management (in 2007). The disintegration was welcomed by shareholders, and the stock price recovered. Based on the data material under consideration, one could conclude that the history of DaimlerChrysler is largely a story of failure and misunderstandings. During the merger period, Chrysler rarely contributed profits to the corporation. At the same time, a total of 16 production plants were closed and a third of the Chrysler workforce lost their jobs. One should not only reduce this poor development to the competitive disadvantages of Chrysler. Flawed decisions were

[152]Cf. Wirtschaftswoche (2003, Issue 8, p. 80) (cf. Appendix).

[153]Cf. Handelsblatt (2004, Issue 177, p. 11) (cf. Appendix).

[154]Cf. Handelsblatt (2007, Issue 33, p. 1) (cf. Appendix).

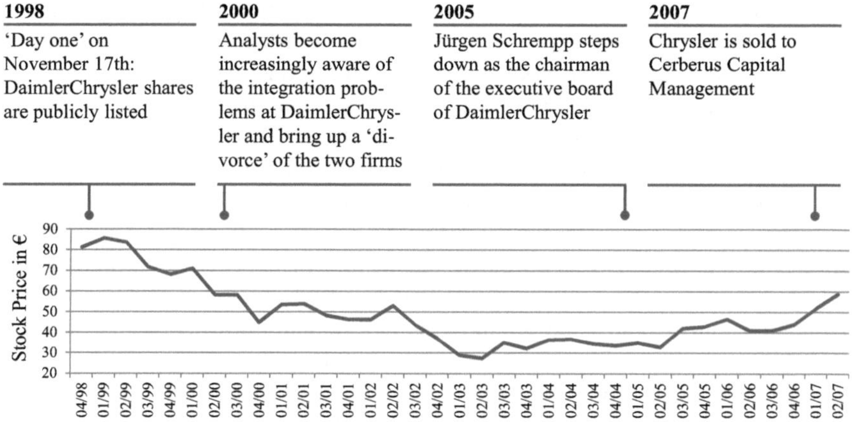

Fig. 4.19 Merger period of DaimlerChrysler and the development of the stock price. Source: Own figure

also taken in Stuttgart, and they contributed to the disappointing turnout of the merger. Much of this, however, was already clear in 2000. Nevertheless, the management of DaimlerChrysler persisted with its course of action for several years until 2007.

4.3.2.2 Production Offshoring to China by Margarete Steiff GmbH (2004–2008)

The family-owned firm Steiff is commonly known for its exquisite plush toys in the high price segment, which enjoy global popularity as collectibles. It is sometimes overlooked, however, that the firm also operates the subsidiary 'ALLIGATOR Ventilfabrik GmbH' (hereafter 'ALLIGATOR') since 1921, which produces valves for all kinds of tires. The toy manufacturer 'Margarete Steiff GmbH' (hereafter 'Margarete Steiff') and ALLIGATOR are pooled under the roof of the holding company 'Steiff Beteiligungsgesellschaft mbH' (hereafter 'Steiff'). As a company with limited liability, Steiff is not required to report financial results for both companies separately. It does, however, disclose the sales figures for toys and valves respectively, which allow for an assumption of the relative importance of Margarete Steiff and ALLIGATOR for the group. According to the reports, Steiff has seen a gradual sales decline in toys from 42.0 million euros in 2006 to 37.8 million euros in 2014. At the same time, however, valve sales increased from 45.9 million euros in 2006 to 62.6 million euros in 2014. These numbers highlight the difficult situation of Margarete Steiff.[155] At the beginning of the century, Steiff

[155] Cf. manager magazin (2006, Issue 8, p. 50) (cf. Appendix).

became increasingly exposed to the fierce price competition in the global toy industry. The sales volumes of the firm's famous plush toys were stagnating and customers preferred cheaper products, which were frequently manufactured in East Asia. At that time, Richard Hussmanns, who was managing director at Steiff (from 2000 to 2007) as well as at Margarete Steiff (from 2001 to 2002 and in 2005), acknowledged that the firm was exposed to severe predatory competition, creating a situation of financial crisis. According to the senior management consultant, who was interviewed for the present case, Steiff's revenue situation deteriorated dramatically at that time. It was primarily thanks to ALLIGATOR that Steiff kept its head above water. The company reacted to this development by appointing Friedhelm Brandau and Uwe Kleinow as new managing directors at Margarete Steiff. The new management took two measures in order to improve the competitive situation of the toy manufacturer. First, the firm decided to diversify its operations via licensing. For example, apparel for children, baby care products, and school supplies were sold under the brand name of Margarete Steiff. Second, the toy manufacturer introduced the product line 'cosy friends', which ought to be produced in East Asia.[156] Against this background, Steiff offshored its manufacturing in 2004 and it began to rely on production partners in China.

What Have Been the Objectives Behind the Offshoring Decision?
Under the pressure of the severe cost competition in the toy industry, Friedhelm Brandau and Uwe Kleinow aimed at lower manufacturing costs particularly with regard to the firm's personnel. The idea was to offer the 'cosy friends' line as a much more attractive option to a cost-sensible clientship. Due to the offshoring of its production to China, Margarete Steiff provided an entry level of about 15 € per toy. In comparison, the traditional Steiff toys that were produced in Portugal, Tunisia, and Germany cost at least 59 €. Until then, production in China was considered unthinkable for the tradition-conscious firm. The decision to move the production line to China was therefore controversial among the owners as well as among the management of the holding, not least because the 'cosy friends' plush toys were primarily made of synthetics and followed a less classic design in comparison to the Margarete Steiff originals. Like many other Western industrial companies, however, the Margarete Steiff management under Brandau and Kleinow considered the offshoring of its manufacturing to be the best answer to the global competition in the toy industry at the time and enforced the new strategy.[157]

What Happened Subsequently to the Offshoring Decision?
According to the consulted interviewee, Margarete Steiff was immediately confronted with the disadvantages of offshore production processes in China in the form of a deficient product quality and long delivery times. The firm realized that the Chinese production partners did not implement the very specific production requirements for its toys as planned, and that they still needed substantial training in order to

[156]Cf. manager magazin (2006, Issue 8, p. 50) (cf. Appendix).
[157]Cf. Handelsblatt (2006, Issue 5, p. 4) (cf. Appendix).

fulfill the high quality standards of Margarete Steiff. Furthermore, coordination between the Margarete Steiff site in Germany and its production partners in China was as much of a challenge as the air cargo costs, which grew significantly. Last but not least, the 'Made in China' line was diluting the high quality perception that Margarete Steiff products commonly enjoyed globally. Based on the data material under consideration, one can state that these experiences are no exception among industrial firms from the Western World that produce in countries shaped by lower production costs. Other German companies with similarly negative experiences abroad include the manufacturer of handheld power equipments Stihl and the producer of kitchen utilities and bathroom furniture Fackelmann, for example.[158] Thus, it is fair to say that many of the problems of Margarete Steiff in China were already known before the management decided to implement its offshoring plan, and that they became even more apparent when the manufacturing processes abroad were finally enacted. Margarete Steiff attempted to control these issues by sending its own quality managers to the production plants in China, but this measure had no significant effect.

Despite this unfavorable development, Margarete Steiff waited until 2008 to announce the recall of its production. The question is why it took the firm so long to draw this conclusion. The consulted interview partner, who worked closely with the managements of the holding as well as of Margarete Steiff, argued that Brandau and Kleinow were more assertive than the management of the holding around Richard Hussmanns—especially before the offshoring plan was implemented. According to his opinion, earlier withdrawal would have been possible, but with increasing purchasing obligations in China a strategic turnaround became difficult. Furthermore, the new capacities in China have also led to a smaller production output in the company's former manufacturing sites in Portugal, Tunisia, and Germany. Therefore, a withdrawal became increasingly difficult once the offshore plan was implemented. As a consequence, opposition within Margarete Steiff declined. The middle management, for example, backed the strategic direction of the top management, on the surface at least. The development of the firm, however, led to a conflict between the management of the holding on the one side and Brandau and Kleinow on the other. As part of this conflict, the two managers did not shy away from keeping external consultants from creating more transparency of Margarete Steiff's production processes. The course of action only changed once the management of the toy manufacturer was replaced. In 2006, Martin Frechen became the new managing director at Margarete Steiff. In 2008, the firm withdrew its production from China.

[158]Also management studies are becoming increasingly aware of this issue and cover the re-integration and backshoring of production processes of firms in the context of, for example, lacking market information as well as poor product quality abroad (cf. Foerstl et al. (2016, pp. 492 ff.) and Dost (2014, p. 22.). Researchers of the Fraunhofer Institute estimated that one out of four to six offshoring decisions is reversed within 4 years (cf. Kinkel and Maloca (2009, p. 154).

4.3.3 Comparative Case Discussion

Considering their negative outcome, the two presented cases certainly highlight the circumstances in which internationalization processes can fail. Yet it is also a question of whether they allow for an assessment of the impact of the forces of escalation of commitment. In order to answer this question, the present section will, as a first step, attempt to diagnose the display of the three stages of the escalation process of Staw and Ross as a common decision-making pattern for both cases.[159] If diagnosed correctly, this should not only illustrate the research topic in a concrete manner, but it should also further substantiate the analysis of the first hypothesis of the present study. Thereafter, the implications of psychic distance and establishment chain progress will be addressed against the background of the presented cases and in the context of the second and third hypotheses.[160]

During the first stage of a process of escalation of commitment, decision-makers are commonly confronted with project economics that allow for an objective evaluation of the decision alternatives.[161] In the case of the merger of Daimler-Benz and Chrysler, the respective managements around Jürgen Schrempp and Robert Eaton had good reason to argue in favor of the decision to pool both businesses. Despite the opinion of a limited number of skeptics both automotive manufacturers seemed to complement each other fairly well (on the surface at least), given the significant growth potential of Chrysler in Europe and of Daimler-Benz in North-America. Likewise at Margarete Steiff, the decision to lower the manufacturing costs via offshoring to China did not seem unreasonable considering the difficult revenue situation of the firm. Thus, for both cases one could argue that the respective internationalization decisions were in a way supported by project economics.

In the second stage of an escalation process, decision-makers are confronted with questionable or negative results. Yet, these setbacks do not lead to a change of the decision-making path because psychological and social forces for persistence, such as self-justification and face-saving, result in a denial of the factual circumstances.[162] By 2001, DaimlerChrysler had missed its self-set targets clearly; a fact that was also reflected in the collapse of the stock price over the following years. This gives reason to assume that project economics turned negative. The management around Schrempp, however, seemed to be in a state of denial as it continuously stressed (inaccurately) the good market position of the firm. Quite similarly at Margarete Steiff, project economics turned negative due to the deficient quality of the products that were manufactured in China and due to the long delivery times. The management around Brandau and Kleinow, however, ignored this issue. It even hindered efforts to create more transparency regarding the manufacturing

[159] Cf. Sect. 3.3.5 for an overview of the three-stage model of escalation of commitment.

[160] Cf. Sect. 3.3.7 for an overview of the hypotheses of the present study.

[161] Cf. Sect. 3.3.4.1.

[162] Cf. Sects. 3.3.4.2 and 3.3.4.3.

processes. Thus, the events at DaimlerChrysler and Margarete Steiff resemble the second stage of Staw's and Ross's three-stage abstraction of an escalation process to some extent.

Their model foresees furthermore structural forces of persistence as a third stage. This means that the failing course of action is somewhat institutionalized in the organization and that it is advocated by multiple decision-making bodies.[163] In the case of DaimlerChrysler, members of the supervisory and executive board stated their support for the vision of the global corporation as well as for the merger of the two firms repeatedly. Furthermore, the annual reports did not specifically discuss the integration efforts any longer after a few years. All of this indicates a certain level of acceptance of the merger within the corporation. Similarly at Margarete Steiff, the management did not face much opposition once the offshoring decision was actually carried out. Purchasing obligations and less production output in the firm's older manufacturing sites in Portugal, Tunisia, and Germany contributed particularly to an increased structural commitment. Admittedly, however, there is also room to question the structural support in the cases of DaimlerChrysler and Margarete Steiff. In both firms there has been sufficient controversy around the corresponding internationalization steps. Primarily, this was on the accounts of the shareholders (at DaimlerChrysler) and of the holding management (at Margarete Steiff). Hence, there are arguments in support and in contradiction to the view that the third stage of Staw's and Ross's model is reflected in the two cases. Yet overall, a certain equivalency between the theoretical model and the two cases is hard to oversee. This allows for the conclusion that escalation of commitment is indeed a matter to consider in internationalization process reality.

Yet what information do the cases provide concerning the implications of psychic distance and establishment chain progress in the context of escalation of commitment in internationalization process decision-making? In Sect. 3.3.7.2, it has been hypothesized that managerial decision-makers, who are under escalation of commitment, will increasingly diverge from the logic of rational choices with an increasing psychic distance to targeted markets. Psychic distance is the "the sum of factors preventing the flow of information from and to the market"[164] and results from differences in language, education, business practices, culture, and industrial development. One could certainly say that the internationalization steps of DaimlerChrysler and of Margarete Steiff presented significant challenges in terms of psychic distance. To a certain extent, the experiences of the two firms indicate the difficulties that arise when highly committed decision-makers have to cope with internationalization decisions in a context of high psychic distance (despite the circumstance that the psychic distance between Germany and the USA is smaller than the psychic distance between Germany and China). For example, in the case of DaimlerChrysler, it was underestimated how the shift of the decision-making power to Stuttgart in Germany (and therefore also the shift of management style

[163]Cf. Sect. 3.3.4.4.

[164]Johanson and Vahlne (1977, p. 24).

presumably) affected the employees in Auburn Hills in Michigan (a matter that ultimately led to the exodus of important figureheads of the Chrysler staff). Similarly in the case of Margarete Steiff, the manufacturing circumstances in China were not sufficiently taken into account. Nevertheless, it is difficult to conduct a fruitful comparison between the two firms. As both of the cases are examples of committed decision-makers in a context of high psychic distance, they allow only for a limited conclusion regarding an interaction effect of psychic distance and escalation of commitment.

Furthermore, it has been stated that managerial decision-makers, who are under escalation of commitment, will increasingly converge towards the logic of rational choices with an increasing establishment chain progress. Here as well, only a limited statement is possible considering that both firms were substantially committed to their international course of action. Certainly, however, the examples showcase the difficulty of decision-makers to withdraw from internationalization paths once significant resource-committing actions (such as the here presented merger or the offshoring decision) have been carried out. Overall, one can conclude that the qualitative-empirical study served its purpose as it illustrated the quantitative-empirical results in international business reality. The cases of DaimlerChrysler as well as of Margarete Steiff provide a reasonable insight into escalation of commitment in actual internationalization processes beyond the theoretical statistical analysis of the previous section, and they underline the relevance of this topic for business reality.

References

Angerer, T., Foscht, T., & Swoboda, B. (2006). Mixed Methods – Ein neuerer Zugang in der empirischen Marketingforschung. *der markt, 45*(3), 115–127.

Ayres, L., Kavanaugh, K., & Knafl, K. A. (2003). Within-case and across-case approaches to qualitative data analysis. *Qualitative Health Research, 13*(6), 871–883.

Backhaus, K., Erichson, B., Plinke, W., & Weiber, R. (2011). *Mulivariate Analysemethoden* (13th ed.). Heidelberg: Springer.

Baxter, P., & Jack, S. (2008). Qualitative case study methodology: Study design and implementation for novice researchers. *The Qualitative Report, 13*(4), 544–559.

Bianchi, C. C., & Ostale, E. (2006). Lessons learned from unsuccessful internationalization attempts: Examples of multinational retailers in Chile. *Journal of Business Research, 59*(1), 140–147.

Blanco Ramírez, G. (2016). Case studies. In C. Marshall & G. B. Rossman (Eds.), *Designing qualitative research* (6th ed., pp. 19–20). London: Sage.

Bortz, J., & Döring, N. (2006). *Forschungsmethoden und Evaluation für Human- und Sozialwissenschaftler* (4th ed.). Heidelberg: Springer.

Brake, A. (2009). Schriftliche Befragung. In S. Kühl, P. Strodtholz, & A. Taffertshofer (Eds.), *Handbuch Methoden der Organisationsforschung* (pp. 392–412). Wiesbaden: VS Verlag für Sozialwissenschaften.

Buckley, P. J., Devinney, T. M., & Louviere, J. J. (2007). Do managers behave the way theory suggests? A choice-theoretic examination of foreign direct investment location decision-making. *Journal of International Business Studies, 38*(7), 1069–1094.

Camerer, C. F., & Hogarth, R. M. (1999). The effects of financial incentives in experiments: A review and capital-labor-production framework. *Journal of Risk and Uncertainty, 19*(1–3), 7–42.

Cameron, R., & Molina-Azorin, J. F. (2011). The acceptance of mixed methods in business and management research. *International Journal of Organizational Analysis, 19*(3), 256–271.

Campbell, D. T., & Stanley, J. C. (1963). *Experimental and quasi-experimental designs for research*. Chicago: Rand McNally.

Creswell, J. W. (2010). Mapping the developing landscape of mixed methods research. In A. Tashakkori & C. Teddlie (Eds.), *SAGE handbook of mixed methods in social and behavioral research* (2nd ed., pp. 45–68). Thousand Oaks: Sage.

Creswell, J. W. (2014). *Research design: Qualitative, quantitative and mixed methods approaches* (4th ed.). Thousand Oaks: Sage.

Creswell, J. W., & Plano Clark, V. L. (2011). *Designing and conducting mixed methods research* (2nd ed.). Thousand Oaks: Sage.

Daimler-Benz. (1998). *Annual report*. Accessed January 7, 2017, from https://www.daimler.com/dokumente/investoren/berichte/geschaeftsberichte/daimler-benz/daimler-ir-geschaefts-bericht-1997.pdf

DaimlerChrysler. (1999). *Annual report*. Accessed January 7, 2017, from https://www.daimler.com/dokumente/investoren/berichte/geschaeftsberichte/daimlerchrysler/daimler-ir-geschaefts-bericht-1998.pdf

Dobbins, G. H., Lane, I. M., & Steiner, D. D. (1988). A note on the role of laboratory methodologies in applied behavioural research: Don't throw out the baby with the bath water. *Journal of Organizational Behavior, 9*(3), 281–286.

Dost, J. R. (2014). *Produktionsverlagerungen deutscher Unternehmen nach China: Eine neo-institutionalistische Perspektive*. Lohmar: Josef Eul Verlag.

Eisenhardt, K. M. (1989). Building theories from case study research. *Academy of Management Review, 14*(4), 532–550.

Eisenhardt, K. M., & Graebner, M. E. (2007). Theory building from cases: Opportunities and challenges. *Academy of Management Journal, 50*(1), 25–32.

Eisenhardt, K. M., & Zbaracki, M. J. (1992). Strategic decision making. *Strategic Management Journal, 13*(S2), 17–37.

Eschweiler, M., Evanschitzky, H., & Woisetschläger, D. (2007). *Laborexperimente in der Marketingwissenschaft: Bestandsaufnahme und Leitfaden bei varianzanalytischen Auswertungen* (Working Paper No. 45). Förderkreis für Industriegütermarketing e.V. an der Westfälischen Wilhelms-Universität Münster (Ed.).

Falk, A., & Heckman, J. J. (2009). Lab experiments are a major source of knowledge in the social sciences. *Science, 326*(5952), 535–538.

Fisch, J. H., & Oesterle, M. -J. (2003). Exploring the globalization of German MNCs with the complex spread and diversity measure. *Schmalenbach Business Review, 55*(1), 2–21.

Fisher, R. A. (1966). *The design of experiments* (8th ed.). New York: Hafner.

Flyvbjerg, B. (2011). Case study. In N. K. Denzin & Y. S. Lincoln (Eds.), *The SAGE handbook of qualitative research* (4th ed., pp. 301–316). Thousand Oaks: Sage.

Foerstl, K., Kirchoff, J. F., & Bals, L. (2016). Reshoring and insourcing: Drivers and future research directions. *International Journal of Physical Distribution and Logistics Management, 46*(5), 492–515.

Forsgren, M. (2002). The concept of learning in the Uppsala internationalization process model: A critical review. *International Business Review, 11*(3), 257–277.

Gerring, J. (2007). *Case study research: Principles and practices*. Cambridge: Cambridge University Press.

Grbich, C. (2013). *Qualitative data analysis* (2nd ed.). London: Sage.

Gulati, R. (2007). Tent poles, tribalism, and boundary spanning: The rigor-relevance debate in management research. *Academy of Management Journal, 50*(4), 775–782.

Hair, J. F., Black, W. C., Babin, B. J., & Anderson, R. E. (2010). *Multivariate data analysis* (7th ed.). Upper Saddle River: Pearson Education.

Homburg, C. (2012). *Marketingmanagement. Strategie – Instrumente – Umsetzung – Unternehmensführung* (4th ed.). Wiesbaden: Gabler.

Huber, F., Meyer, F., & Lenzen, M. (2014). *Grundlagen der Varianzanalyse*. Wiesbaden: Gabler.

Hurmerinta-Peltomäki, L., & Nummela, N. (2006). Mixed methods in international business research: A value-added perspective. *Management International Review, 46*(4), 439–459.

Hutzschenreuter, T., Pedersen, T., & Volberda, H. W. (2007). The role of path dependency and managerial intentionality: A perspective on international business research. *Journal of International Business Studies, 38*(7), 1055–1068.

Jick, T. D. (1979). Mixing qualitative and quantitative methods: Triangulation in action. *Administrative Science Quarterly, 24*(4), 602–611.

Johanson, J., & Vahlne, J.-E. (1977). The internationalization process of the firm – A model of knowledge development and increasing foreign market commitments. *Journal of International Business Studies, 8*(1), 23–32.

Johnson, R. B., & Onwuegbuzie, A. J. (2004). Mixed methods research: A research paradigm whose time has come. *Educational Researcher, 33*(7), 14–26.

Johnson, R. B., Onwuegbuzie, A. J., & Turner, L. A. (2007). Toward a definition of mixed methods research. *Journal of Mixed Methods Research, 1*(2), 112–133.

Keselman, H. J., Huberty, C. J., Lix, L. M., Olejnik, S., Cribbie, R. A., Donahue, B., et al. (1998). Statistical practices of educational researchers: An analysis of their ANOVA, MANOVA, and ANCOVA analyses. *Review of Educational Research, 68*(3), 350–386.

Kinkel, S., & Maloca, S. (2009). Drivers and antecedents of manufacturing offshoring and backshoring – A German perspective. *Journal of Purchasing and Supply Management, 15*(3), 154–165.

Kobrak, C., & Oesterle, M.-J. (1999). Nationalism and internationalism in corporate governance: The case of Daimier Chrysler. In *Entreprises et Histoire* (Vol. 21, pp. 70–89).

Kühl, S. (2009). Experiment. In S. Kühl, P. Strodtholz, & A. Taffertshofer (Eds.), *Handbuch Methoden der Organisationsforschung* (pp. 534–557). Wiesbaden: VS Verlag für Sozialwissenschaften.

Kuhn, T. S. (2012). *The structure of scientific revolutions*. Chicago: University of Chicago Press.

Langer, T. (2007). Experimentelle Forschung. In R. Köhler, H.-U. Küpper, & A. Pfingsten (Eds.), *Handwörterbuch der Betriebswirtschaft* (col. 421–430). Stuttgart: Schäffer-Poeschel.

Lawrence, B. S. (1997). Perspective – The black box of organizational demography. *Organization Science, 8*(1), 1–22.

Leigh, J. H., & Kinnear, T. C. (1980). On interaction classification. *Educational and Psychological Measurement, 40*(4), 841–843.

Leonard-Barton, D. (1990). A dual methodology for case studies: Synergistic use of a longitudinal single site with replicated multiple sites. *Organization Science, 1*(3), 248–266.

Manning, W. G., Newhouse, J. P., Duan, N., Keeler, E. B., & Leibowitz, A. (1987). Health insurance and the demand for medical care: Evidence from a randomized experiment. *The American Economic Review, 77*(3), 251–277.

Maxwell, J. A. (2013). *Qualitative research design: An interactive approach* (3rd ed.). Thousand Oaks: Sage.

Mayring, P. (2001). Combination and integration of qualitative and quantitative analysis. *Forum Qualitative Sozialforschung (FQS), 2*(1), 1–14.

Miles, M. B., Huberman, A. M., & Saldaña, J. (2014). *Qualitative data analysis: A methods sourcebook* (3rd ed.). Thousand Oaks: Sage.

Oesterle, M.-J., Schick, E. M., & Lang, E.-M. (2011). Daimler trucks in India – Foreign market entry modes and location decisions. In J. Zentes, B. Swoboda, & D. Morschett (Eds.), *Fallstudien zum Internationalen Management* (4th ed., pp. 192–210). Wiesbaden: Gabler.

Patton, M. Q. (2015). *Qualitative evaluation and research methods* (4th ed.). Thousand Oaks: Sage.

Pauwels, P., & Matthyssens, P. (2004). The architecture of multiple case study research in international business. In R. Marschan-Piekkari & C. Welch (Eds.), *Handbook of qualitative research methods for international business* (pp. 125–143). Cheltenham: Edward Elgar.

Petersen, B., Pedersen, T., & Sharma, D. D. (2003). The role of knowledge in firms' internationalization process: Wherefrom and whereto. In A. Blomstermo & D. D. Sharma (Eds.), *Learning in the internationalization process of firms*. Cheltenham: Edward Elgar.

Peterson, R. A. (2001). On the use of college students in social science research: Insights from a second-order meta-analysis. *Journal of Consumer Research, 2*(3), 450–461.

Piekkari, R., Welch, C., & Paavilainen, E. (2009). The case study as disciplinary convention: Evidence from international business journals. *Organizational Research Methods, 12*(3), 567–589.

Podsakoff, P. M., MacKenzie, S. B., Lee, J. Y., & Podsakoff, N. P. (2003). Common method biases in behavioral research: A critical review of the literature and recommended remedies. *Journal of Applied Psychology, 88*(5), 879–903.

Reeb, D., Sakakibara, M., & Mahmood, I. P. (2012). Endogeneity in international business research. *Journal of International Business Studies, 43*(3), 211–218.

Roethlisberger, F. J., & Dickson, W. J. (1949). *Management and the worker: An account of a research program conducted by the western electric company*. Chicago: Hawthorne Works. 9th Print, Cambridge.

Rubin, D. B. (1974). Estimating causal effects of treatments in randomized and nonrandomized studies. *Journal of Educational Psychology, 66*(5), 688–701.

Schram, A. (2005). Artificiality: The tension between internal and external validity in economic experiments. *Journal of Economic Methodology, 12*(2), 225–237.

Sherif, M. (1936). *The psychology of social norms*. New York: Harper.

Starr, M. A. (2012). Qualitative and mixed-methods research in economics: Surprising growth, promising future. *Journal of Economic Surveys, 28*(2), 238–264.

Statista. (2016). *Ranking of the most circulated financial and business newspapers in Germany for the first quarter of 2016*. Accessed June 19, 2016, from http://de.statista.com/statistik/daten/studie/271298/umfrage/verkaufte-auflage-der-wirtschaftsmaga-zine-in-deutschland/

Staw, B. M. (1976). Knee-deep in the big muddy: A study of escalating commitment to a chosen course of action. *Organizational Behavior and Human Performance, 16*(1), 27–44.

Staw, B. M. (2010). The trouble with JDM: Some limitations to the influence of JDM on organizational research. *Industrial and Organizational Psychology, 3*(4), 411–416.

Tashakkori, A., & Creswell, J. W. (2007). The new era of mixed methods. *Journal of Mixed Methods Research, 1*(1), 3–7.

Thomas, R. W. (2011). When student samples make sense in logistics research. *Journal of Business Logistics, 32*(3), 287–290.

Voss, C., Tsikriktsis, N., & Frohlich, M. (2002). Case research in operations management. *International Journal of Operations and Production Management, 22*(2), 195–219.

Wiso. (2016). *Die Online-Datenbank für Studium und Wissenschaft*. Accessed June 17, 2016, from https://www.wiso-net.de/popup/ueber_wiso

Woodside, A. G. (2010). *Case study research: Theory, methods, practice*. Bingley: Emerald.

Yang, Z., Wang, X., & Su, C. (2006). A review of research methodologies in international business. *International Business Review, 15*(6), 601–617.

Yin, R. K. (2012). *Applications of case study research* (3rd ed.). Thousand Oaks: Sage.

Yin, R. K. (2014). *Case study research* (5th ed.). Thousand Oaks: Sage.

Zellmer-Bruhn, M., Caligiuri, P., & Thomas, D. C. (2016). Experimental designs in international business research. *Journal of International Business Studies, 47*(4), 399–407.

Chapter 5
Disparity Between Theory and Practice in Internationalization Process Research: Lessons Learned

The empirical analysis of escalation of commitment in internationalization process decision-making and the theoretical foundations that have been outlined upfront allow the drawing of a number of concluding remarks. First, the key findings will be summarized and the most important implications from a theoretical point of view will be outlined (Sect. 5.1). Second, some practical implications will be presented (Sect. 5.2). Finally, research limitations will be addressed and potential areas for further study—which partially result from the limitations—will be identified (Sect. 5.3).

5.1 Key Findings of the Present Study and Theoretical Implications

Point of departure of the present study was the realization that bounded rationality is not recognized sufficiently in internationalization process research today. Unlike researchers in many other economic disciplines, international business scholars have often only turned partially away from orthodox economic beliefs as they limited the notion of bounded rationality to the consideration of incomplete information availability for decision-makers. This, however, neglects the consequences of limited cognitive capabilities of decision-makers as a second important dimension of bounded rationality. Even the popular U-Model, which is usually already seen as a rather realistic approach due to its recognition of organizational learning and incomplete information availability, is no exception in this regard. The current state, however, presents a major shortcoming. Bounded rationality in its full extent poses a significant challenge to the judgment and decision-making powers of managers in internationalization processes. It has the potential to entail significant performance-compromising consequences. Against the background of this state of neglect, the aim of the present study was to contribute to IB literature with an exploration of bounded rationality in the context of internationalization processes.

B. Röber, *Escalation of Commitment in Internationalization Processes*, MIR Series in International Business, https://doi.org/10.1007/978-3-319-69102-2_5

For this purpose, the much cited U-Model was submitted to a critical review with the help of escalation of commitment as a concrete example for the cognitive dispositions that constitute the side of bounded rationality that is currently somewhat neglected in theory. The underlying research question was whether there is substantial evidence for the display of an escalation bias among decision-makers in internationalization process decision-making, due to which they allocate further resources to an already initiated course of action despite ongoing negative results. Such a bias would present a contradiction to the U-Model as it would falsify its implicit behavioral assumptions to a certain extent. Essentially, the theory implies that decision-makers in internationalization processes respond with a step by step proceeding to the incomplete information, with which they are confronted. As part of this process, they are expected to balance perceived and tolerable market risks, irrespective of possible cognitive dispositions that are not further addressed. Such a rational decision-making behavior would be incompatible to a display of escalation of commitment. In the course of the investigation, it was also asked whether escalation of commitment had specific IB-related consequences due to the singular context factors of internationalization processes. In this regard, the implications of psychic distance and establishment chain variations have been checked for a moderating effect on the impact of escalation of commitment.

The study presented the reader with a disclosure of an underlying understanding of rationality in Sect. 2.1 as well as with an introduction of a classification framework for JDM approaches in Sect. 2.2. Against this backdrop, the U-Model's stance on rational choice and bounded rationality contents was assessed in Sect. 3.2. It was possible to confirm that the U-Model is somewhat ambiguous with regard to its prescriptive and descriptive perspective as well as to its behavioral assumptions. For example, its processual understanding and its empirical foundation are indicative for descriptive models. At the same time, it also expects decision-makers to follow a certain formal (and therefore prescriptive) logic, which is defined by their perceived and tolerable market risks. The U-Model respects limited information availability while neither cognitive limitations nor respective behavioral biases are addressed. Thus, the assessment of the U-Model yielded the insight that it is neither unequivocally attributable to the sphere of bounded rationality nor to that of rational choice theories. Quite factually, however, it does expect decision-makers to act purposefully and consistently under the restriction of limited information availability. The lacking consideration of cognitive dispositions and behavioral biases entitles the statement that the U-Model implies—at least inter alia—rational managers, who possess the cognitive capacity to assess their actions. Thus, the U-Model must also allow for a critical testing in this regard (with the aid of escalation of commitment).

For such a test, a mixed-methods research approach has been applied in the present study. It consisted of a consolidated design in the form of a randomized IP decision-making experiment as a quantitative-empirical approach as well as of a cross case analysis of two pertinent examples of IP-failure as a qualitative-empirical method. This procedure allowed the drawing of a comprehensive picture of the role of bounded rationality in the form of escalation of commitment in internationalization processes. During the simulated internationalization process of the randomized experiment, test subjects reacted in a hypothesis-confirming manner to the psychological, social, and structural forces for persistence, to which they were exposed. Unlike a non-committed peer group, they continued to raise internationalization investments irrespective of the negative feedback that they received to their actions during the simulated IP. This effect aggravated with increasing levels of psychic distance to target markets. Test subjects acted increasingly against the U-Model's implicit assumption of rational decision-makers as they seemed to have misjudged the increased risk that resulted from the higher level of uncertainty in corresponding situations. As a result, the treatment group of the randomized experiment persisted with its course of action, while the respective control group opted relatively more often for an IP-exit. On the downside, it was not possible to demonstrate a similar effect for the context of little establishment chain progress. Based on the statistical results, there is no ground to conclude that committed decision-makers in internationalization processes fail to recognize the opportunity to withdraw from failing internationalization processes during the early stages of an establishment chain (when the withdrawal costs are still relatively low). Eventually, this was due to the experiment's 'item characteristic' of the establishment chain progress, which included a direct monetary incentive to withdraw from the IP and which may have worked 'too well'. Such a common method bias could at least partially explain the rejection of the respective hypothesis of the present study. At large, however, the randomized experiment provided the insight that escalation of commitment as a representative of bounded rationality can unfold quite a specific impact on internationalization processes—a matter that is currently not reflected in the U-Model. This insight was additionally illustrated with the descriptive case study on the merger of Daimler-Benz and Chrysler as well as on Margarete Steiff GmbH in China. Both examples showed that bounded rationality in the form of escalation of commitment is a relevant matter in internationalization process reality and highlighted that cognitive dispositions present an issue that IP-theories—including the U-Model—should account for.

The key finding of the present study could be summarized with the statement that bounded rationality in the form of cognitive limitations is currently somewhat neglected in the U-Model. It underlines the problem of a disparity between theory and practice in IP-research that is not sufficiently addressed by scholars. Certainly, some areas of the U-Model and IP-research in general are critically addressed by scholars.[1] Yet, the very fundamental question of whether the theoretical abstractions match the reality of internationalization processes remains an issue that is rarely covered. One cannot help but have the impression that this very essential matter of the IB discipline is not sufficiently put to the test by concerned scholars. As a result, research covering the internationalization processes of firms has to cope with a questionable applicability of its results in reality. Oesterle highlighted this matter already relatively early. In a nutshell, his line of thought is built on the argument that better insights into internationalization process reality lead to a

[1]Hadjikhani (1997, pp. 47–49).

complicated development of fitting abstractions of selfsame.[2] Thus, the challenge for IP-research lies in the establishment of explanatory theories, which succeed to reflect the complexity of reality accurately. Yet, also with the results of the present study in mind, one might have doubts regarding the feasibility of a comprehensive and extensive abstraction of internationalization process reality. Technically, the implications of bounded rationality alone can entail numerous theoretical constraints. Nonetheless, the answer to this challenge cannot lie in factoring out these issues of reality because such a response could, in the worst case, lead to a "fictitious character" of the field of research.[3]

5.2 Implications for Business Practice

As it has already been stated in the introduction to this study, internationalization processes consist of consecutive JDM situations. Managers, who deal with matters of internationalization, are often confronted with crucial decisions such as the choice of promising foreign market locations and respective market entry modes. Obviously, such crucial questions come along with equally important decisions once the firm has finally decided to go international. Many of these can be summed up by the choice between a continued internationalization process (and further expansion) or a reduction of the international engagement. Respective questions surface regardless of the intent behind single internationalization steps, and they are in fact quite manifold. 'How long should a firm continue to support a foreign sales subsidiary in a specific market despite continuously negative revenue results?' 'Should a firm maintain R&D facilities in a country, which do not contribute to the firm's innovation base as it has once been hoped for?' These are just two examples for the broad scope of issues that managers can face in the context of internationalization processes. The results of the present study highlight that IP-administrators are likely to be impacted by escalation of commitment in situations such as in the given examples. This means that internationalization processes can be maintained for the wrong reasons due to the escalation problem, which usually goes unnoticed by the managers and which often involves the entire organization at a structural level.

Yet, how should managers (and organizations) react in business practice now that they know about their possible cognitive disposition (from a theoretical stance at least)? This crucial question from a practitioner's perspective was not directly addressed by the present study. Therefore, it would not be adequate to deduce respective implications on the basis of the here outlined study results alone. In fact, most research on escalation of commitment "generally stops at the point at which an

[2]Cf. Oesterle (1999, pp. 219 ff.).

[3]Oesterle (1999, p. 221).

organization is still locked in a losing situation".[4] There are, however, a small number of publications (primarily authored by Staw and Ross) that try to give concrete advice that can help to control the consequences of the impact of escalation of commitment.[5] With the help of these proposed measures, some practical implications of the present study can be stated.

The possible actions that managers can take against escalating internationalization processes present themselves in a dichotomous structure. On the one hand, there are measures that potentially affected decision-makers can see after for themselves; on the other hand, organizational changes can be necessary. The biggest challenge for concerned managers lies in recognizing that they themselves are actually affected by escalation of commitment. In this regard, the findings of the present study can contribute to an increased awareness of managerial decision-makers for the escalation bias. For concerned administrators, it could help to distance oneself from internationalization steps in which one is heavily involved (e.g., by critically reflecting one's own decisions or by a proactive request for critical feedback). Regularly reflecting upon the causes and consequences of a failing internationalization process as well as upon other people's opinions could increase the cognitive transparency for managers. Obviously, this is easier said than done. Staw and Ross also realized that the "line between an optimistic, can-do attitude and overcommitment is very thin".[6] Therefore, the risk is high that managers do not see their disposition for what it is. Such a situation limits the measures that they can take for themselves and it increases the need for organizational responses to escalation of commitment. This is evermore the case, as failing internationalization processes can be institutionalized and as they can present a concern for the entire organization. So, how can firms react to the threat of escalating internationalization processes in an effective way? At least four measures can be identified.

Administrative turnovers: An exchange of responsible managers could help to reduce the vulnerability to escalation of commitment because newly appointed administrators are not personally responsible for a chosen course of action. Thus, they are less likely to be prone to social and psychological forces for persistence in internationalization processes.[7] Certainly, such a measure comes at the price of potentially high replacement costs while it also brings disruptive effects to the organization. Not just in the context of internationalization processes, the knowledge of a firm will always be a derivative of the knowledge of its administrators. Therefore, too much reliance on administrative turnovers can also undermine the knowledge base of a firm.

Separation of decision-makers: It could be more feasible and less costly to separate initial and subsequent managers in internationalization processes instead

[4] Ross and Staw (1993, p. 724).

[5] Cf. Staw and Ross (1987a, pp. 72–74, b, pp. 71–74).

[6] Staw and Ross (1987b, p. 72).

[7] As discussed in Sect. 3.3.4 of the present study.

of building upon administrative turnovers straightaway. This could also help to overcome psychological and social forces for persistence, while there would be no replacement costs. Disruptive effects, however, will still be a problem.

Improvement of the information system: Better data preparation concerning the costs of failing internationalization processes could enhance the consciousness of managers for their decisions and, hence, counteract the escalation bias due to the sobering effect of bare figures.

Less risk of failure and de-institutionalization: A withdrawal from a failing course of action could be connected with a severe threat to the career of the responsible manager. Better support mechanisms and less draconic consequences in the case of a failing internationalization process may increase the chances of a timely withdrawal. In addition, the de-institutionalizing of internationalization processes could present a remedy. Labeling the internationalization strategy of a firm as peripheral or insignificant, for example, could increase the likelihood of managers accepting withdrawal as a good decision alternative. In fact, both of these measures have been empirically confirmed indirectly by Hayward and Shimizu in the pages of Strategic Management Journal not too long ago.[8] The authors investigated the conditions in which managers de-commit from failing projects. The study showed that they end poorly performing projects when the cause of failure does not incriminate them or when the overall firm performance allows the admittance of failure. On this matter, the results of the present study can contribute as well. One should recall the previously discussed case of the failed merger between Daimler-Benz and Chrysler. Only after the head of the DaimlerChrysler executive board Jürgen Schrempp was replaced with a less incriminated management around Dieter Zetsche and only after the Daimler division was better off financially, the management put an end to the integration process of the two firms. Similarly at Steiff, a less incriminated management had to be installed first before the offshoring decision was finally reversed. Thus, the stories of DaimlerChrysler and Steiff confirm the importance of a reduced risk of failure and de-institutionalization.[9]

Considering the presented (organizational) measures against escalation of commitment, one cannot help but assume certain implementation difficulties due to the possibility of intra-firm opposition (administrative turnovers, separation of decision-makers), technology expenditures (improvement of the information system), and doubtful managerial incentives (less risk of failure and de-institutionalization). These potential difficulties underline the significant challenge that escalation of commitment—and other cognitive dispositions in the sphere of bounded rationality—impose upon managers and firms. In order to confront these dispositions effectively, it would be a good start for practitioners in international business to account for their cognitive decision-making limitations and to know of the full extent of their bounded rationality.

[8]Cf. Hayward and Shimizu (2006, pp. 541 ff.).

[9]As disclosed in Sect. 4.3.2 of the present study.

5.3 Research Limitations and Areas for Further Research

The present study is marked by certain research limitations, which will be disclosed in the following and which open up the possibility for further investigations. These limitations can roughly be distinguished by content and methodological issues.

Content-wise, the present study contributed to IB-literature with an exploration of bounded rationality in the context of internationalization processes. For this purpose, the general impact of escalation of commitment in IP decision-making has been elaborated, and the moderating effects of psychic distance and establishment chain progress variations have been discussed. These two moderators have been chosen because of their great theoretical and practical significance in the researched area. Certainly, however, there is a multitude of other factors that have the potential to affect the impact of escalation of commitment in internationalization process decision-making. As an example, one could consider the relative decision-making power of different decision-making bodies within a firm. The present study applied a very broad and universal understanding of decision-makers and did not distinguish very much between different degrees of decision-making power, which can vary significantly in dependence of regional corporate governance standards. This has been a permissible simplification because the research problem of the present study addressed a display of escalation of commitment in a rather general internationalization process context. Now that respective research results have been established, it can be sensible to differentiate between the roles of decision-makers as well as to consider different degrees of decision-making power. The differences between decision-makers present researchers with further complexities. A closer look upon such complexities can reveal additional interesting research insights. One could consider the different legal decision-making competencies of US-American 'chief executive officers' and German 'chairmen of executive boards', for example. While the former function as the heads of monistic top managements, which may control themselves, the latter are part of a dual top management, which is legally restricted by a supervisory board ('*Aufsichtsrat*') that provides a control function over the executive board (theoretically at least). One could easily assume that US-American corporations are more prone to behavioral biases (such as escalation of commitment) because of their monistic governance structure. This assumption, however, holds only from a de jure perspective. De facto, there is a convergence tendency between US-American and German governance structures.[10] Nevertheless, this matter exemplifies how a closer look at decision-makers and their respective decision-making powers from an IB perspective could help to provide more accurate insights into the matter of escalation of commitment in internationalization process decision-making. Furthermore, one might question whether the idea of individual decision-makers is still adequate today. One could argue that joint decision-making bodies are much more of a contemporary reality. Most likely, this would imply that the third stage of an escalation process (i.e., structural forces

[10]Cf. Oesterle and Krause (2004, pp. 274–276) and Oesterle (2003, p. 199).

for persistence) unfolds its impact much sooner than assumed by the model of Staw and Ross. To sum up the content limitations of this study, further research on the moderating factors of escalation of commitment in internationalization process decision-making could bring additional, fruitful insights to light.

With regard to the methodological limitations of the present study, further research concerning the rejected third hypothesis (addressing the moderating effect of the establishment chain progress) is required. In Sect. 4.2.4.3 it has been referred to common method biases as a potential cause for the rejection (particularly concerning the 'item characteristics' of the establishment chain progress). Thus, further research could test a different operationalization of the establishment chain or, alternatively, reconsider the hypothesis altogether. Furthermore, it must be noted critically that the argumentative explanation behind the moderating effect of psychic distance variations requires further empirical analysis. The present study merely demonstrated that decision-makers respond differently to psychic distance changes in dependence of their commitment. Yet, it remained (empirically at least) unanswered why the changes of psychic distance evoked different effects among test subjects. In Sect. 3.3.7.2 it has been argued in this regard that decision-makers under escalation of commitment have to cope with a lower risk assessment capacity and that they are therefore blind for the corresponding negative implications of high psychic distance (such as a higher degree of uncertainty and an increased risk of failure). Implicitly, this line of argumentation served as the explanation for the moderating effect of psychic distance. It is, however, only based on plausibility and theory and not on empirics; therefore, it needs further justification. Thus, the present study could serve as a basis for a follow-up study that covers the relation between psychic distance and the risk assessment capacity of committed decision-makers empirically.

Altogether—and despite the here disclosed limitations—one can conclude that the present study managed to deliver further insights into the role of bounded rationality in internationalization processes. It has been demonstrated that escalation of commitment—as a representative of cognitive limitations and bounded rationality—presents a serious cause for erroneous judgments in the internationalization process decision-making of firms. This means that the commitment dimension is more complex than postulated by the Uppsala School of Thought. Managers and their cognitive dispositions can constitute a contradiction to the implicit assumption of rationally proceeding administrators of the U-Model. This result supports the limited number of earlier published studies that raise awareness to the matter of bounded rationality in the context of internationalization processes.[11] Furthermore, it highlights the importance that managers and firms consider the full extent of their bounded rationality—and therefore also escalation of commitment—as a cause for failure in IB-reality.

---

[11] Most notably, Matthyssens and Pauwels (2000, pp. 697 ff.), raise attention to the subject matter as part of their study on international market-exit decision-making.

References

Hadjikhani, A. (1997). A note on the criticisms against the internationalization process model. *Management International Review, 37*(S2), 43–66.

Hayward, M. L., & Shimizu, K. (2006). De-commitment to losing strategic action: Evidence from the divestiture of poorly performing acquisitions. *Strategic Management Journal, 27*(6), 541–557.

Matthyssens, P., & Pauwels, P. (2000). Uncovering international market-exit processes: A comparative case study. *Psychology and Marketing, 17*(8), 697–719.

Oesterle, M.-J. (1999). Fiktionen der Internationalisierungsforschung. In J. Engelhard & W. A. Oechsler (Eds.), *Internationales Management* (pp. 219–245). Wiesbaden: Gabler.

Oesterle, M.-J. (2003). Entscheidungsfindung im Vorstand großer deutscher Aktiengesellschaften. *Zeitschrift für Führung und Organisation, 72*(4), 199–209.

Oesterle, M.-J., & Krause, D. (2004). Leitungsorganisation des Vorstands in deutschen Aktiengesellschaften. *WiSt-Wirtschaftswissenschaftliches Studium, 33*(5), 272–277.

Ross, J., & Staw, B. M. (1993). Organizational escalation and exit: Lessons from the Shoreham nuclear power plant. *Academy of Management Journal, 36*(4), 701–732.

Staw, B. M., & Ross, J. (1987a). Behavior in escalation situations: Antecedents, prototypes, and solutions. In *Research in organizational behavior* (Vol. 9, pp. 39–78). Greenwich: JAI Press.

Staw, B. M., & Ross, J. (1987b). Knowing when to pull the plug. *Harvard Business Review, 65*(2), 68–74.

References

Appendix

Consulted Articles for the Case Study on DaimlerChrysler

No.	Article	Date	Source	Issue	Pages
1	Gewerkschaften sehen Daimler-Chrysler-Fusion durchaus mit gemischten Gefühlen	08.05.1998	Handelsblatt	88	p. 12
2	Unterschiedliche Rechtskulturen müssen miteinander versöhnt werden	11.05.1998	Handelsblatt	89	p. 2
3	Daimler-Chrysler: Völlig neue Regeln	14.05.1998	Wirtschaftswoche	21	p. 50
4	Gewaltiger Kursschub erwartet	19.05.1998	Handelsblatt	95	p. 39
5	Zum Chrysler-Deal gab es wenig Handfestes	28.05.1998	Handelsblatt	101	p. 15
6	Höhere Gewinneinschätzung für Daimler-Chrysler	06.08.1998	Handelsblatt	149	p. 23
7	This way, please	21.08.1998	manager magazin	9	p. 68
8	Daimler-Chrysler: Schlaflose Nächte	16.09.1998	Wirtschaftswoche	39	p. 57
9	Analysten sind von der Fusion überzeugt	17.09.1998	Handelsblatt	179	p. 14
10	Daimler-Chrysler-Fusion schafft Potential für Kurssteigerungen	29.09.1998	Handelsblatt	187	p. 41
11	Weg für neue Daimler-Chrysler AG ist frei – Umtauschquote von 97 Prozent Doppeldividende für Chrysler-Aktionäre	27.10.1998	Handelsblatt	207	p. 1
12	Absatzrekord vor der Fusion	04.11.1998	Handelsblatt	213	p. 22
13	Daimler-Chrysler ist startklar	10.11.1998	Handelsblatt	217	p. 17
14	Daimler-Chrysler mit 13 Prozent Umsatzplus	28.12.1998	Handelsblatt	250	p. 11

(continued)

B. Röber, *Escalation of Commitment in Internationalization Processes*, MIR Series in International Business, https://doi.org/10.1007/978-3-319-69102-2

No.	Article	Date	Source	Issue	Pages
15	Daimler-Chrysler ist gut in Form	26.02.1999	Handelsblatt	40	p. 13
16	Fusion in Fahrt	01.04.1999	Handelsblatt	64	p. 2
17	Schrempp: Bestbezahlter deutscher Manager	05.05.1999	Handelsblatt	88	p. 15
18	DaimlerChrysler: Prinzip Schrempp	06.05.1999	Wirtschaftswoche	19	p. 56
19	Daimler-Chrysler will Umsatz in zehn jahren verdoppeln	19.05.1999	Handelsblatt	95	p. 1
20	Daimler-Chrysler realisiert Synergien	27.05.1999	Handelsblatt	100	p. 19
21	Kollision der Kulturen	01.06.1999	manager magazin	6	p. 96
22	Daimler-Chrysler	18.06.1999	Handelsblatt	115	p. i03
23	DaimlerChrysler: Jubel verflogen	05.08.1999	Wirtschaftswoche	32	p. 8
24	Die Fusion muss noch in den Köpfen stattfinden	24.08.1999	Handelsblatt	162	p. 15
25	Der große Kehraus	01.10.1999	manager magazin	10	p. 12
26	Erfolg bleibt aus	28.01.2000	Handelsblatt	20	p. 2
27	DaimlerChrysler	01.03.2000	manager magazin	3	p. 78
28	Daimler-Chrysler will die Nummer Eins werden	20.04.2000	Handelsblatt	79	p. 17
29	Der Angriff rollt	01.07.2000	manager magazin	7	p. 63
30	Schrempps Welt	10.08.2000	Capital	17	p. 54
31	DaimlerChrysler: Gefallener Engel	05.10.2000	Wirtschaftswoche	41	p. 90
32	DaimlerChrysler: "Abrechnung in drei Jahren"	02.11.2000	FOCUS Money	45	p. 12
33	Schrempp feuert Chrysler-Chef	15.11.2000	Handelsblatt	221	p. 1
34	Aktie von Daimler-Chrysler fällt und fällt	21.11.2000	Handelsblatt	225	p. 37
35	Chrysler ist ein Schrottladen	29.11.2000	Handelsblatt	231	p. 16
36	Marathon-Mann	01.12.2000	manager magazin	12	p. 64
37	"Arrogant und diktatorisch": DaimlerChrysler	14.12.2000	Capital	26	p. 246
38	Der Rettungsplan DaimlerChrysler	14.12.2000	Capital	26	p. 58
39	Chrysler bremst Daimler aus	19.12.2000	Handelsblatt	245	p. 1
40	Konsolidierung: Die Welt verteilen	21.12.2000	Wirtschaftswoche	52	p. 128
41	Chrysler rutscht in die roten Zahlen	29.01.2001	Handelsblatt	20	p. 14
42	Platzt Daimler-Chrysler?	15.02.2001	Wirtschaftswoche	8	p. 24
43	DaimlerChrysler – Klares Signal	22.02.2001	FOCUS Money	9	pp. 18–20
44	DaimlerChrysler: Schrempps Elchtest	22.02.2001	Wirtschaftswoche	9	p. 50
45	Schmerzlose Lösung	08.03.2001	Wirtschaftswoche	11	p. 26
46	DaimlerChrysler: Die Chrysler-Sanierung wird schwieriger als erwartet	15.03.2001	Wirtschaftswoche	12	p. 230

(continued)

No.	Article	Date	Source	Issue	Pages
47	DaimlerChrysler: Der Frontmann	10.05.2001	Wirtschaftswoche	20	p. 58
48	DaimlerChrysler: Kurzes Aufatmen	19.07.2001	FOCUS Money	30	pp. 22–23
49	Chrysler macht Daimler neue Sorgen	12.10.2001	Handelsblatt	197	p. 20
50	DaimlerChrysler: Vollbremsung	15.11.2001	Wirtschaftswoche	47	p. 222
51	DaimlerChrysler: Auf dünnem Eis	10.01.2002	Wirtschaftswoche	3	p. 44
52	Auch Chrysler gibt jetzt großzügig Rabatt	01.02.2002	Handelsblatt	23	p. 13
53	DaimlerChrysler: Die Stunde der Wahrheit	14.02.2002	FOCUS Money	8	pp. 24–25
54	DaimlerChrysler: Die Wahrheit – was die geheime Konzernplanung verrät	02.05.2002	Capital	9	p. 149
55	DaimlerChrysler: Neues Image für Chrysler	23.05.2002	Wirtschaftswoche	22	p. 12
56	Chrysler bereitet Daimler wieder echte Freude	25.06.2002	Handelsblatt	119	p. 16
57	DaimlerChrysler: Amerika über Plan	04.07.2002	FOCUS Money	28	pp. 20–21
58	DaimlerChrysler	01.08.2002	FOCUS Money	32	p. 94
59	Daimler hat Chrysler wieder im Griff	05.02.2003	Handelsblatt	25	p. 13
60	DaimlerChrysler: "Wir sind durch"	13.02.2003	Wirtschaftswoche	8	p. 80
61	DaimlerChrysler: Viele Fragezeichen	20.02.2003	Wirtschaftswoche	9	p. 40
62	Schrempp sieht Chrysler auf gutem Kurs	21.02.2003	Handelsblatt	37	p. 2
63	Daimler leidet unter US-Markt	10.04.2003	Handelsblatt	71	p. 15
64	Chrysler fährt auf holprigem Weg	25.04.2003	Handelsblatt	80	p. 13
65	Gretchenfrage Chrysler	05.06.2003	Handelsblatt	107	p. 1
66	Der große Irrtum	12.06.2003	Capital	12	p. 10
67	Viel zu tun bei Chrysler	18.07.2003	Handelsblatt	136	p. 18
68	DaimlerChrysler: Die drei Fragezeichen	07.08.2003	FOCUS Money	33	pp. 14–15
69	"Wir sind einmalig"	01.11.2003	manager magazin	11	p. 58
70	Ohne Daimler wäre Chrysler pleite	21.01.2004	Handelsblatt	14	p. 12
71	DaimlerChrysler: Letzte Chance	22.01.2004	FOCUS Money	5	pp. 12–14
72	Chrysler-Krise wirft Daimler nicht um	05.02.2004	Handelsblatt	25	p. 11
73	Vision gescheitert: DaimlerChrysler	15.04.2004	Capital	9	p. 110
74	Für Chrysler wird die Luft dünner	26.04.2004	Handelsblatt	80	p. 2
75	Braucht Daimler Schrempp?	29.04.2004	Wirtschaftswoche	19	p. 42
76	DaimlerChrysler: Zwei paar Stiefel	29.04.2004	FOCUS Money	19	pp. 16–17

(continued)

No.	Article	Date	Source	Issue	Pages
77	Chrysler sieht sich auf Erfolgskurs	13.09.2004	Handelsblatt	177	p. 11
78	Die Versprechen der Fusion erfüllen sich	13.09.2004	Handelsblatt	177	p. 11
79	Mercedes belastet Daimler-Chrysler	07.04.2005	Handelsblatt	67	p. 15
80	Daimler gewinnt gegen Kerkorian	11.04.2005	Handelsblatt	69	p. 14
81	Daimler-Chrysler: Lohnt sich eine Zerschlagung?	20.04.2005	FOCUS Money	17	p. 11
82	Chrysler gerät wieder in den Abwärtssog	29.04.2005	Handelsblatt	83	p. 17
83	DaimlerChrysler: Hat die Welt-AG überhaupt eine Zukunft?	04.05.2005	FOCUS Money	19	p. 8
84	DaimlerChrysler – Schlechte Zeiten, gute Zeiten	22.06.2005	FOCUS Money	26	pp. 12–15
85	Schrempp geht, Zetsche kommt, Börse feiert Wechsel bei Daimler	29.07.2005	Handelsblatt	145	p. 1
86	"Zetsche-Effekt" treibt den Daimler-Kurs	25.10.2005	Handelsblatt	206	p. 36
87	Daimler-Chrysler überzeugt Investoren mit Gewinnsprung	27.10.2005	Handelsblatt	208	p. 17
88	Erdung eines Weltkonzerns	25.01.2006	Handelsblatt	18	p. 8
89	Zetsche stutzt die Daimler-Zentrale	25.01.2006	Handelsblatt	18	p. 1
90	Daimlers Achillesferse heißt Chrysler	07.06.2006	Handelsblatt	108	p. 11
91	Daimler kämpft mit Problemen bei Chrysler	06.07.2006	Handelsblatt	128	p. 14
92	Mercedes überstrahlt Chrysler-Einbruch	28.07.2006	Handelsblatt	144	p. 17
93	Die US-Tochter belastet Daimler-Chrysler	08.08.2006	Handelsblatt	151	p. 12
94	Heißer Atem	21.08.2006	Wirtschaftswoche	34	p. 116
95	Chrysler fährt auf Sparflamme	20.09.2006	Handelsblatt	182	p. 13
96	Chrysler plant noch keinen Abbau	29.09.2006	Handelsblatt	189	p. 15
97	Daimler-Chef Zetsche rückt Chrysler bei der Sanierung enger an Mercedes	06.02.2007	Handelsblatt	26	p. 15
98	Letzte Chance	13.02.2007	Handelsblatt	31	p. 8
99	Daimler und der Ikarus	15.02.2007	Handelsblatt	33	p. 1
100	Nichts ist unmöglich – Daimler	15.02.2007	Handelsblatt	33	p. 10
101	Zetsche zieht Notbremse bei Chrysler	15.02.2007	Handelsblatt	33	p. 1
102	Chrysler-Entscheidung noch 2007	19.02.2007	Handelsblatt	35	p. 11
103	Scheiden tut nicht weh	23.02.2007	manager magazin	3	p. 12
104	Pistole auf die Brust	26.02.2007	Wirtschaftswoche	9	p. 64

(continued)

No.	Article	Date	Source	Issue	Pages
105	Ohne Chrysler auf der Hauptversammlung von Daimlerchrysler gibt es ein großes Thema: Was passiert mit der US-Tochter?	29.03.2007	Capital	8	p. 176
106	Zetsche forciert Chrysler-Verkauf	05.04.2007	Handelsblatt	68	p. 1
107	Daimler liebäugelt mit Minderheit an Chrysler	16.04.2007	Handelsblatt	73	p. 18
108	Chrysler-Zukunft bald geklärt	25.04.2007	Handelsblatt	80	p. 15
109	Daimler befreit sich von Chrysler	15.05.2007	Handelsblatt	93	p. 1
110	Neun verflixte Jahre Machosprüche, Maßlosigkeit und Milliardenverluste	15.05.2007	Handelsblatt	93	p. 10
111	Erfolg oder Exit	16.05.2007	Handelsblatt	94	p. 8
112	Ohne Chrysler kann Daimler durchstarten	16.05.2007	Handelsblatt	94	p. 1
113	Daimler hat viel Substanz verloren	21.05.2007	Handelsblatt	96	p. 16
114	Chrysler verhagelt Daimler-Bilanz	22.05.2007	Handelsblatt	97	p. 1
115	DaimlerChrysler: Doppelter Freudensprung	24.05.2007	Capital	12	p. Börse
116	"Wir schneiden einen Konzern in zwei Teile"	05.06.2007	Handelsblatt	106	p. 17
117	Daimler und Chrysler vollziehen ihre Scheidung endgültig	06.08.2007	Handelsblatt	149	p. 12
118	Daimler öffnet die Schatulle	30.08.2007	Handelsblatt	176	p. 1
119	Scheidung von Chrysler wird billiger	30.08.2007	Handelsblatt	167	p. 16
120	Name neu, Strategie neu	05.10.2007	Handelsblatt	192	p. 18
121	Chrysler erwartet hohen Verlust	07.12.2007	Handelsblatt	237	p. 18
122	Jahr der Entscheidung	22.08.2008	manager magazin	9	p. 5
123	Zetsche gibt den Rest	26.09.2008	manager magazin	10	p. 10

Consulted Articles for the Case Study on Margarete Steiff GmbH

No.	Article	Date	Source	Issue	Pages
1	Verlorenes Terrain	29.09.2005	Wirtschaftswoche	40	p. 16
2	Das Ländle fällt zurück	06.01.2006	Handelsblatt	5	p. 4
3	Der Problembär	21.07.2006	manager magazin	8	p. 50
4	Strenger prüfen	20.08.2007	Wirtschaftswoche	34	p. 16
5	Steiff holt Produktion aus China zurück	02.07.2008	Handelsblatt	126	p. 14

(continued)

No.	Article	Date	Source	Issue	Pages
6	Jeder fünfte Betrieb bereut Gang ins Ausland	04.07.2008	Handelsblatt	128	p. 21
7	Frachtraten steigen dramatisch	08.07.2008	Handelsblatt	130	p. 16
8	Standorte der Zukunft	08.07.2008	Handelsblatt	130	p. 7
9	Politik, Ökonomie, Management—Globalisierung Wandel im Handel	30.07.2008	Focus-Money	32	pp. 76–79
10	Politik, Ökonomie, Management—China Teddys, Träume, Triebwerke	06.08.2008	Focus-Money	33	pp. 74–77
11	In der Krise nicht an Qualität sparen	10.11.2008	Handelsblatt	218	p.2
12	Arbeitsplätze Innere Stärke	12.11.2008	Focus-Money	47	pp. 76–78
13	Spielregeln	18.12.2008	Capital	1	pp. 26–32
14	Das tapfere Schneiderlein	20.03.2009	Handelsblatt	56	p. 11
15	Etliche Betriebe kommen zurück	19.11.2009	Handelsblatt	224	p. 31

MIX
Papier aus verantwortungsvollen Quellen
Paper from responsible sources
FSC® C105338

If you have any concerns about our products,
you can contact us on
ProductSafety@springernature.com

In case Publisher is established outside the EU,
the EU authorized representative is:
Springer Nature Customer Service Center GmbH
Europaplatz 3, 69115 Heidelberg, Germany

Printed by Libri Plureos GmbH
in Hamburg, Germany